ARCHITECTURAL ANTIQUES

BETA-PLUS

ARCHITECTURAL ANTIQUES

February 2008
ISBN 13: 978 90 77213 94 0

p. 2
Architectural
antiques in a house
in the U.S. designed
by Bruce Bananto.

p. 4-5
A project by
Themenos.

CONTENTS

11 | Foreword

14 | PART I: INSPIRATIONAL INTERIORS

16   A complete facelift for a country farmhouse
28   An eclectic style for a Flemish maison de maître
48   The metamorphosis of the Château de Vierset
60   Distinctive total interiors tailored to the client
68   In harmony
80   Interior and exterior unite to form a whole
96   A mix of cultures
110   An intimate atmosphere
126   An ode to country living
140   Passionate and rebellious, traditional and innovative

146	Part II:	THE ARCHITECTURAL ANTIQUE DEALERS

148   A pioneer with a cast-iron reputation
152   A creative symbiosis between past and present
158   A passion for historic wooden floors
164   The timeless cachet of unusual wooden floors
180   A huge stock and a wide variety of old construction materials
190   A passion for antique construction materials since 1965
202   A glimpse of times gone by
210   A specialist in antique Victorian tiled floors and walls
214   Antique style at the top end of the market
226   Perfection right down to the smallest detail
230   A passion for antique materials
234   A specialist in old fireplaces and floors

243 | Addresses

248 | Credits

FOREWORD

In our modern, high-tech society, traditional craftsmanship has increasingly had to give way to mass production. Synthetic materials have taken over from natural ones, and the world of construction in 2008 appears to revolve around efficiency, standardisation and cost optimisation.

However, a growing number of individuals are reacting against these tendencies by working to create authentic and personal living environments.

This new home-design philosophy has had an impact in many areas: a lot of distinctive old residences, farms, country houses and other homes are undergoing careful restoration; industrially manufactured furniture is being replaced by unique, handmade pieces; and preference is given to natural materials and finishes, rather than mass production.

Within this context, it is easy to see why valuable construction materials and pieces from the past are being reclaimed, restored and reintegrated into properties: these "architectural antiques" ensure that every home can have a unique cachet.

Whether it's an 18th-century wooden floor, reclaimed Burgundy slabs, authentic handmade roof tiles and slates, antique fireplaces, or other historic features, these construction materials always offer the opportunity for every home project to have an authentic character, as is clearly illustrated by the many inspiring projects featured in this book.

Dealers in antique construction materials also occupy a very important place in these developments, convincingly demonstrating how their unique discoveries, often to be found in a variety of warehouses and showrooms, can be integrated into magnificent homes. The growing professionalism within this sector has in recent years ensured that an increasing number of architects, interior specialists and private individuals have been able to find materials that suit them perfectly within the ever-expanding assortment of architectural antiques.

Wim Pauwels
Publisher

A project by Themenos.

p. 12-13
A country house created by Porte Bonheur in collaboration with Natalie Haegeman Interiors.

PART I

INSPIRATIONAL INTERIORS

A COMPLETE FACELIFT
FOR A COUNTRY FARMHOUSE

This house in the countryside has undergone a very thorough renovation. However, every effort has been made to leave the original charm of the building intact.

The owner of the house started landscaping the garden as soon as he purchased the property. The complete renovation of the house took three years.
The interior design is by antique dealer Axel Pairon.

The old residential section of the former farmhouse has been left in its original state as far as possible. The red colour of the bricks has been restored to its former glory.

The roof has been completely replaced, but the dip in the roof has been retained so as to respect the authentic atmosphere. The new weatherboarding has been made grey to blend in with the house and its surroundings.

The interior was given a completely new layout to satisfy the owners' living requirements. All of the rooms flow into each other and have beautiful views. This house has all modern comforts.

Large glass windows have been installed where the original stable doors stood. This allows in a lot of light and means that the owners can enjoy the beautiful views of the garden and surrounding landscape. Warm colours were selected to give the rooms a bright and sunny atmosphere. The curtains and furniture fabrics are in natural linen to harmonise with the country surroundings. The robust kitchen table is a perfect match, in terms of its style and size, with the original wooden construction of the farmhouse.

A sleeping alcove for the children has been made in the slope of the roof.

AXEL PAIRON
Antiques and interiors
Leopoldstraat 35
B – 2000 Antwerp
T/F +32 (0)498 102 815

AN ECLECTIC STYLE FOR A FLEMISH MAISON DE MAÎTRE

Architect Stéphane Boens took the Flemish "maison de maître", or grand townhouse, as the source of inspiration for this distinctive country house in wooded surroundings.

This newly built house has a very rural location, but still retains all the charm and style of a majestic maison de maître: an unusual combination and an eclectic approach that has been raised to the highest level in the work of Stéphane Boens.

This is the first house for which Stéphane Boens has employed a "beurré" (buttered) finish in the pale rendering of the facades.

The sumptuous atmosphere of the Flemish maison de maître, with high ceilings, exclusive natural stone and parquet floors.

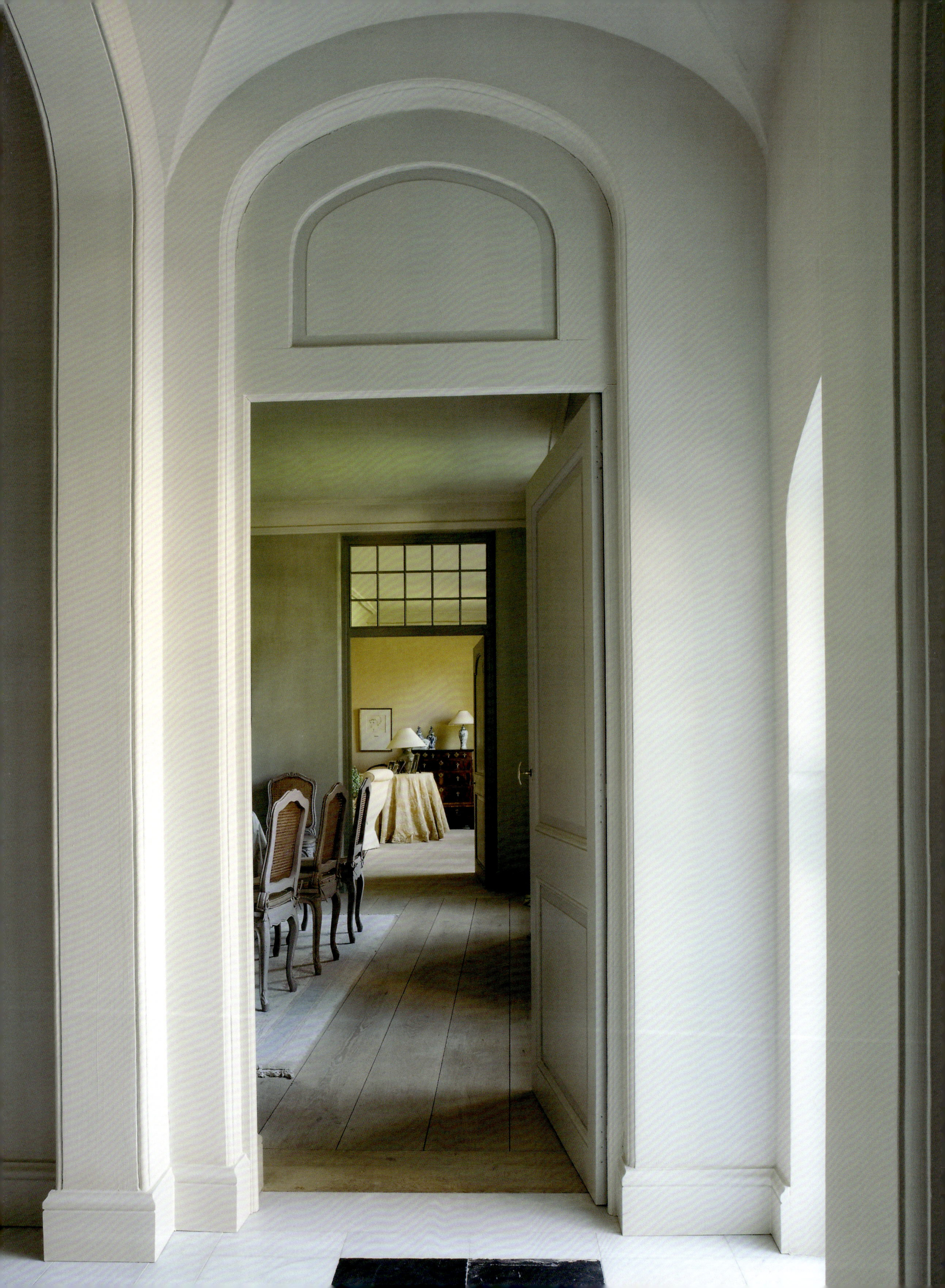

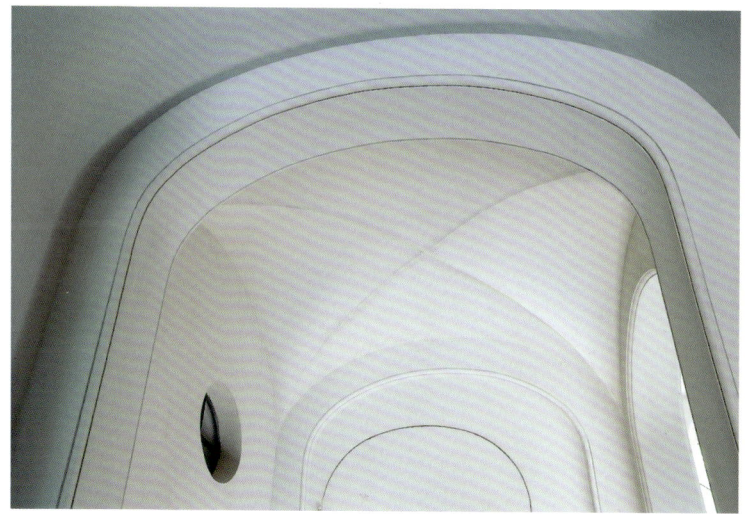

The timeless atmosphere is reinforced by the aged oak wooden floors and the reclaimed flagstones.

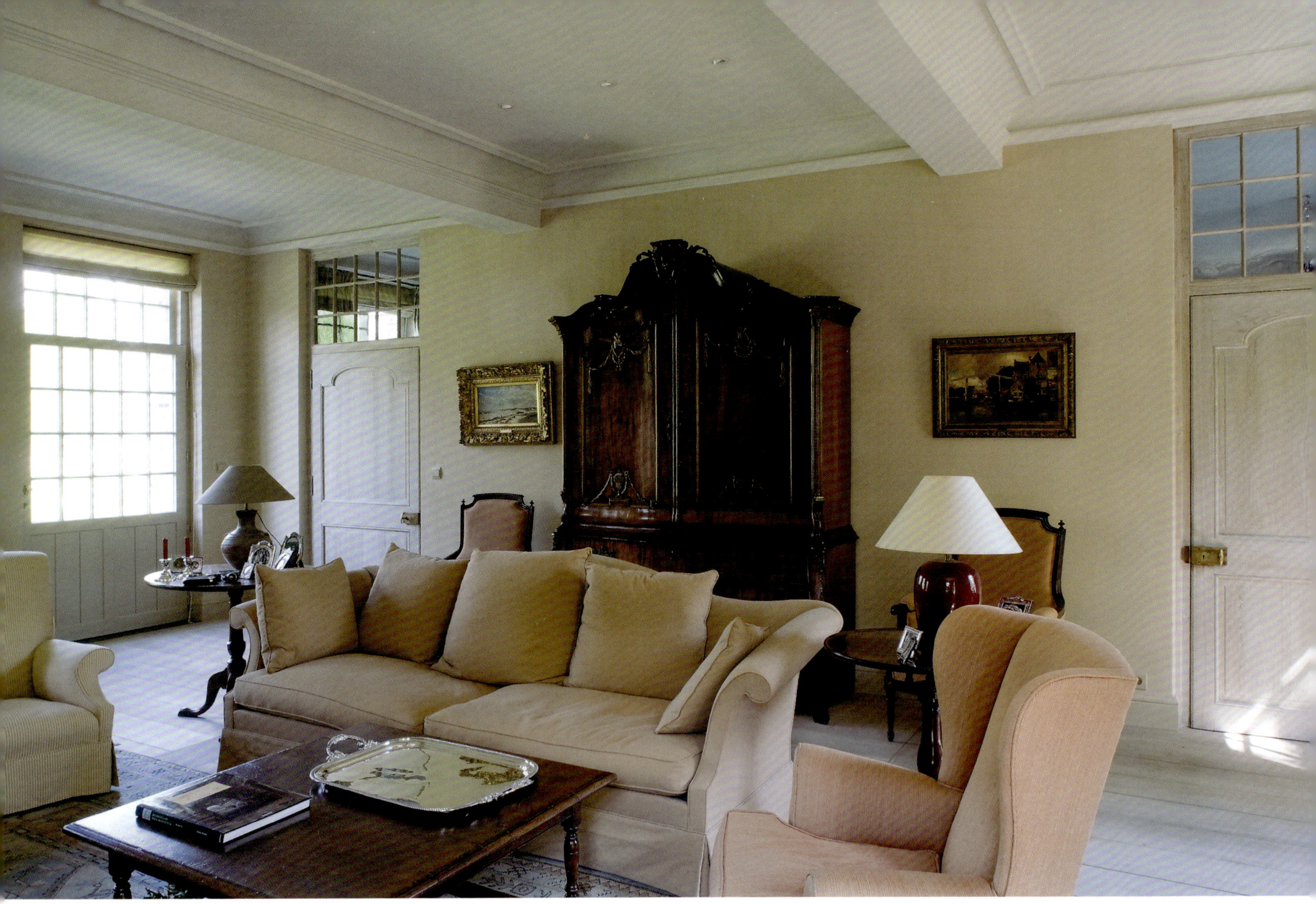

An oak floor with an aged grey finish was also selected for the sitting room.
The mouldings and the grand antique furniture are a reminder of the source of inspiration for this house: the Flemish maison de maître.

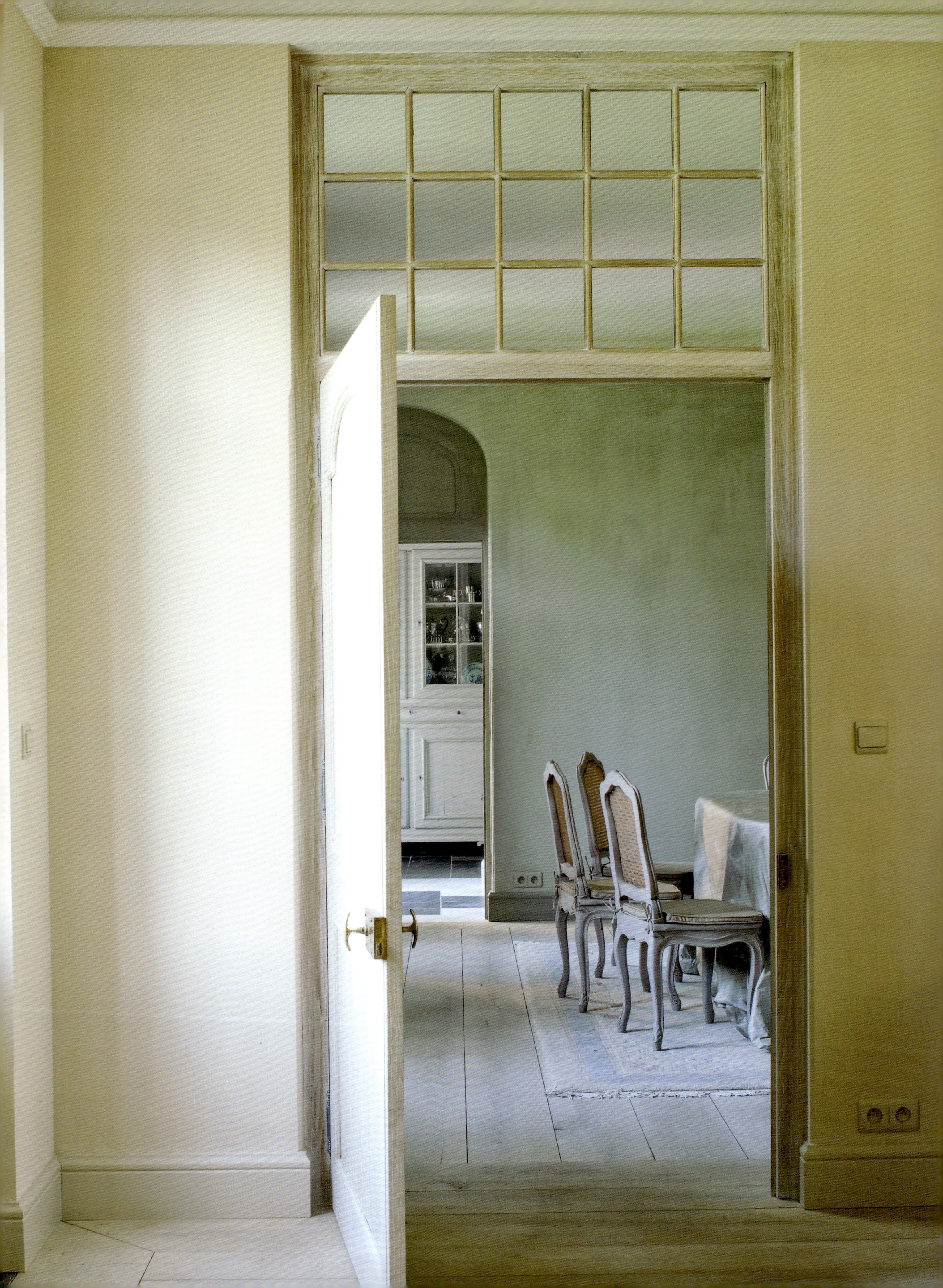

A harmony of limewashed walls, doors and an aged oak wooden floor.

42

Floors in reclaimed bluestone.

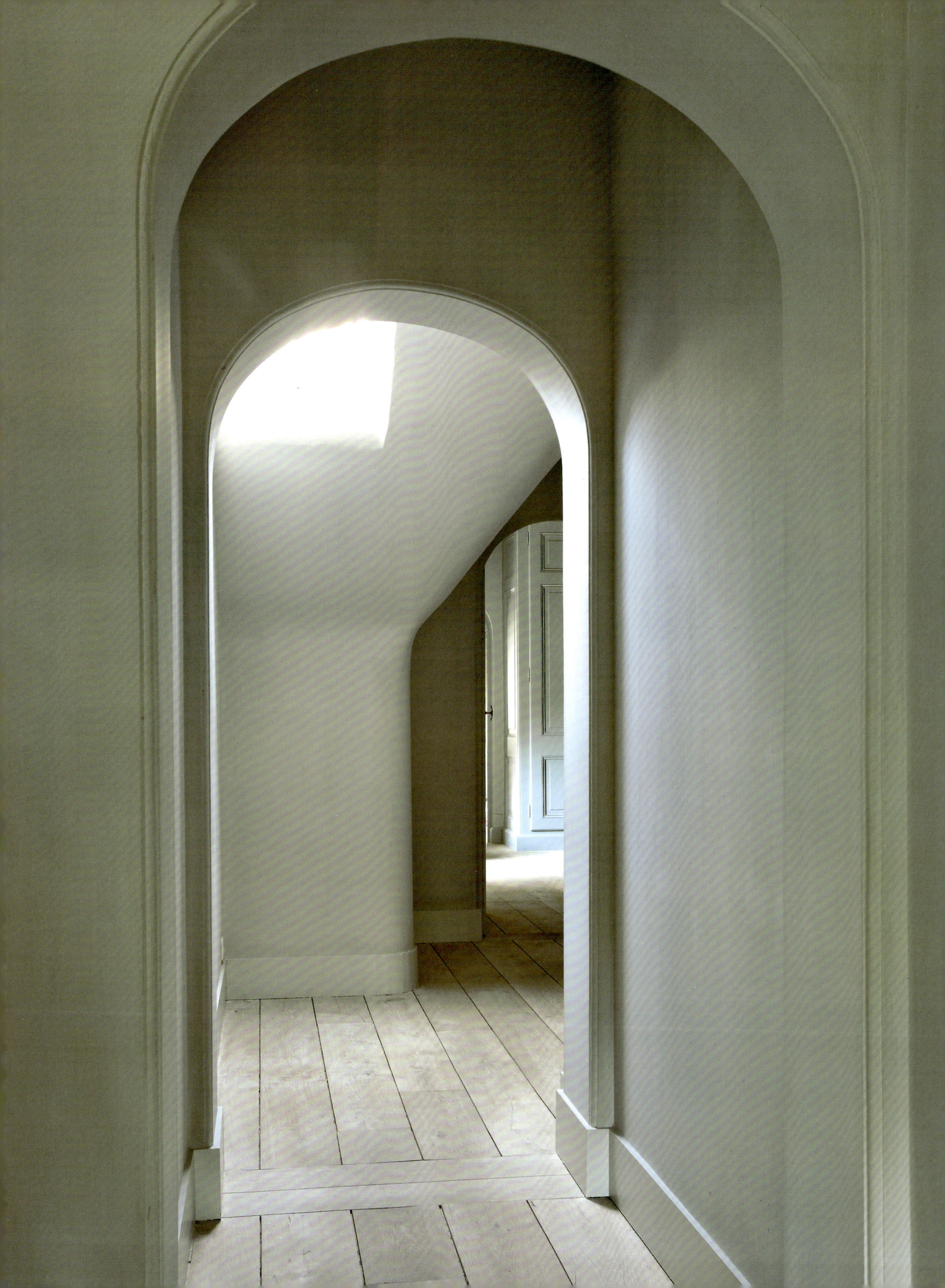

The upstairs corridor bathes in an atmosphere of monastic calm.
The oak planks have been given an aged grey finish here as well.

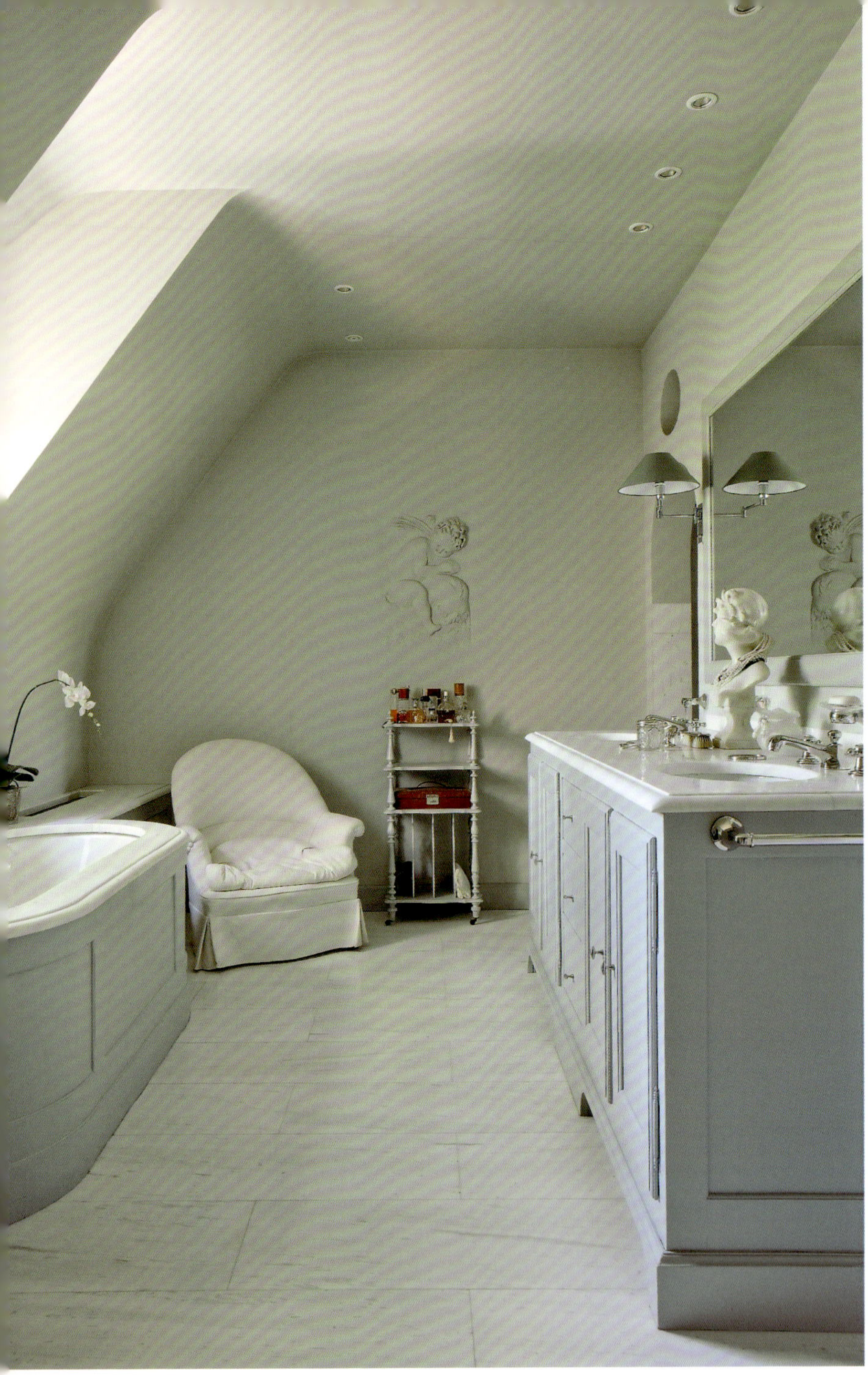

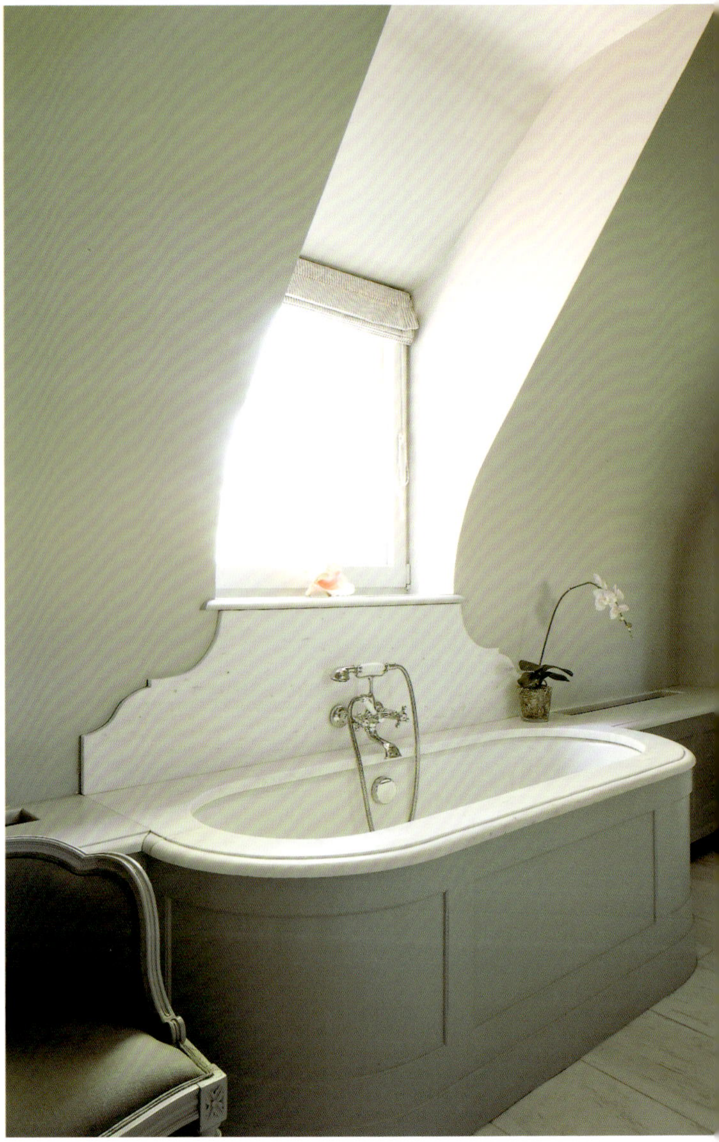

BOENS STEPHANE

Architect

    Latemstraat 118

    B – 9830 Sint-Martens-Latem

    T +32 (0)9 281 02 24

    F +32 (0)9 282 99 16

    stephane.boens@skynet.be

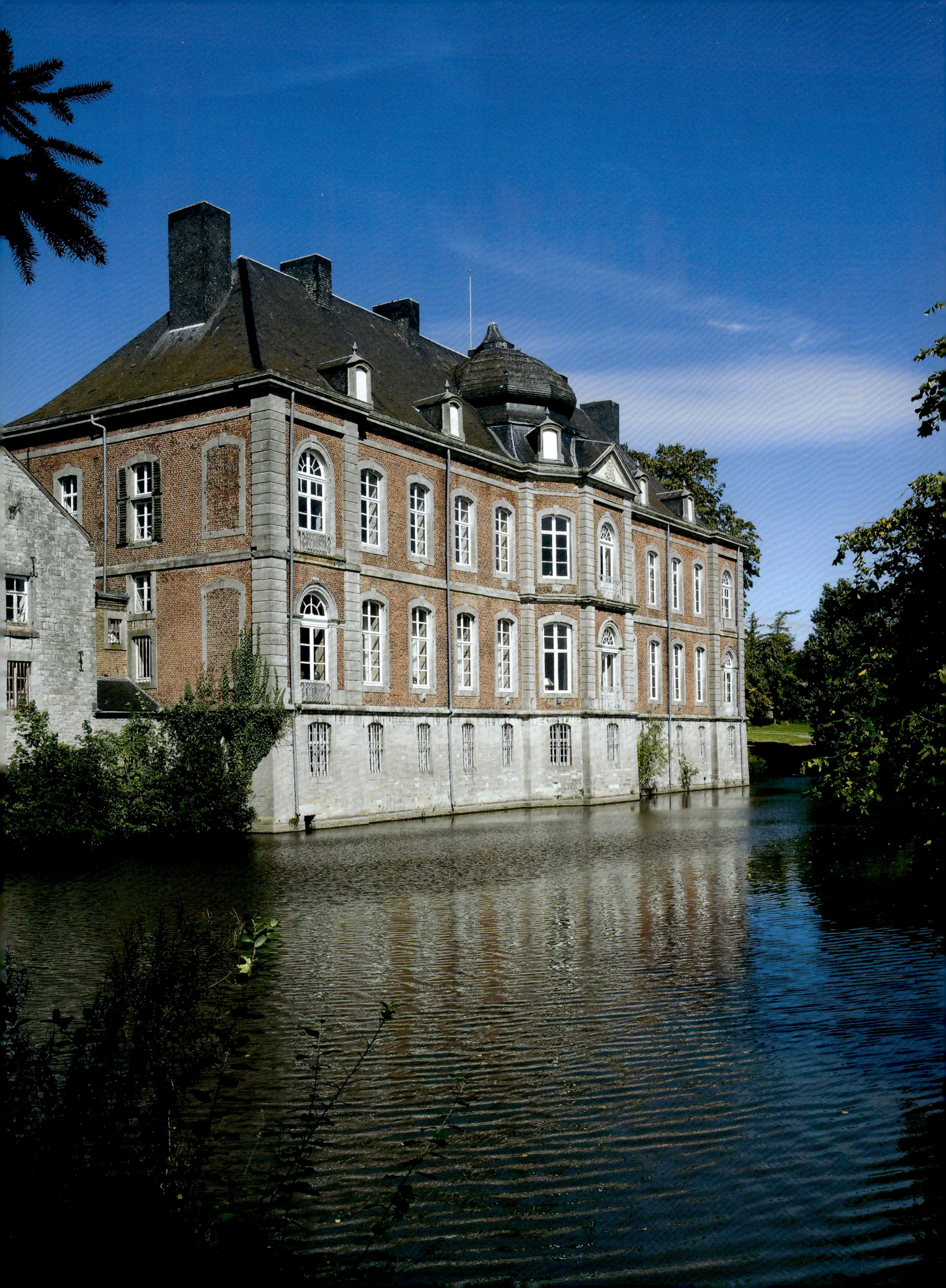

THE METAMORPHOSIS OF THE CHÂTEAU DE VIERSET

The Château de Vierset has an eventful history.
The building, a fortified castle and farm with four towers, was mentioned for the first time in 1090, under the name of "Versaih". It was torched by Prince Bishop Henri van Gelder and later, in around 1775, rebuilt by General de Billehé, knight of the Order of Malta and owner of the famous Vierset regiment, which was in Austrian service.
In 1818, the castle passed into the hands of François-Charles de Mercy-Argenteau, Napoleon's chamberlain. It remained in the family until 1877.
A number of different families subsequently owned the property: d'Overschie de Neerysche, Lamarche and Lamalle.

The current owner, René Bruggeman, an architect who is familiar with restorations, is very keen to carry out a lot of the work himself. He takes his quest for authenticity very seriously. His wife Marleen takes care of the decoration.

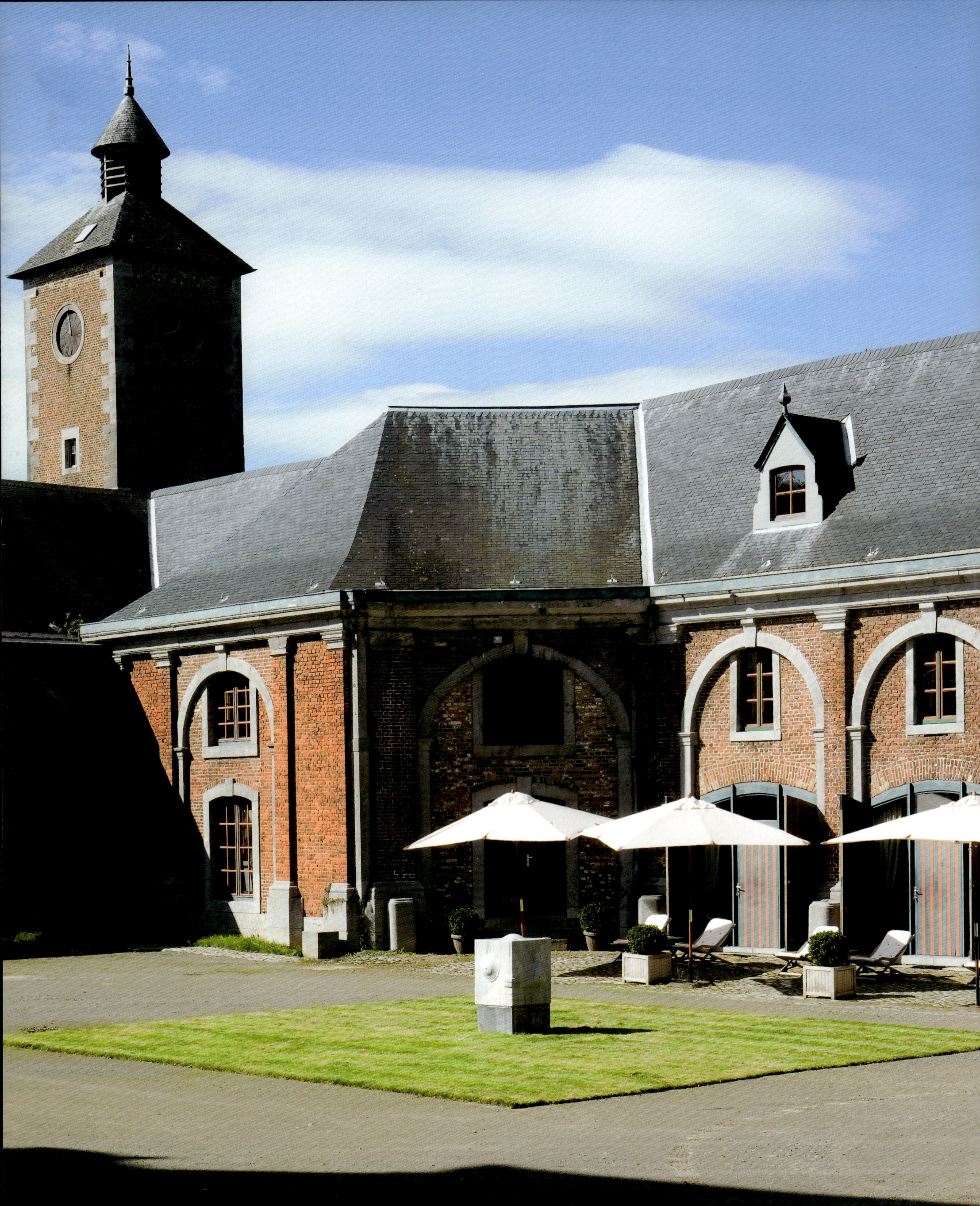

The Château de Vierset is a prestigious setting for business and leisure time, for bed and breakfast, events, seminars and cultural activities.

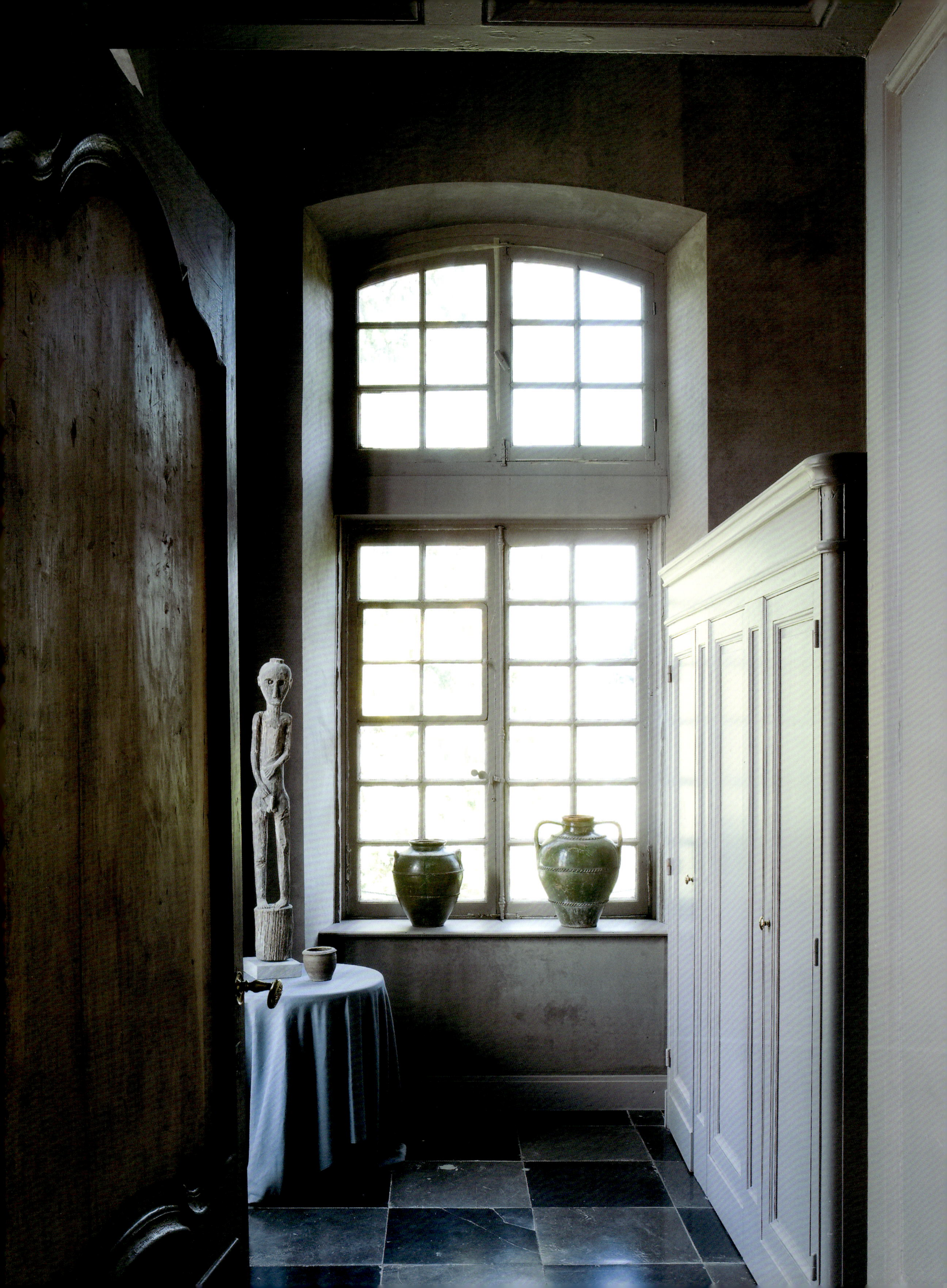

The salon with its authentic, ceiling-height panelling. The ceiling paintings were hidden beneath layers of paint: the owner, architect René Bruggeman, restored them and applied the gold leaf himself.

The oldest window in the castle. An old cabinet has been adapted to conceal the toilets.

A chessboard floor in Vinalmont and Basècle natural stone.

A number of sitting rooms in authentic materials. These rooms are set aside for seminars and other events.

The floor and kitchen work surface are in the same stone (Vinalmont), but with a time difference of 240 years.

55

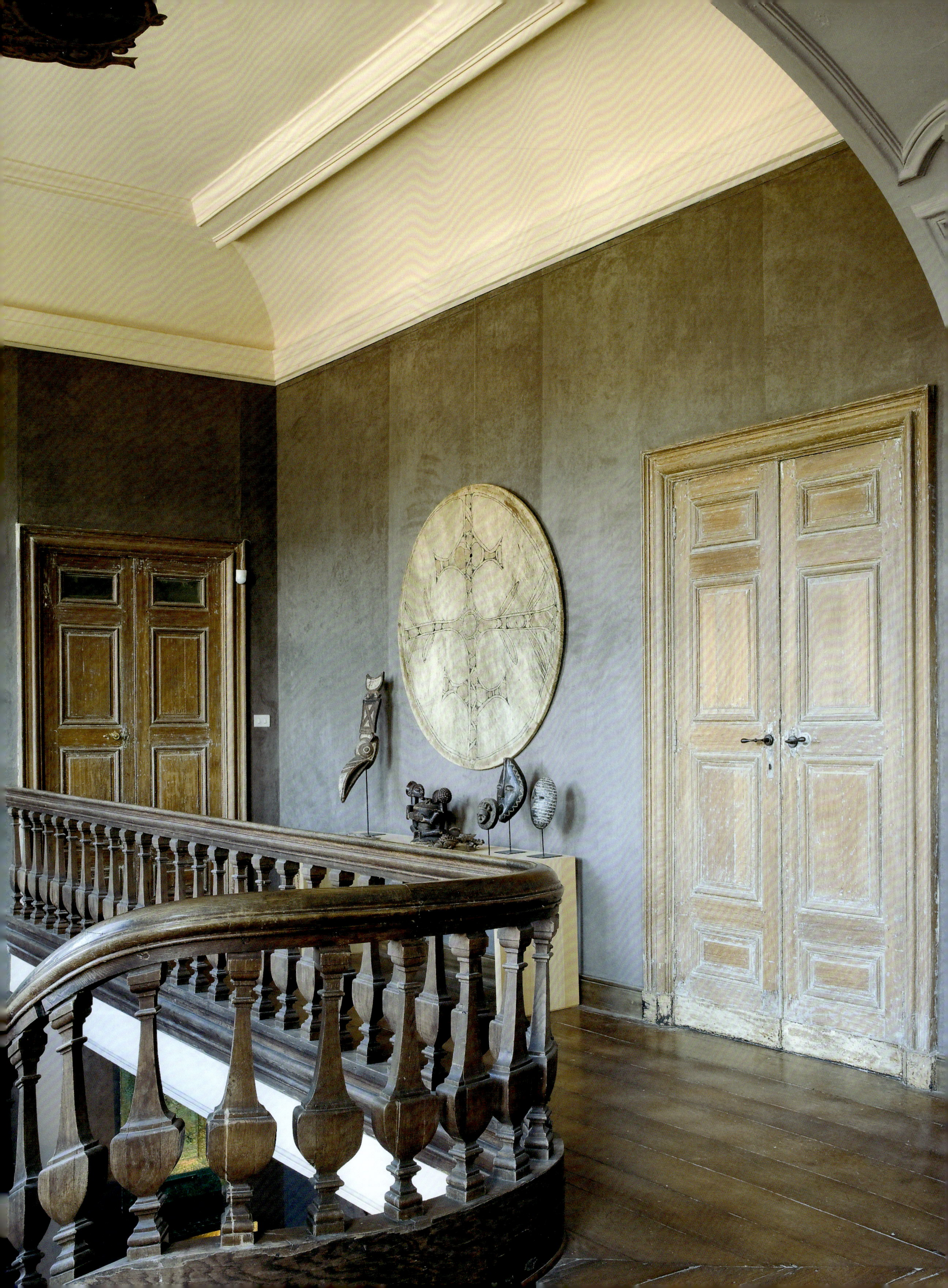

The hallway and the upstairs sitting room with fabric walls and ethnic art. Old Brazilian jugs on a table with an Indian oxcart as a base.

Salon with patinated panelling.

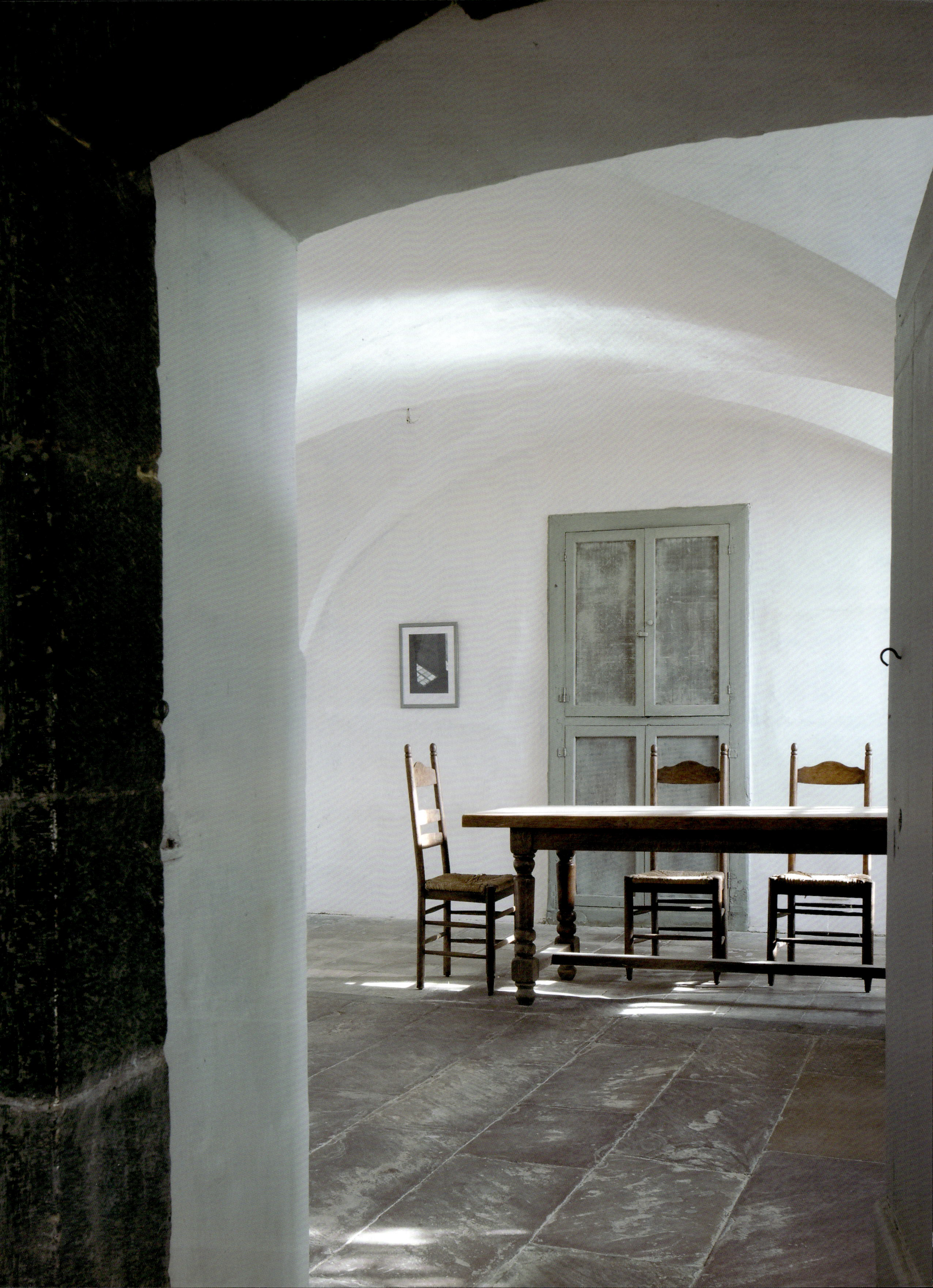

The historic eleventh-century cellars were transformed in the eighteenth century and have recently been thoroughly renovated for the organisation of events.

CHÂTEAU DE VIERSET
Rue la Coulée 1
B – 4577 Vierset
T +32 (0)85 41 01 70
F +32 (0)85 41 01 50
www.chateaudevierset.be

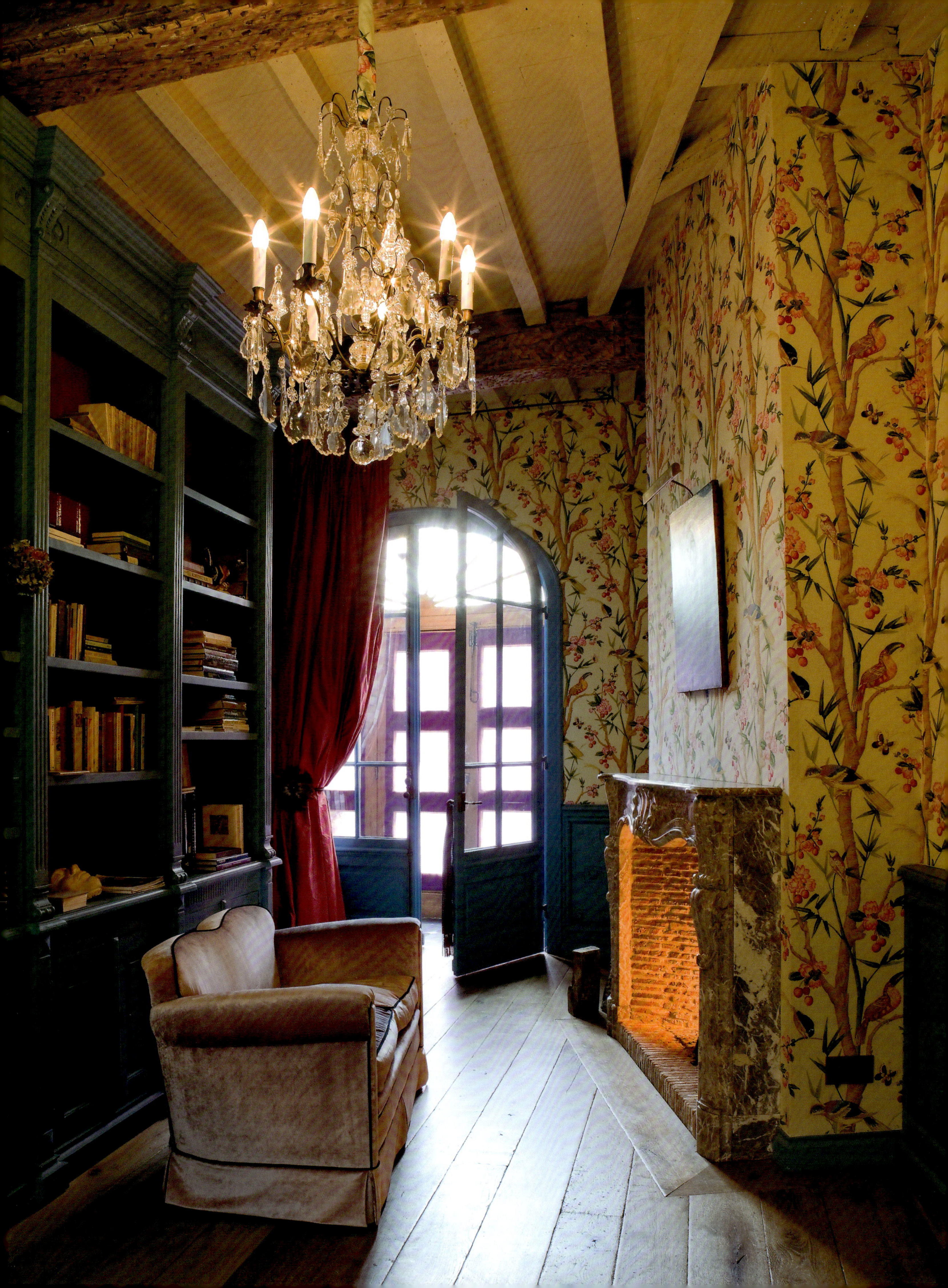

DISTINCTIVE TOTAL INTERIORS TAILORED TO THE CLIENT

In business for thirty years, Antiques & Design has grown to become the port of call for the renovation and adaptation of custom-made antique pine furniture.

This Kempen company's profile was raised after it provided interiors for the branches of the well-known bakery and café chain Le Pain Quotidien, including worldwide shops in the United States.
In recent years, Antiques & Design has increasingly focused on creating private interiors: from design to construction.

Every Antiques & Design interior is unique, whether it involves a kitchen, bathroom, dressing room, library or any other space. The combination of the client's wishes with the ideas of the design team and the use of one-off old elements lends each creation a personal, distinctive feel.

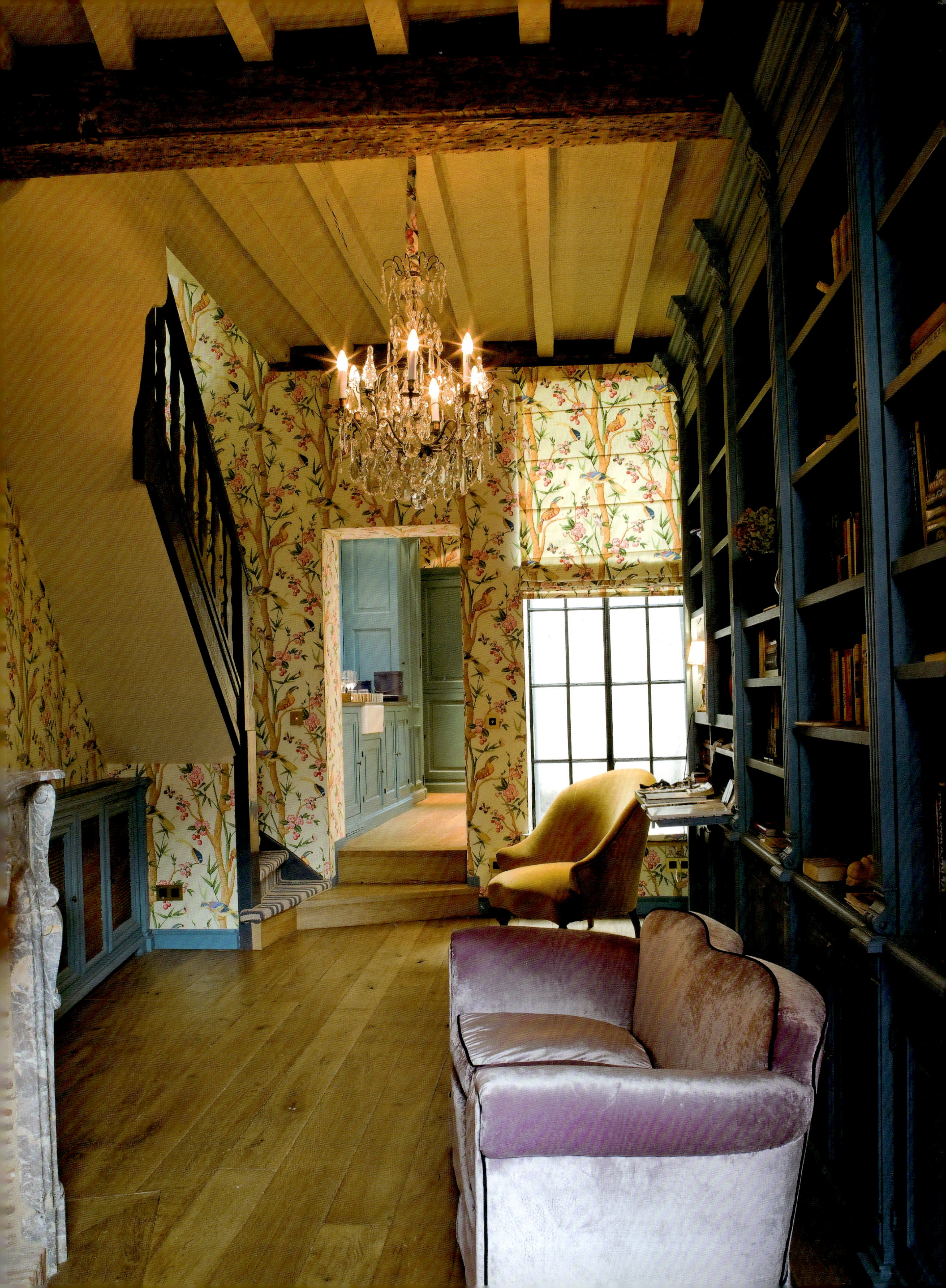

This project in the historic centre of Ghent perfectly displays the know-how of Antiques & Design: a harmonious combination of old and new elements, coupled with modern home comforts in a timeless setting.

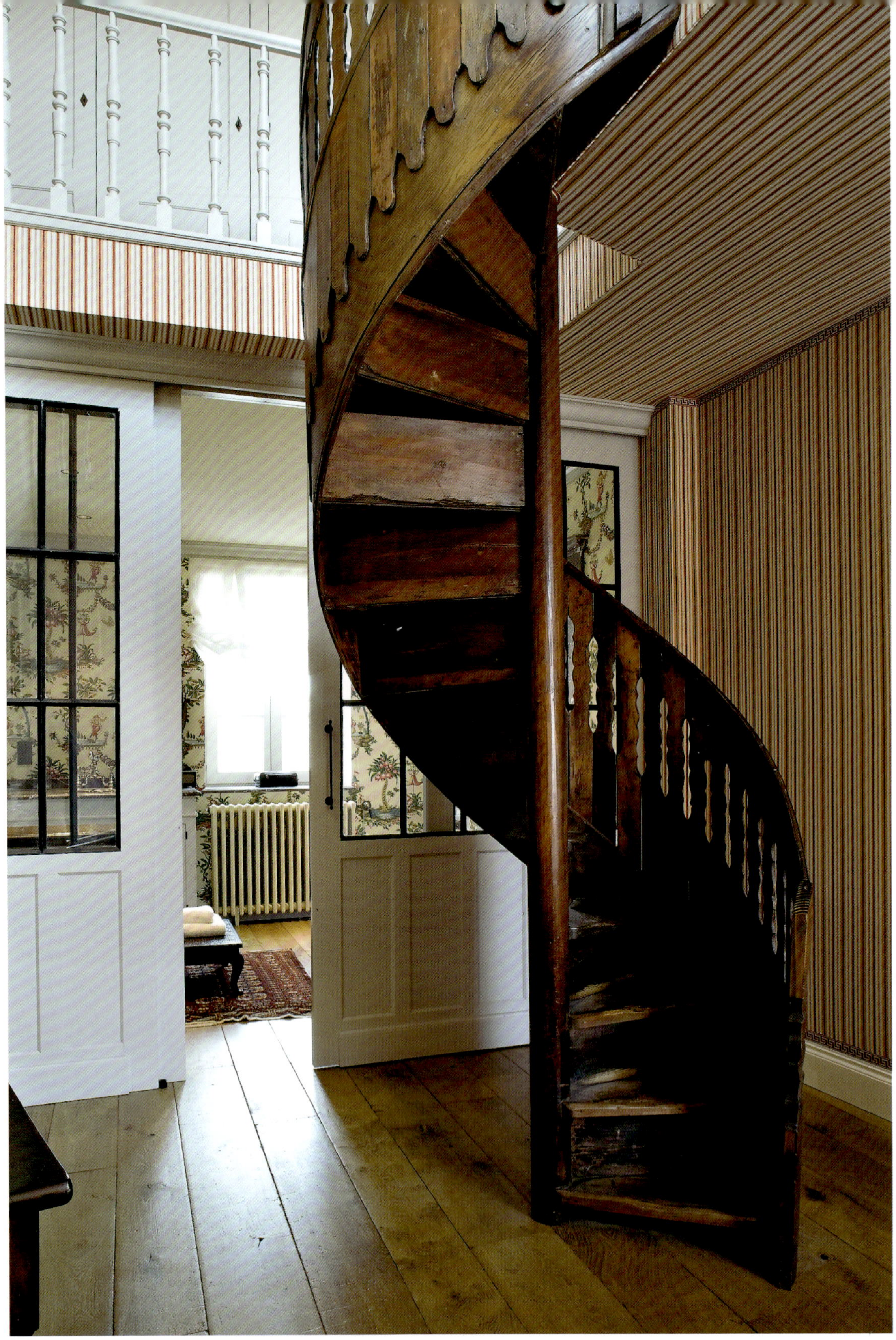

65

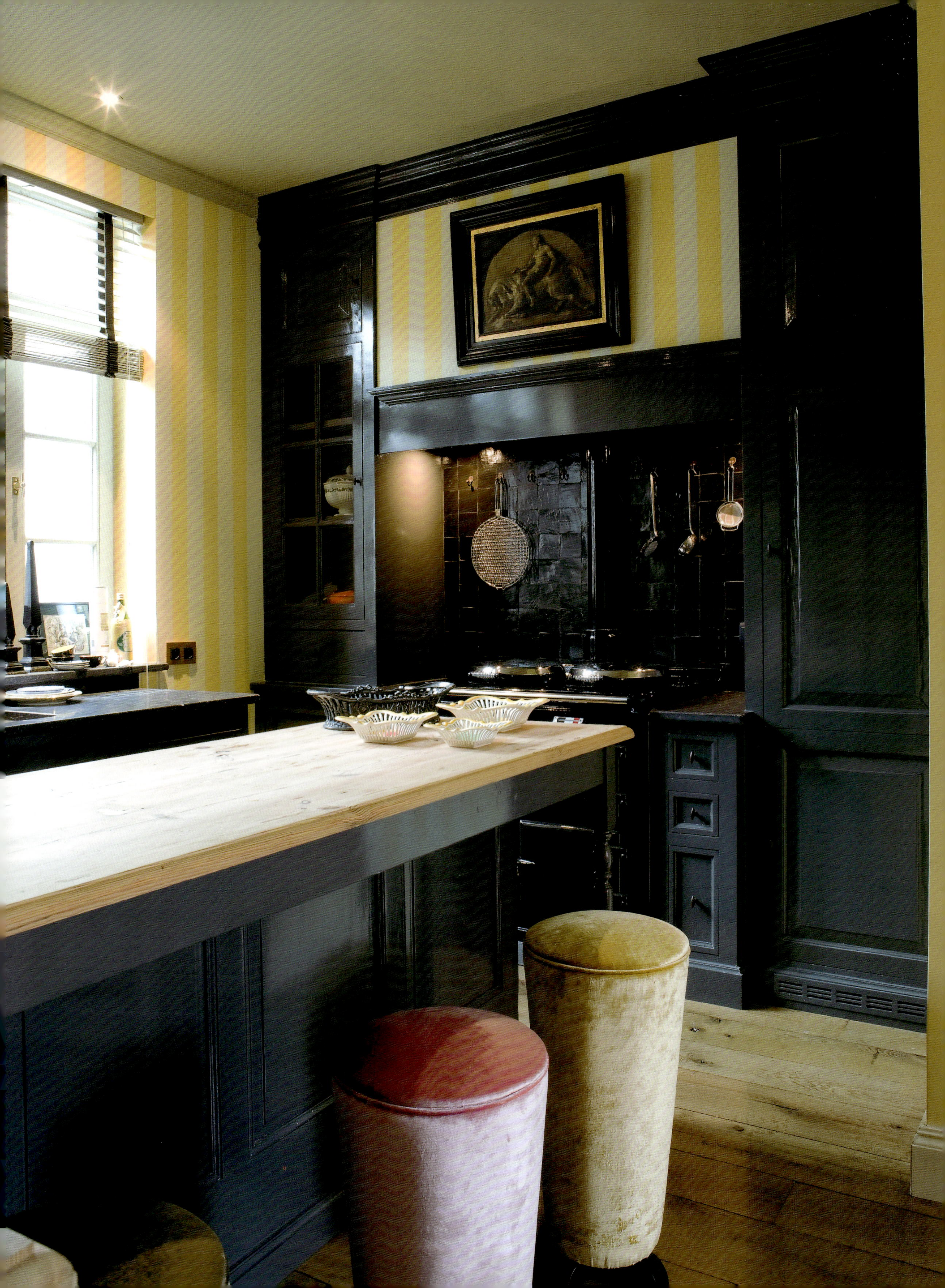

ANTIQUES & DESIGN nv
Karel Van Beek / Gert Verhees
Vossendaal 3
B – 2440 Geel
T +32 (0)14 58 42 42
F +32 (0)14 58 15 49
www.antiques-design.be
info@antiques-design.be

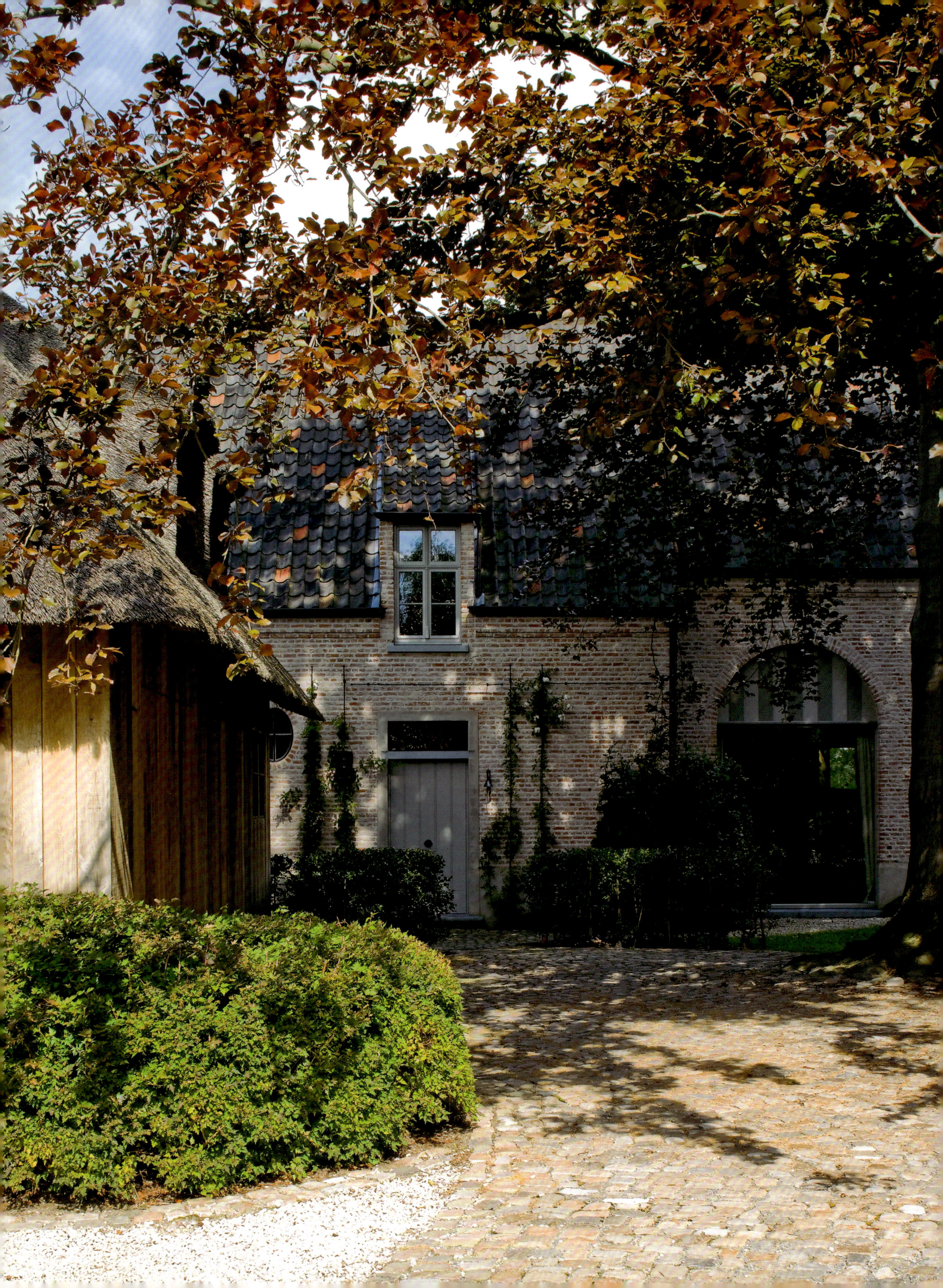

IN HARMONY

"Without emotion, there is no beauty" is the definition of elegance for the Themenos design studio.
The Themenos designers believe that a classic interior suits all kinds of architecture: the essential starting point should always be a house with good proportions, regardless of its size or style.

Houses can always be elegant if proper consideration is given to the use of the space: they should not contain too many things, and the pieces that are chosen should harmonise with each other and with the home.

To create a successful combination, it is essential to find the theme running through the property itself and the desired look. Oak wood is often the perfect basis for a project when there is a need for warmth and cosiness. This is not only true of the plain wood: oak also retains its warm character when it is painted.

The Themenos design studio does not create interiors with one single style.
Home surroundings are, after all, a reflection of the life of the people who live there. The important thing is to ensure that the interior design is in harmony with the owners.

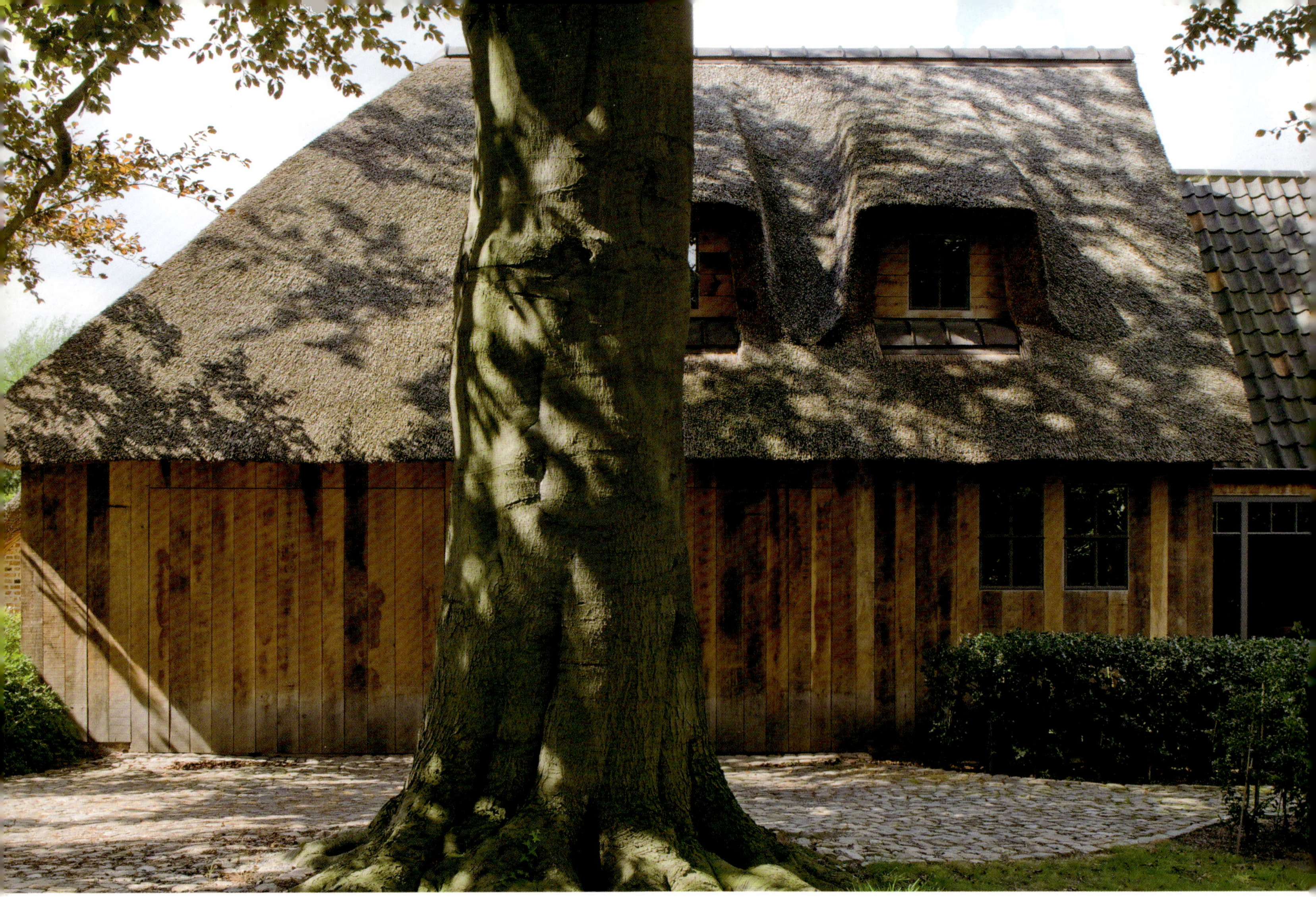

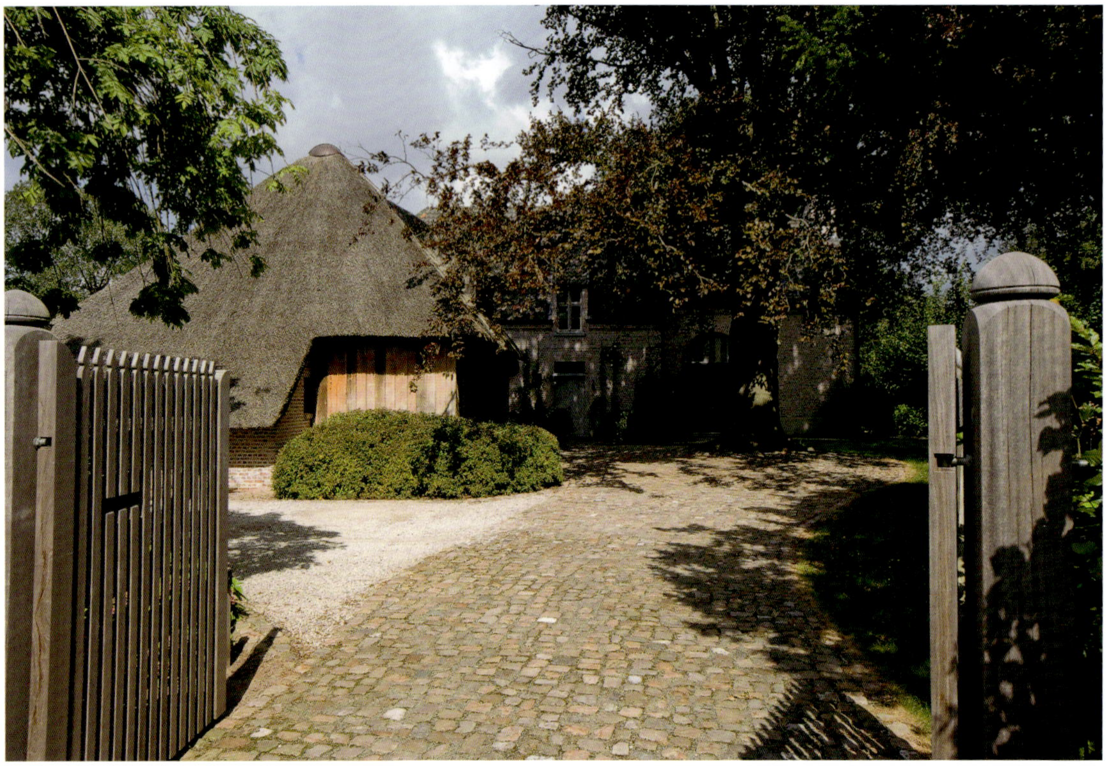

71

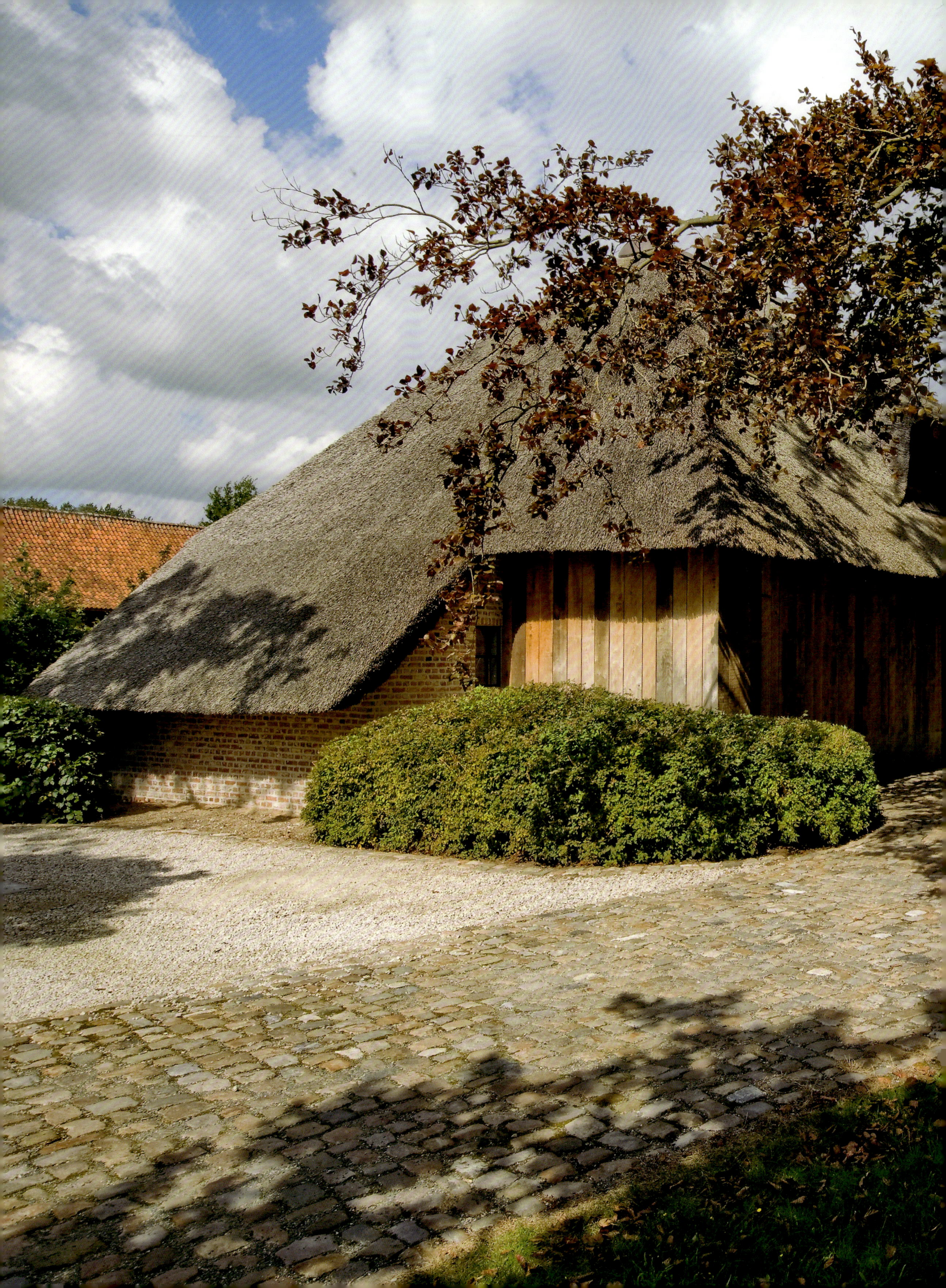

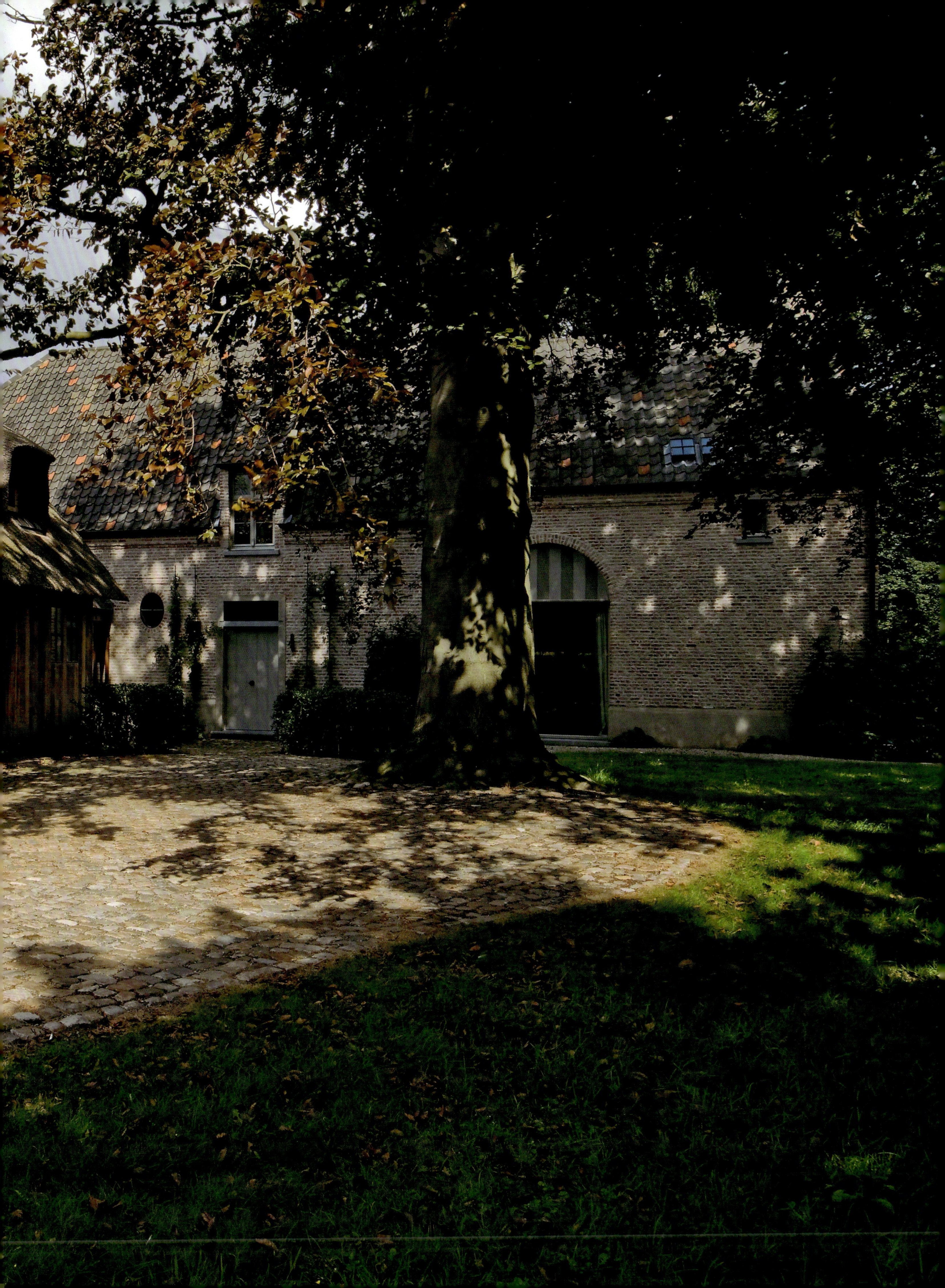

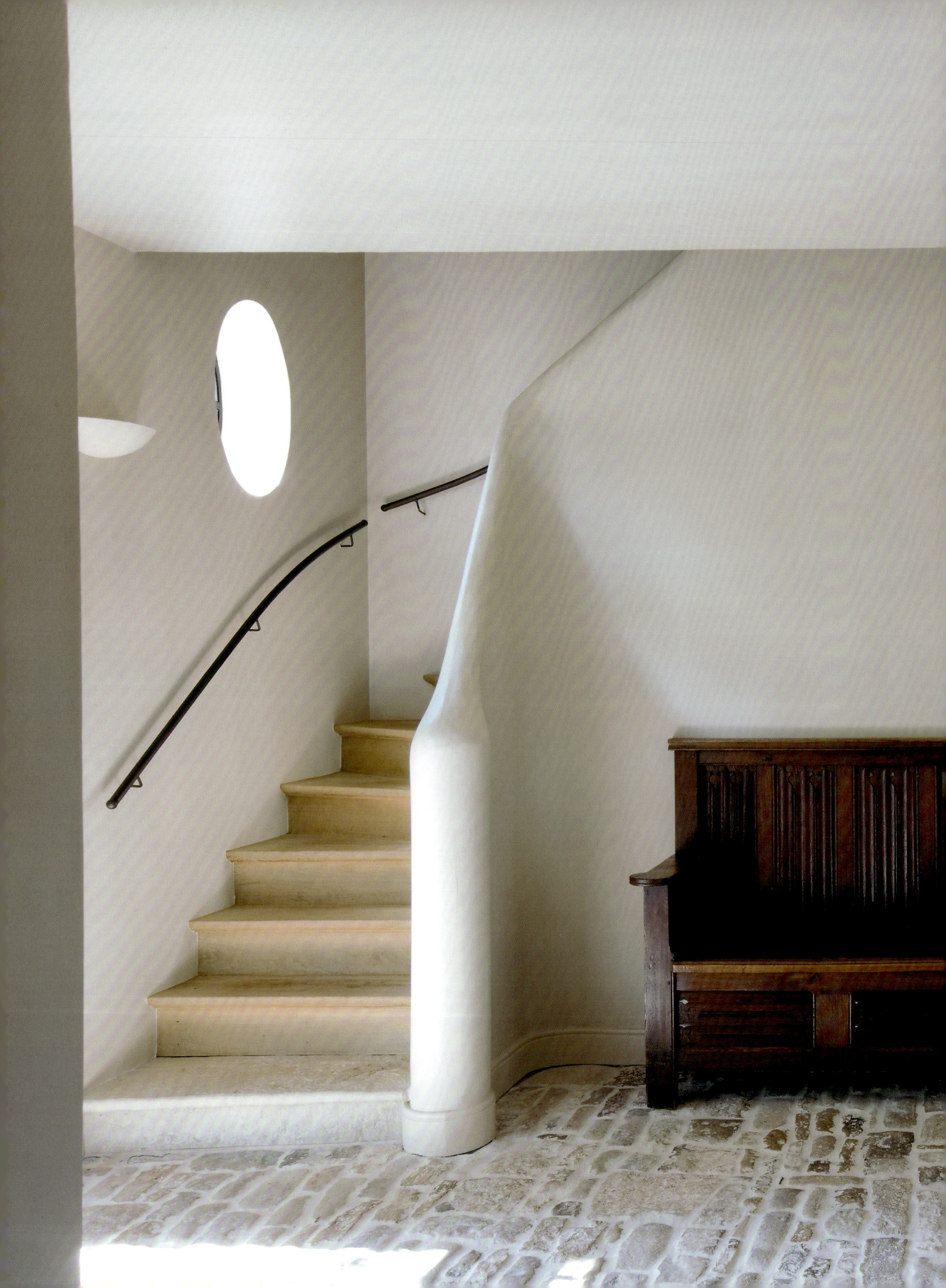

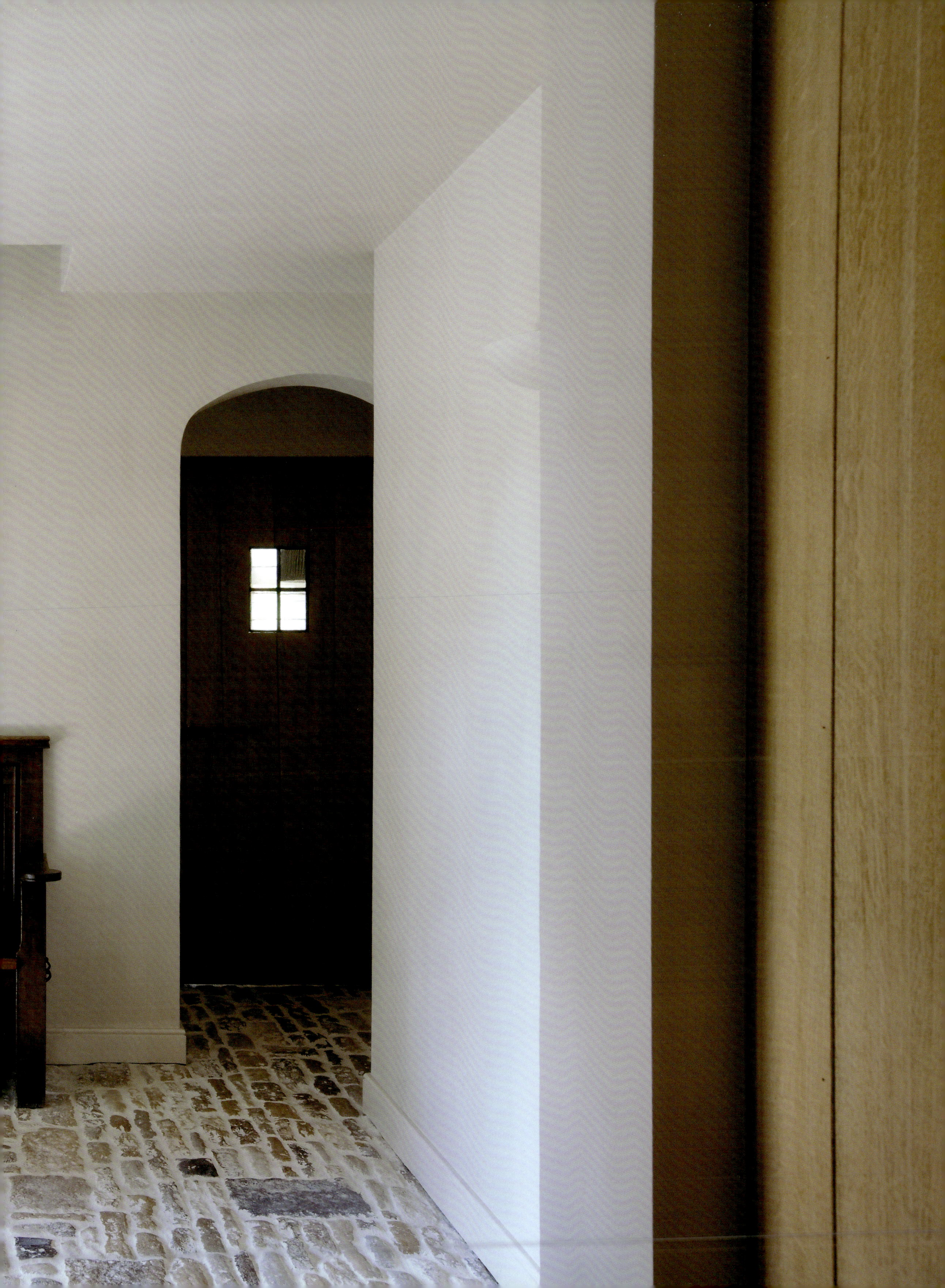

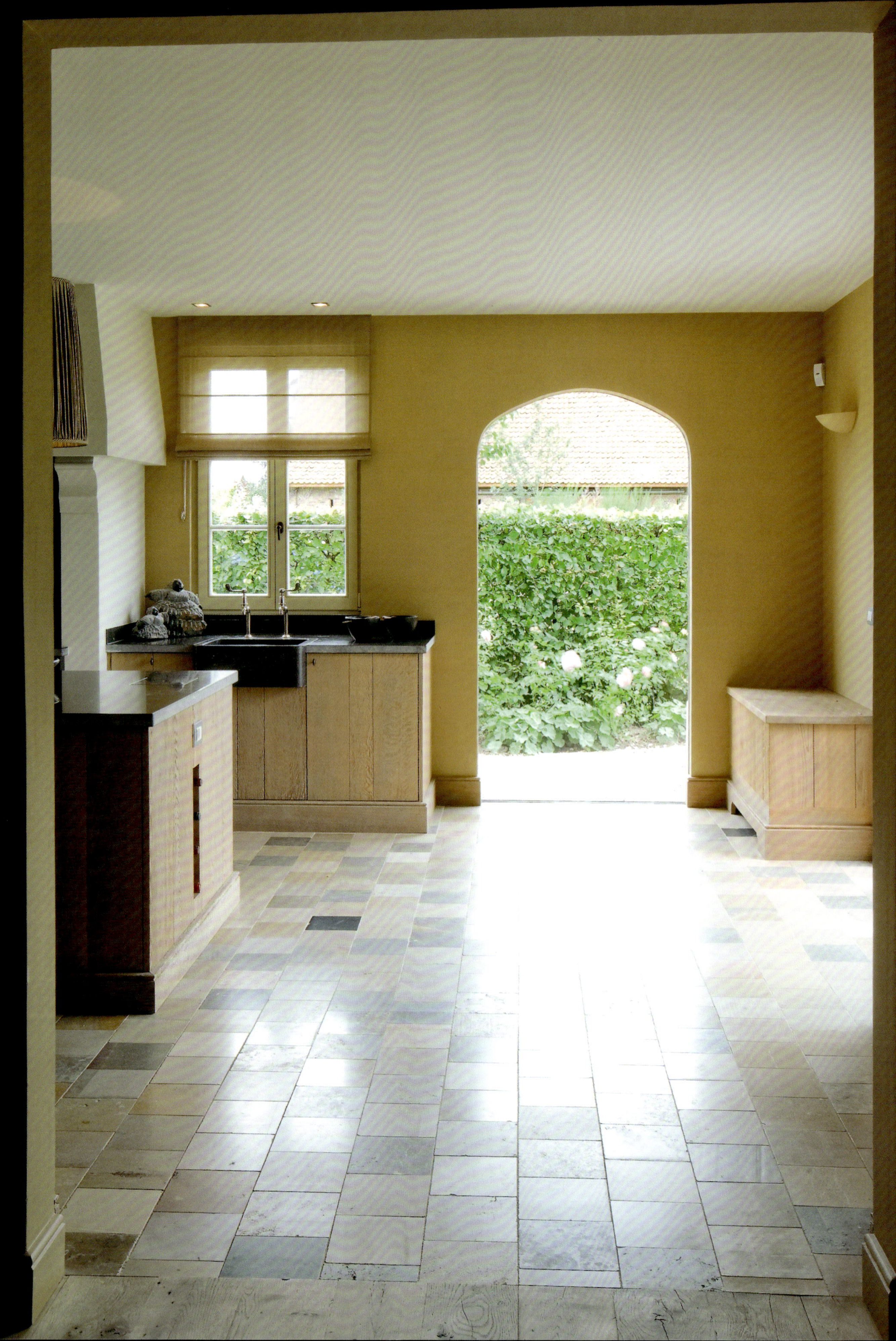

THEMENOS cvba
  Sint-Jansvliet 8
  B – 2000 Antwerp
  T +32 (0)3 248 49 93
  F +32 (0)3 248 56 23
  www.themenos.be

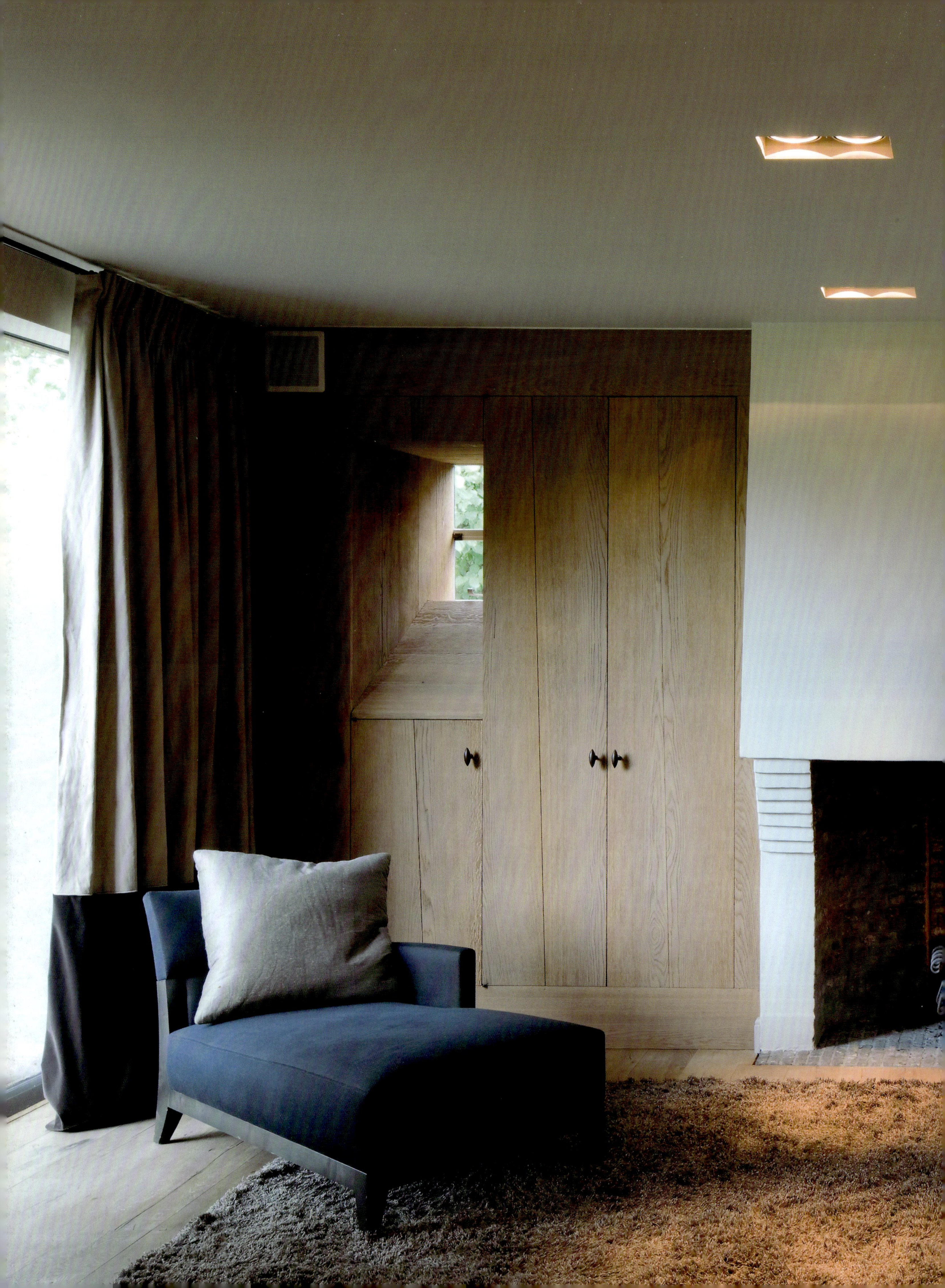

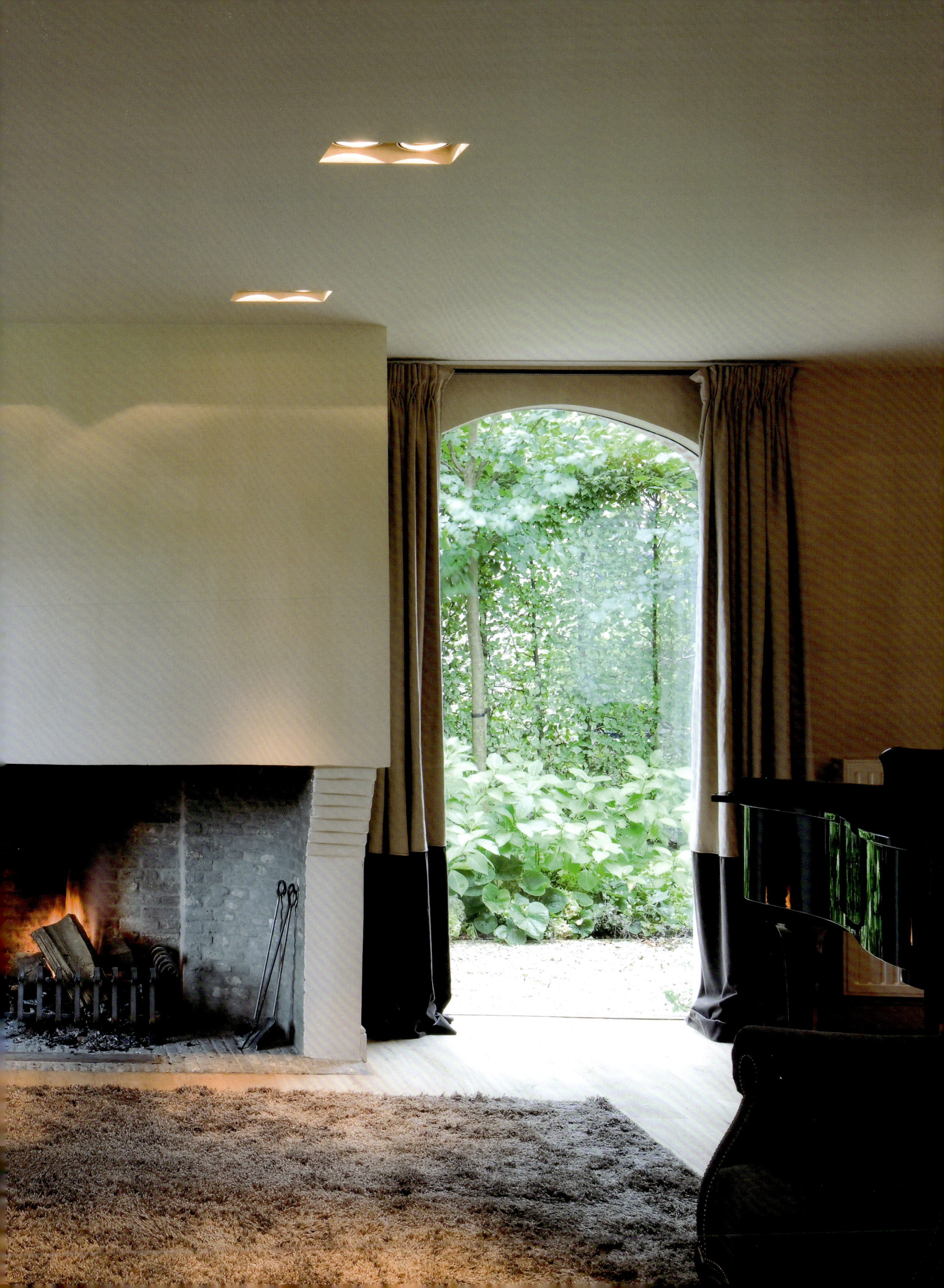

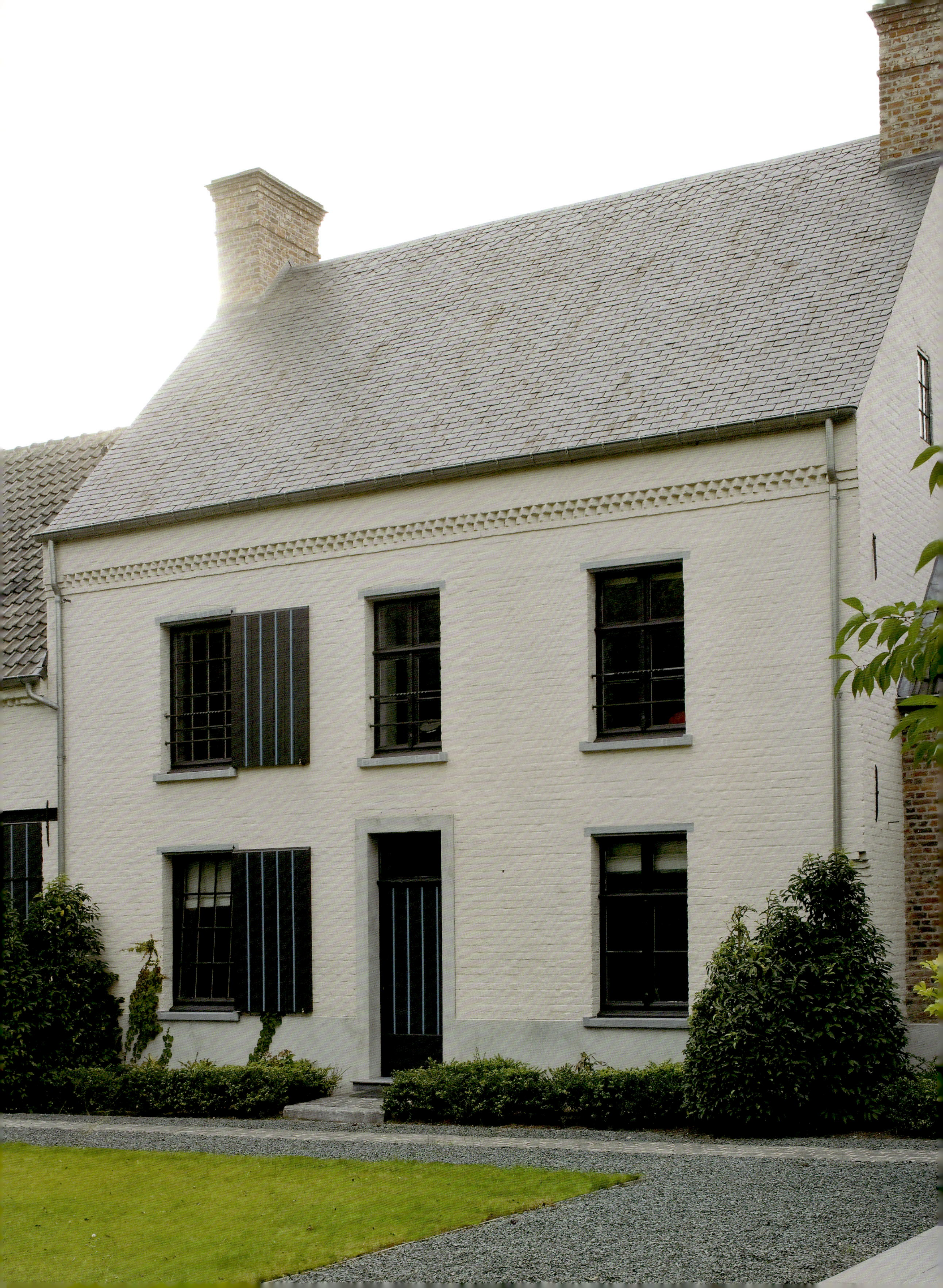

INTERIOR AND EXTERIOR UNITE TO FORM A WHOLE

The Themenos architectural studio was set up in 2002, based on the principle that the dynamic of a group is more than the sum of the individuals.
Architect Bart Pycke brought together interior architects Pascale Broos, Stijn De Cock and Dimitri Bratkowski. The interplay between interior and exterior is of prime importance to this group of designers, even after more than five years.

The added value of the group lies mainly in its creativity, which leads to an enhanced interaction between architect, interior designer and client.

The name Themenos is an allusion to ancient Greek architectural texts and may be loosely translated as "the most beautiful place in a home", perfectly reflecting the projects created by this studio.
To achieve the desired result, it is of course first necessary to create a setting into which this space can be incorporated. This architectural partnership therefore aims to deliver complete projects in which interior and exterior unite to form a whole.

The project in this report is a striking illustration of their approach.

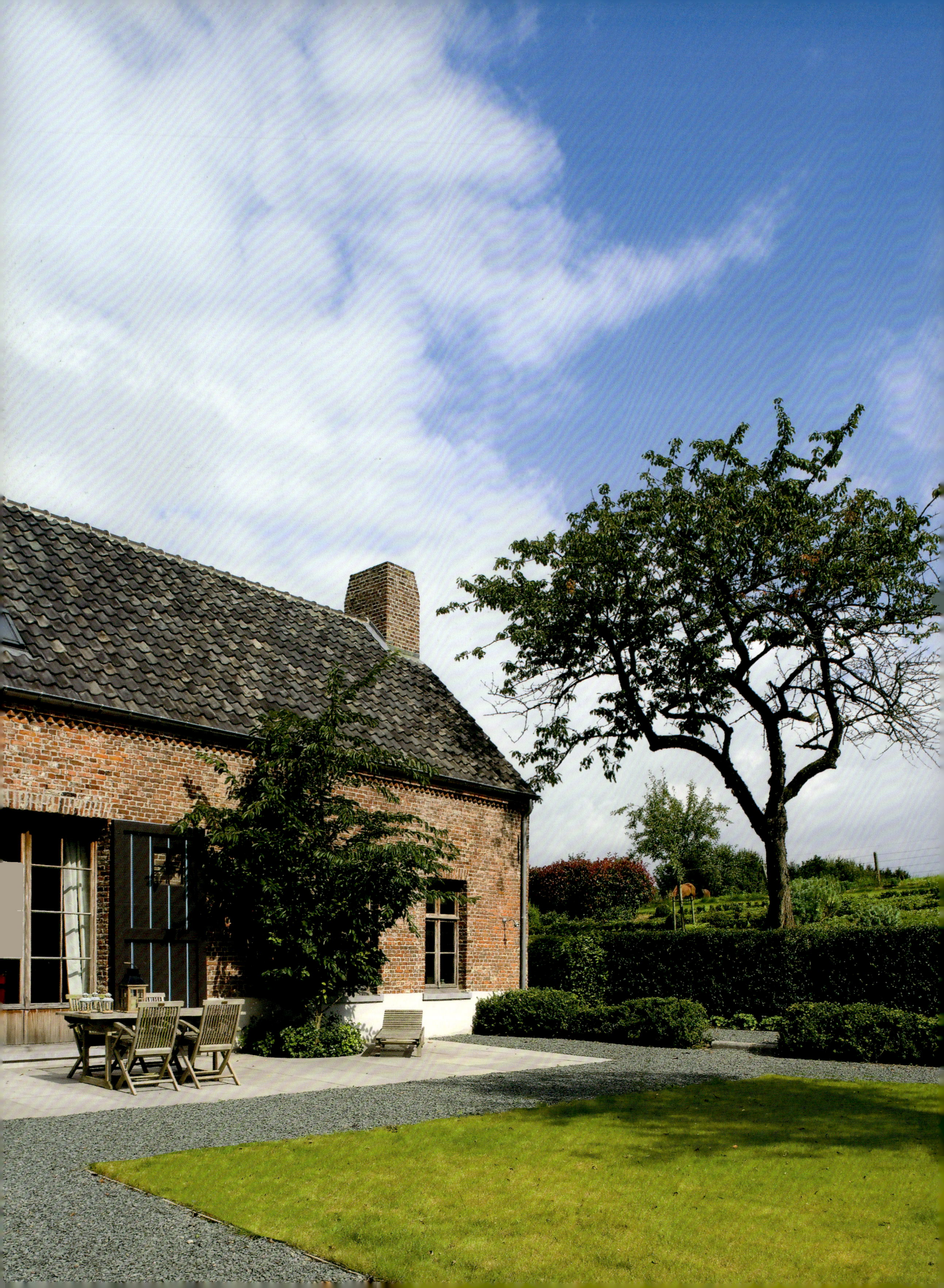

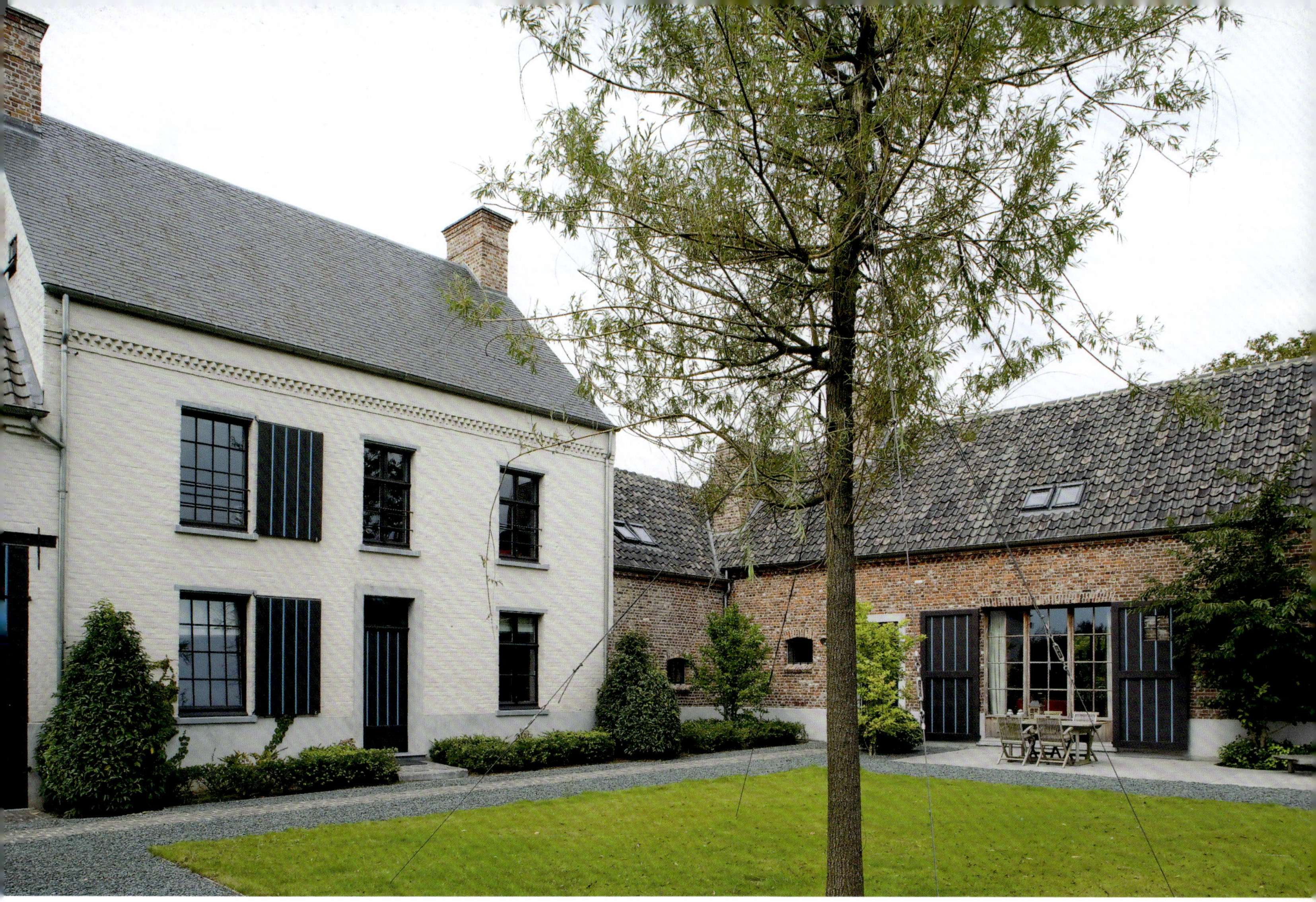

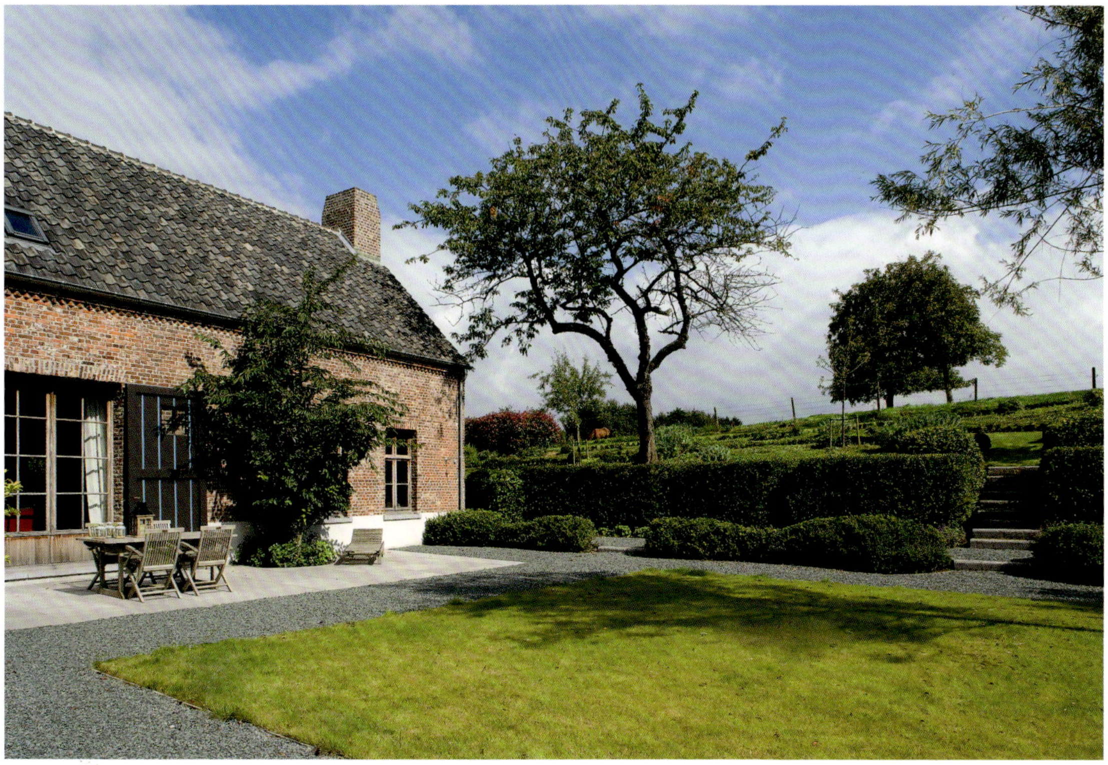

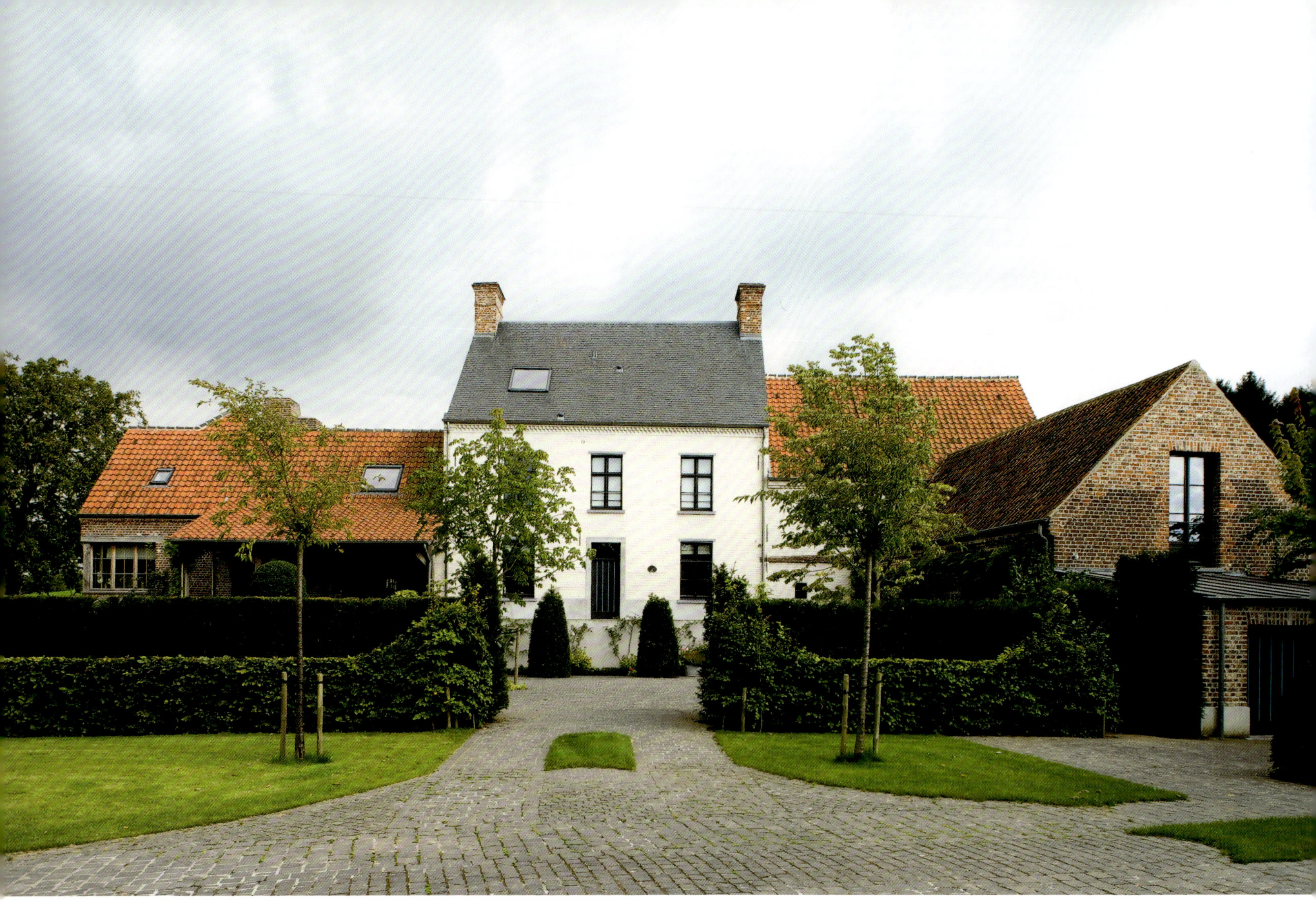

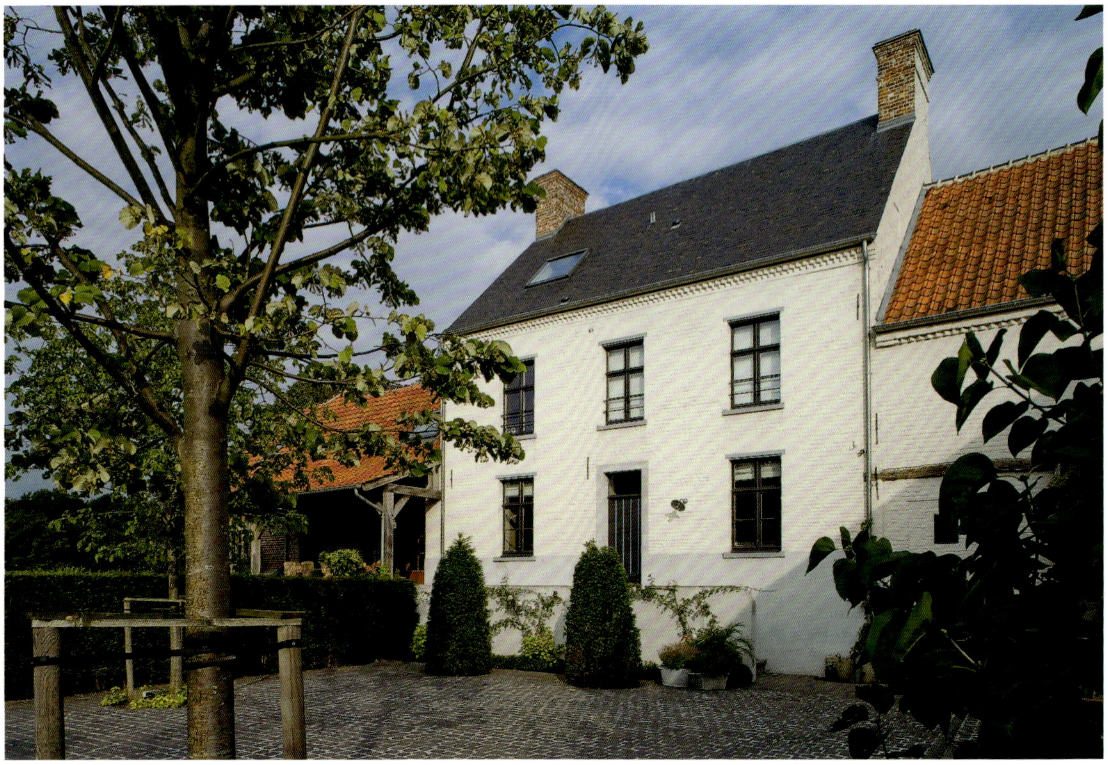

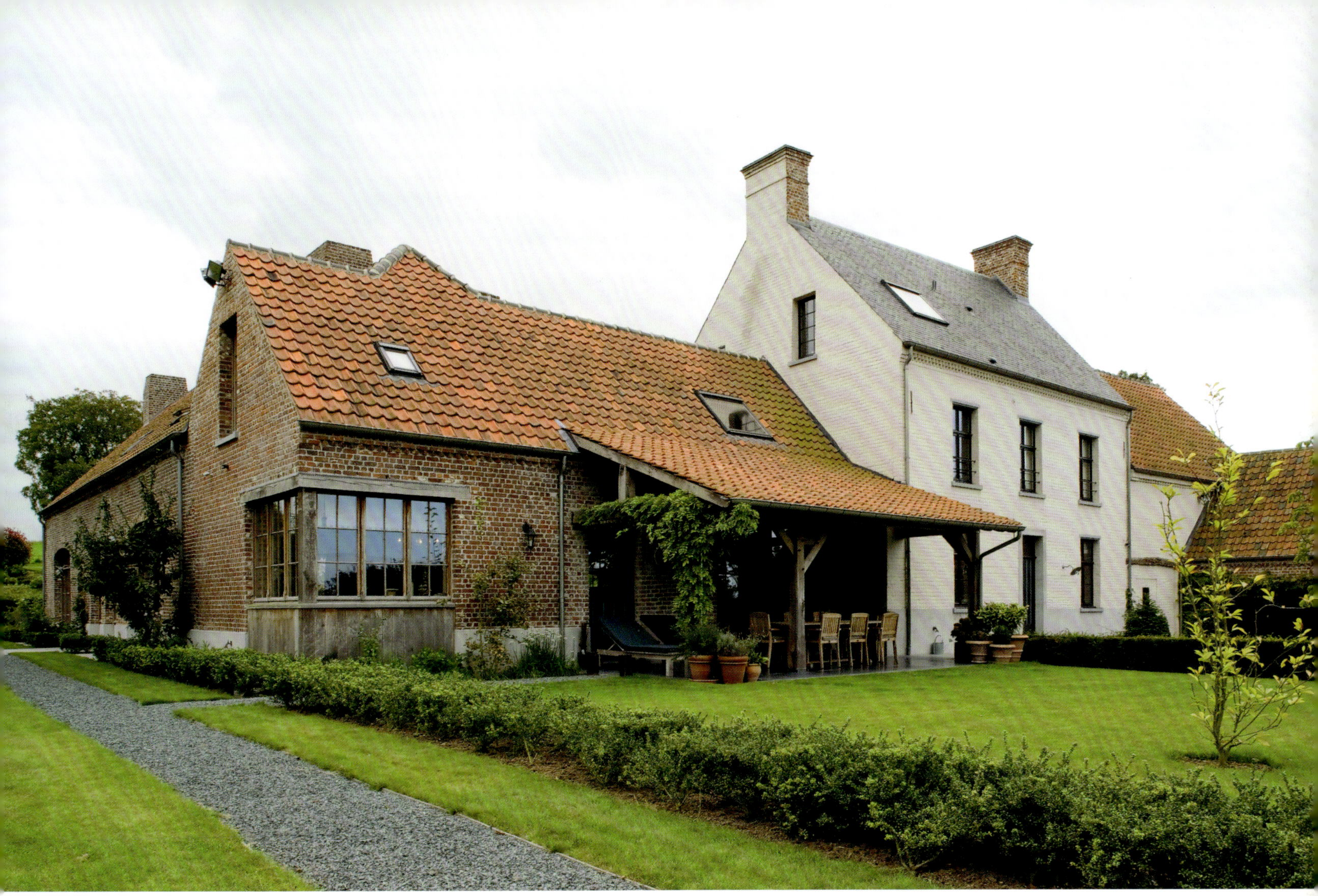

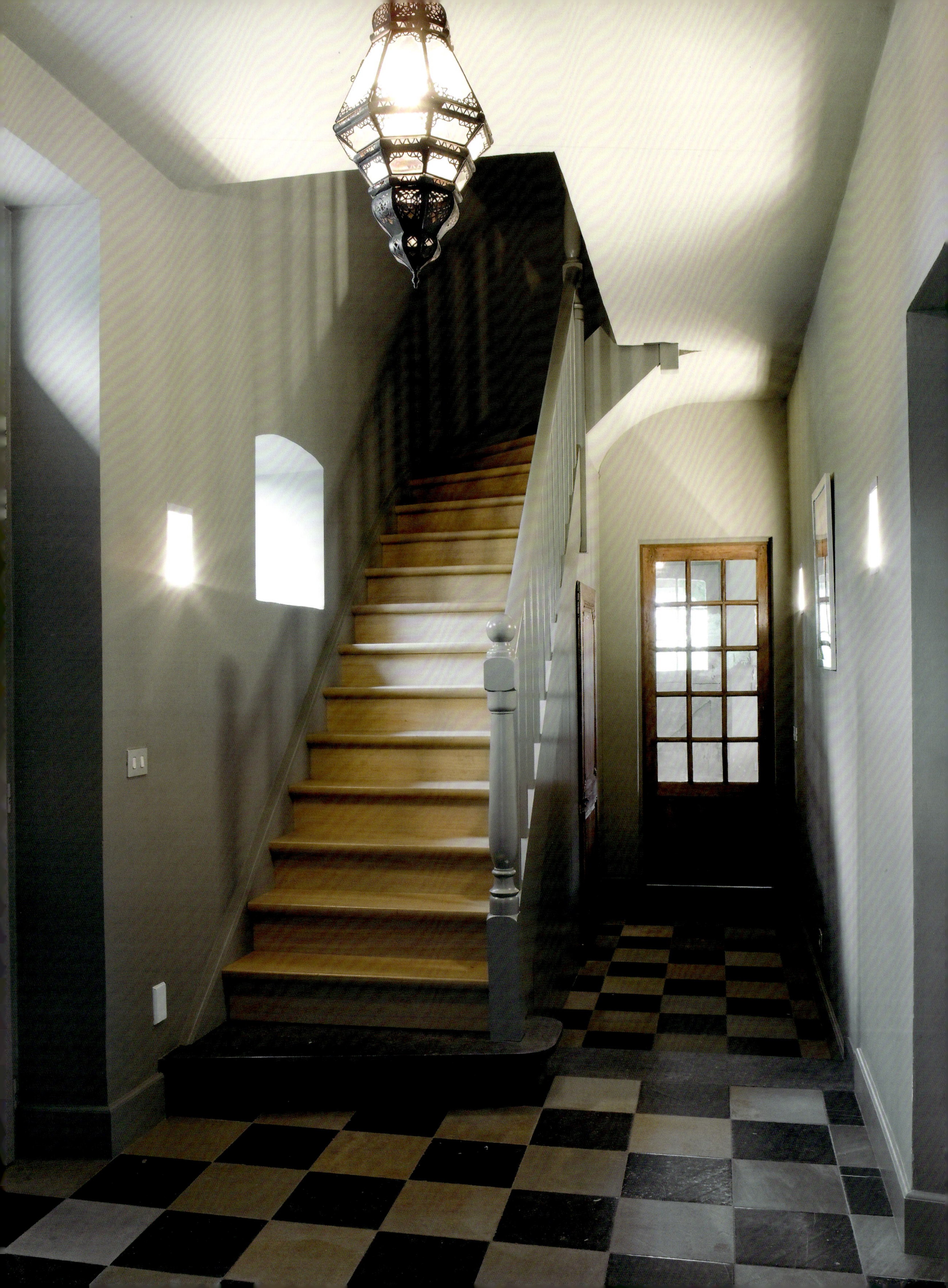

87

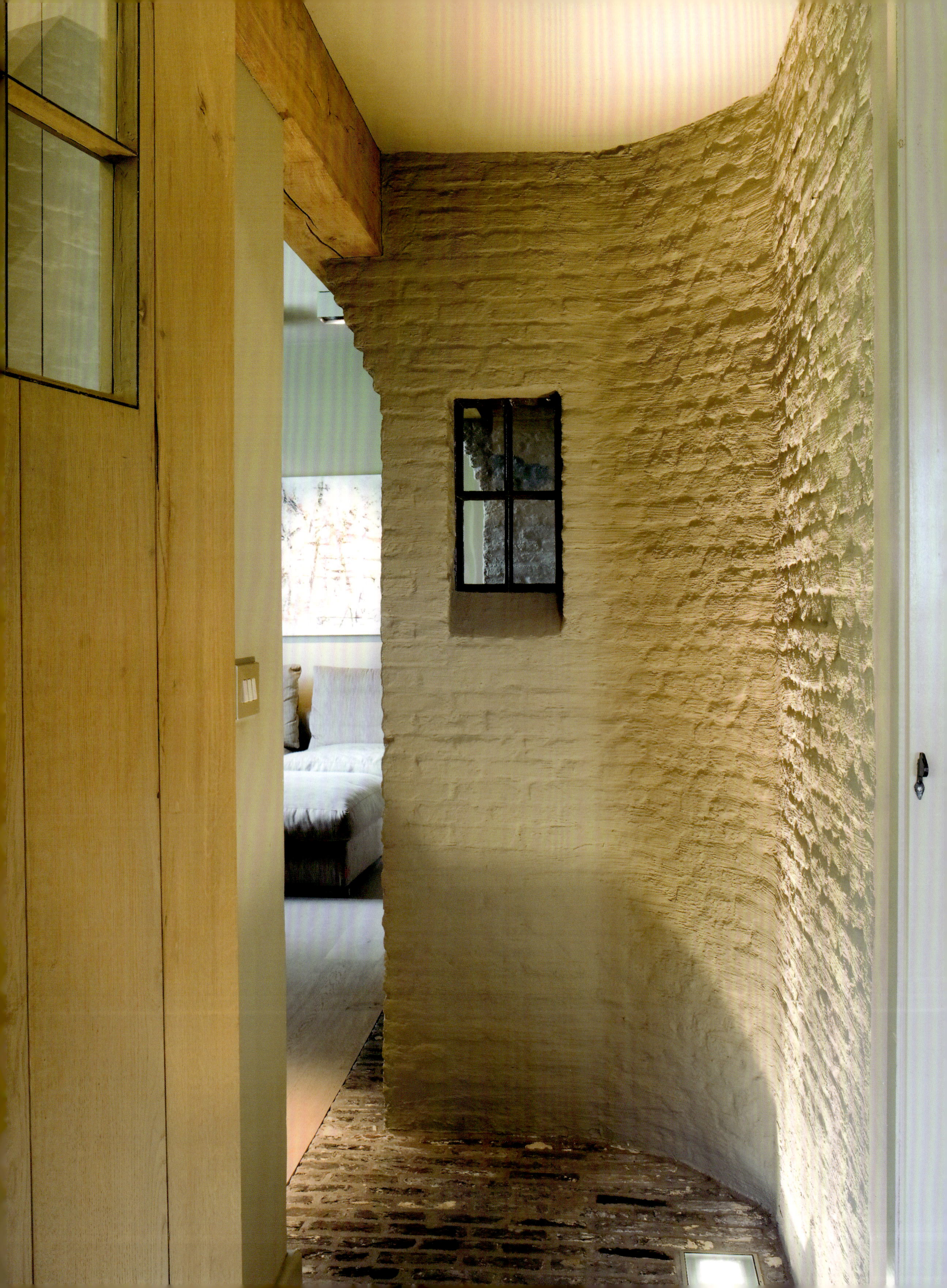

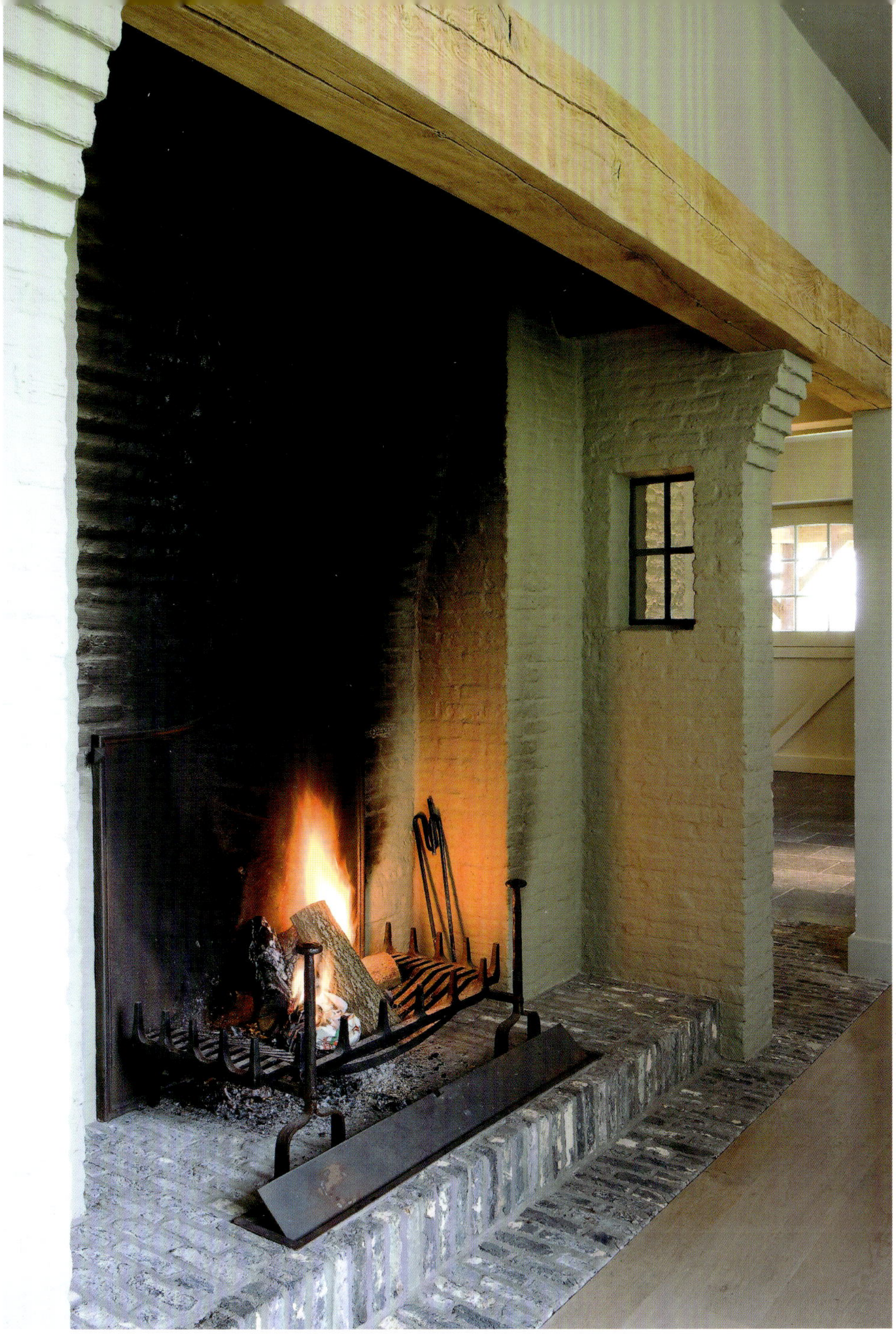

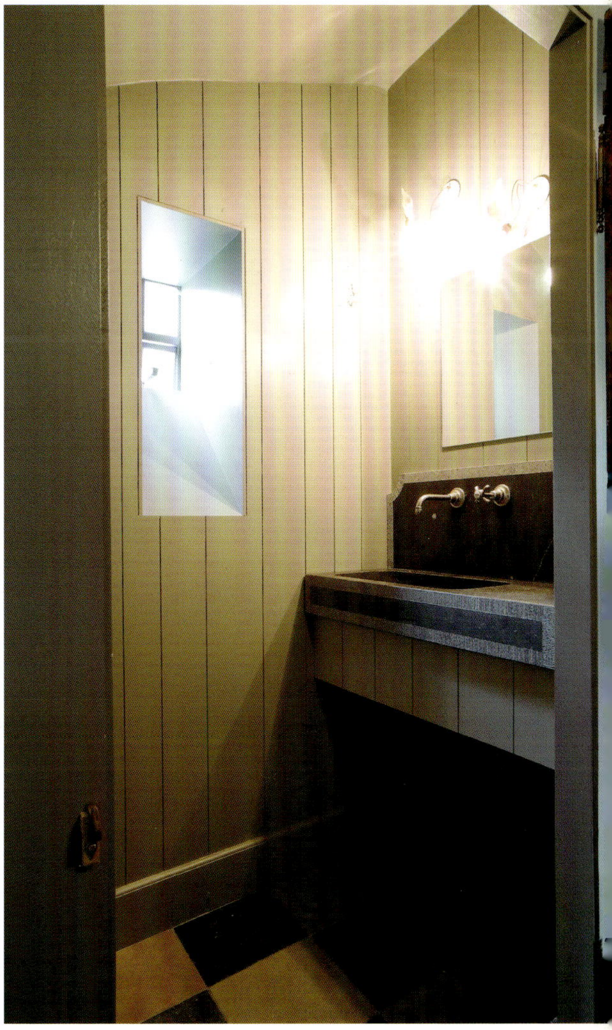

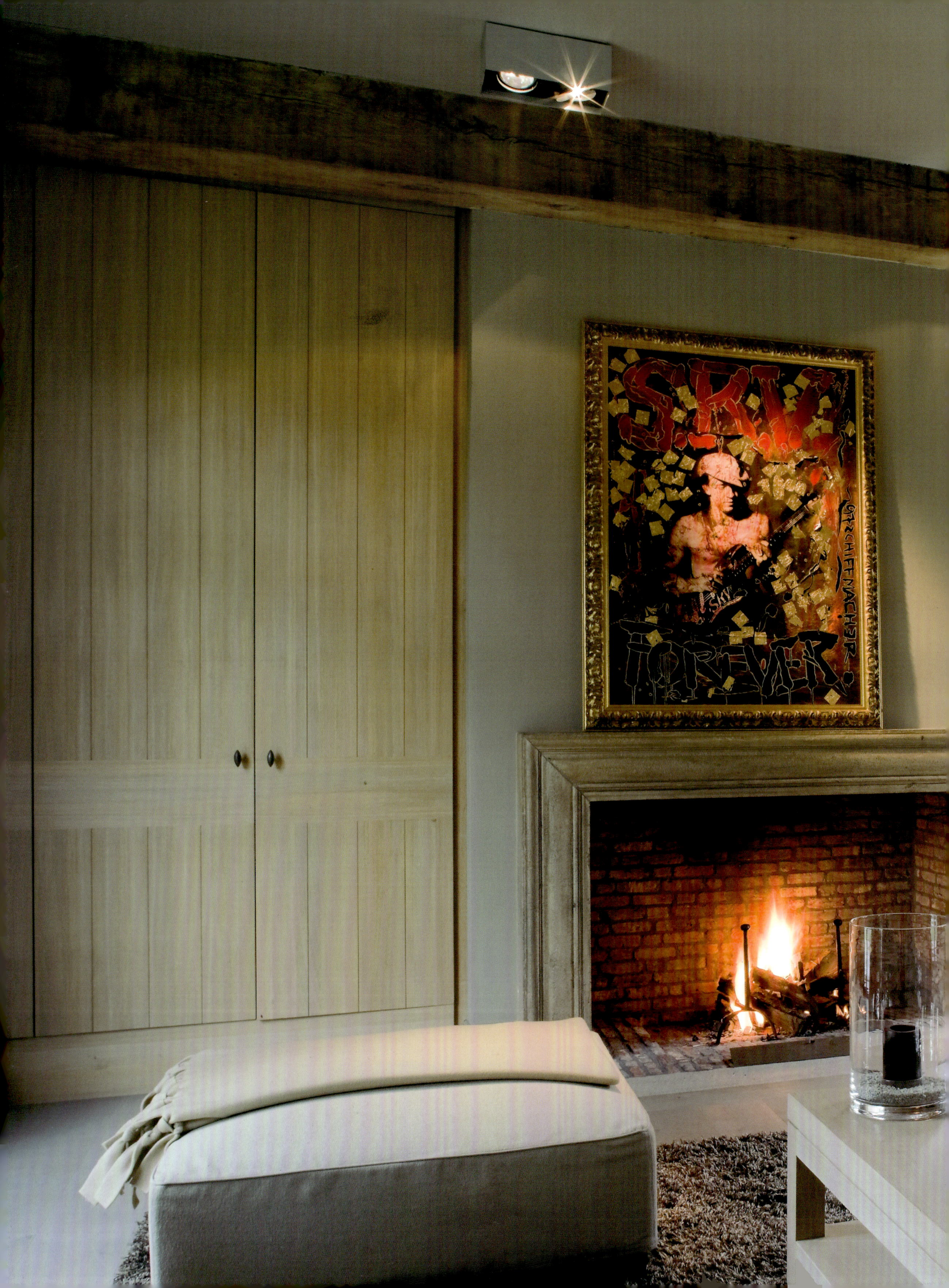
FOREVER.

MAGRITTE
MERCATOR
LE SPECTACLE DE LA TERRE
DE AARDE VANUIT DE HEMEL

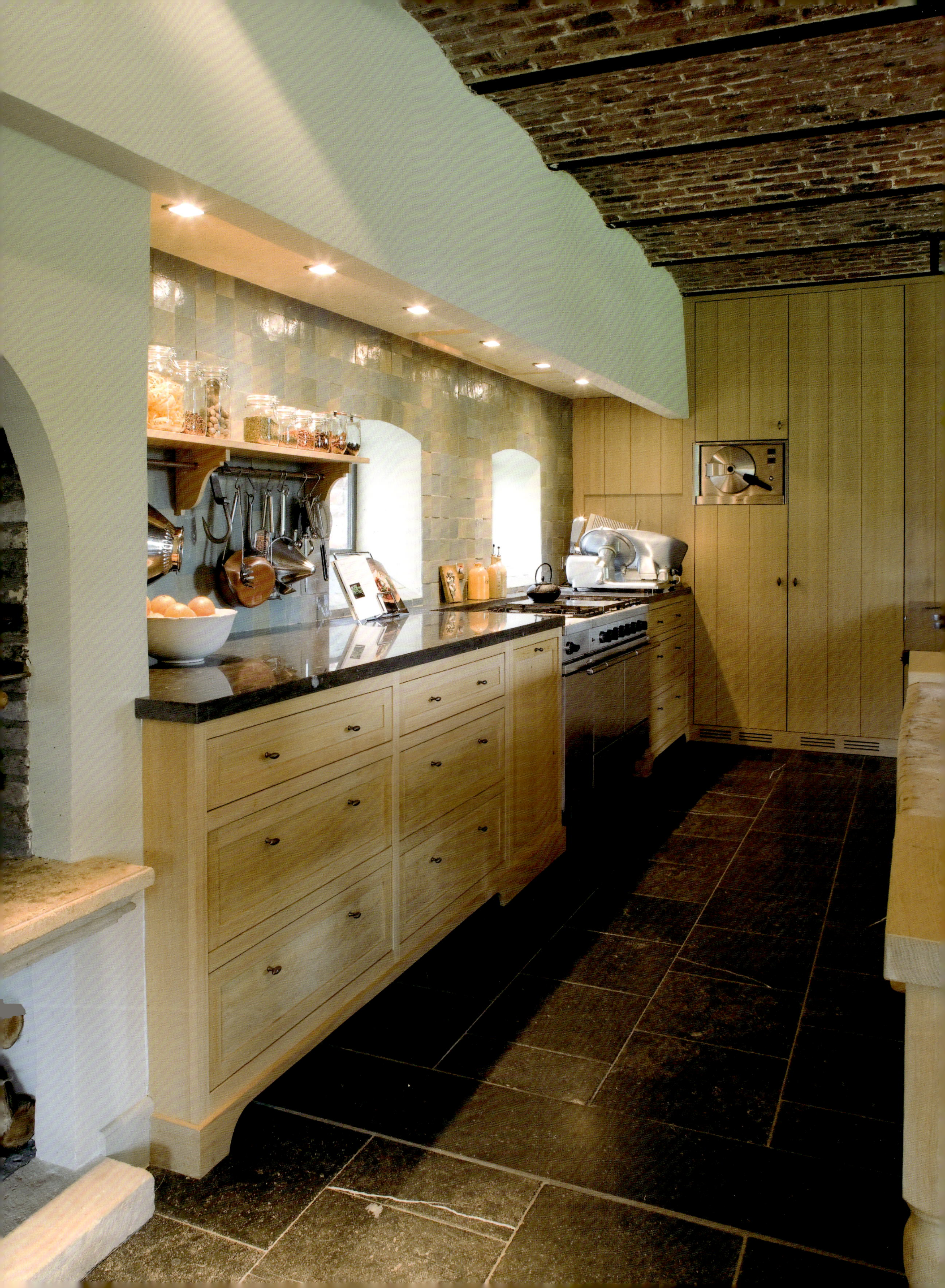

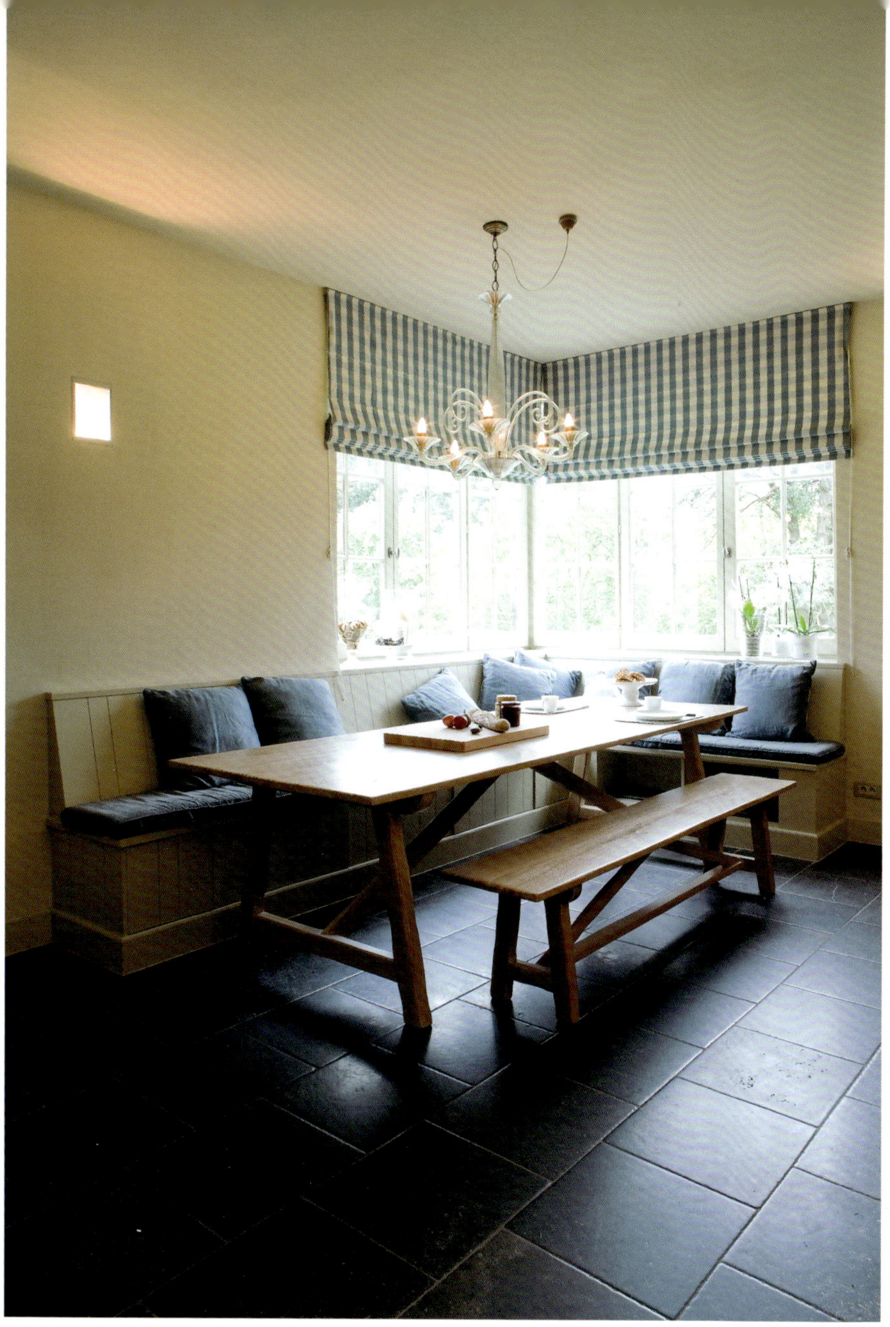

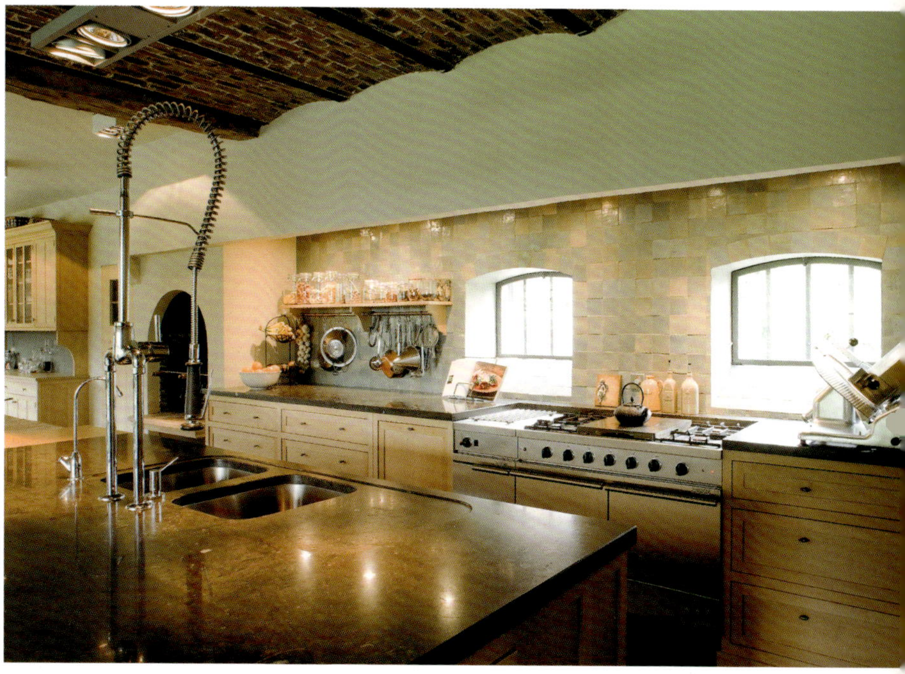

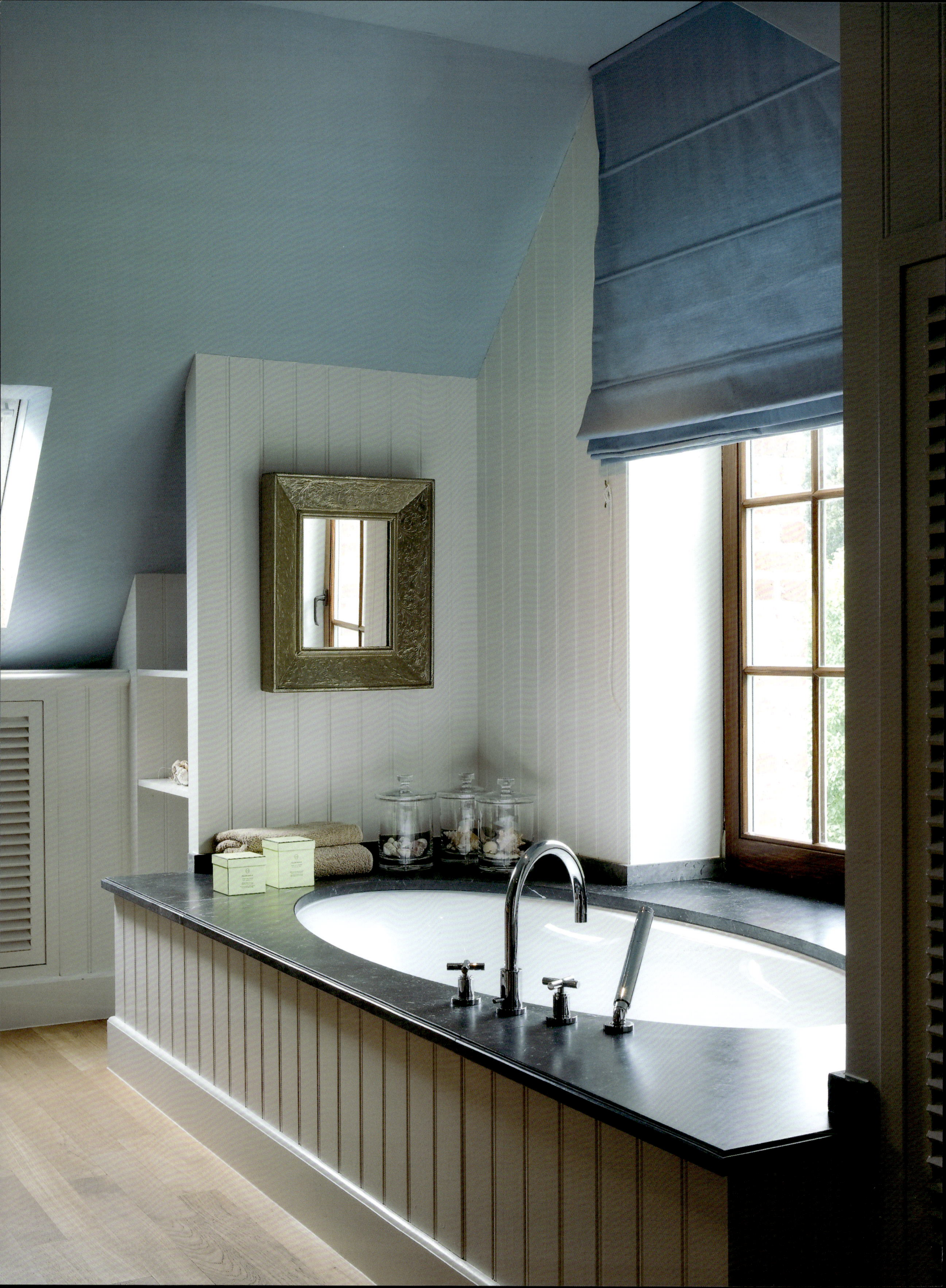

THEMENOS cvba
    Sint-Jansvliet 8
    B – 2000 Antwerp
    T +32 (0)3 248 49 93
    F +32 (0)3 248 56 23
    www.themenos.be

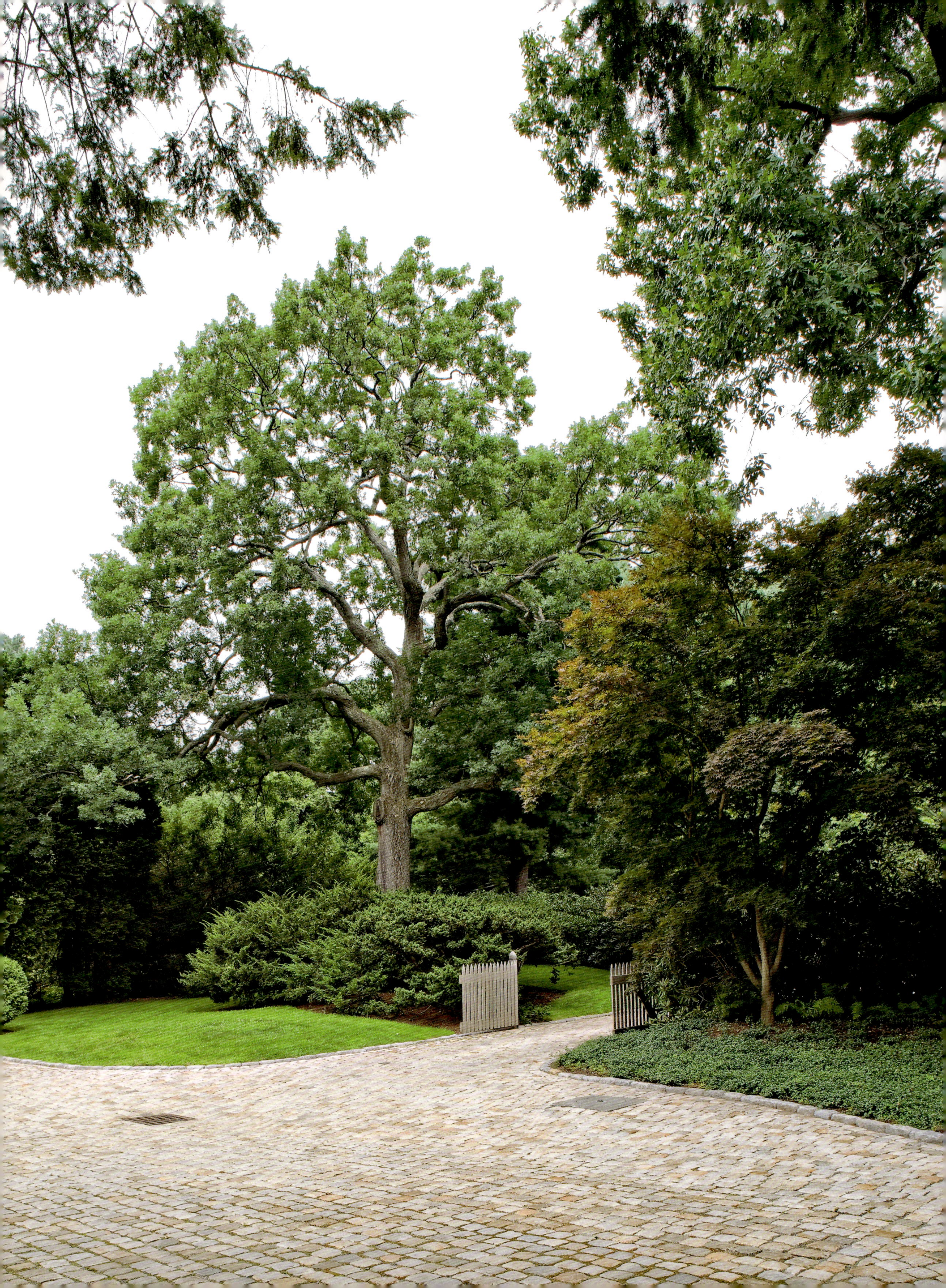

A MIX OF CULTURES

The design of this grand country house in the United States is by the renowned New York designer Bruce Bananto.

He worked on the project for over three years, in consultation with the owners.

During this period, while visiting Belgium, he got to know Koen Van Loo from EA2 (European Architectural Antiques), who was ultimately to work with him on this project and whose recommendations, as a specialist in historic building materials, were to prove invaluable.

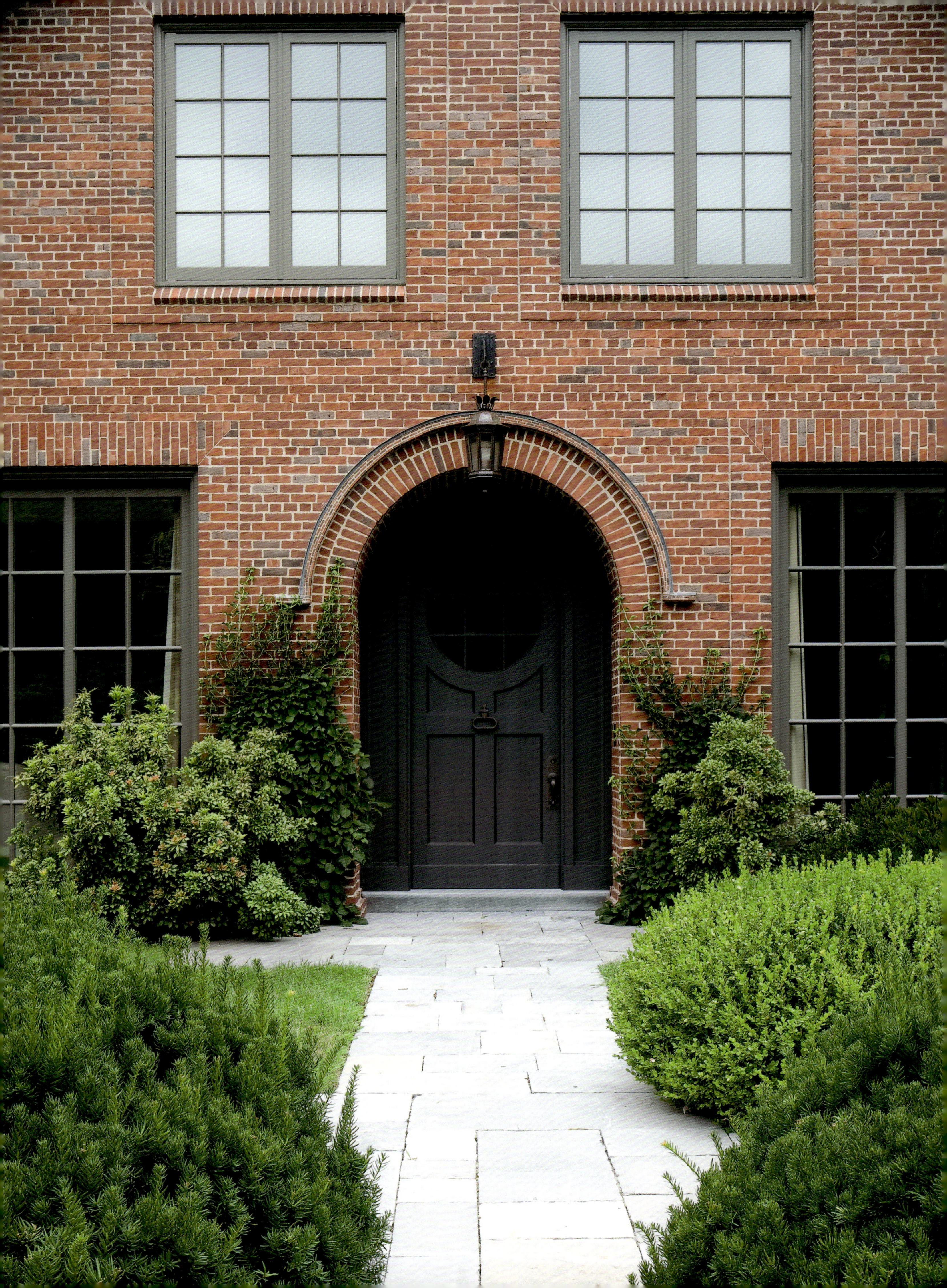

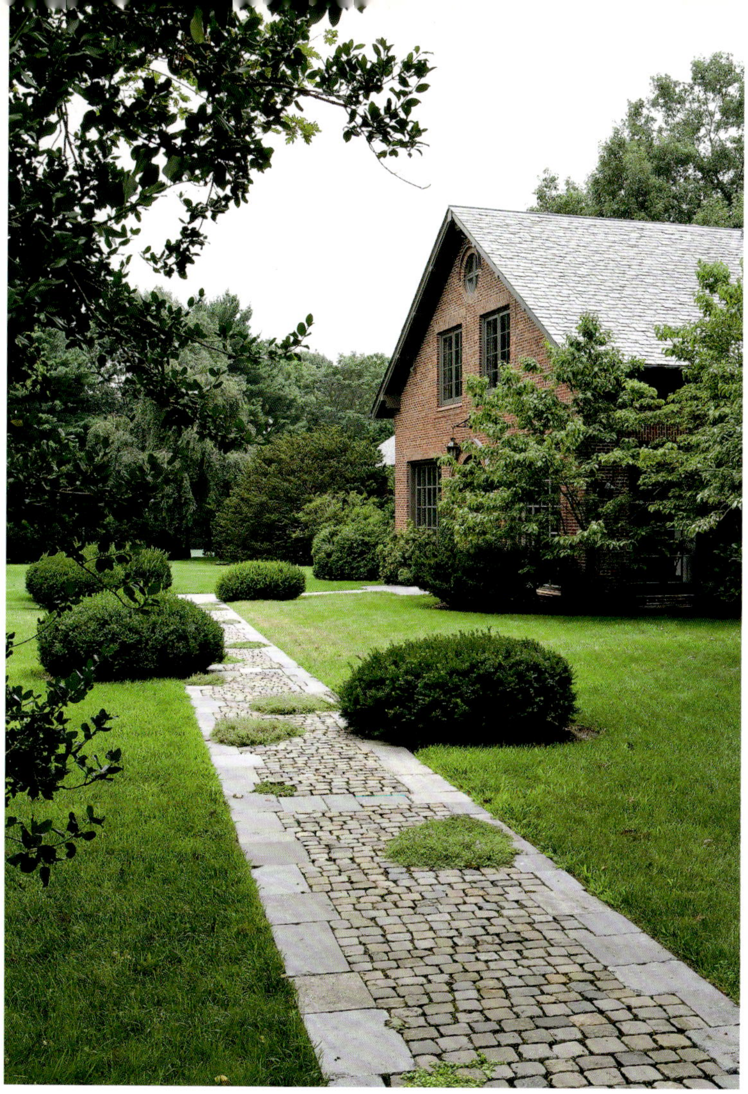

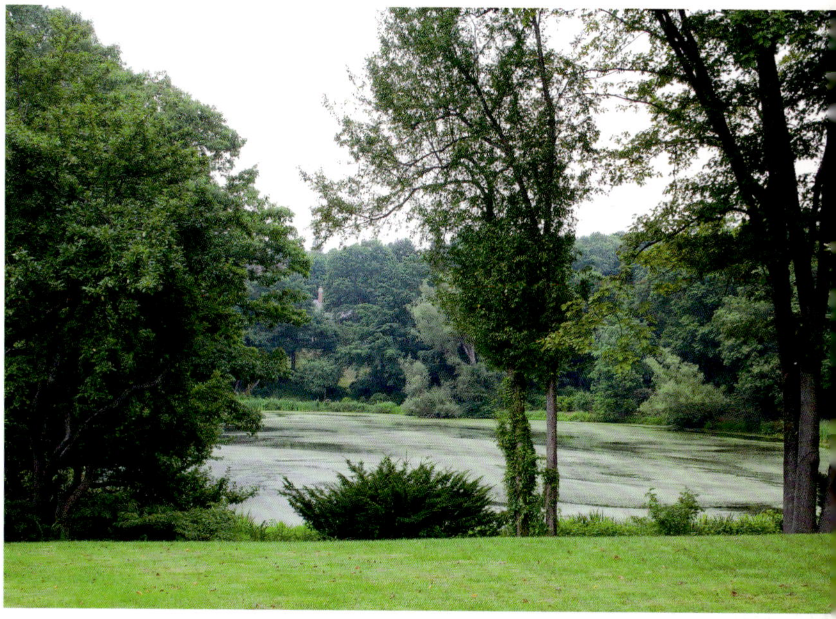

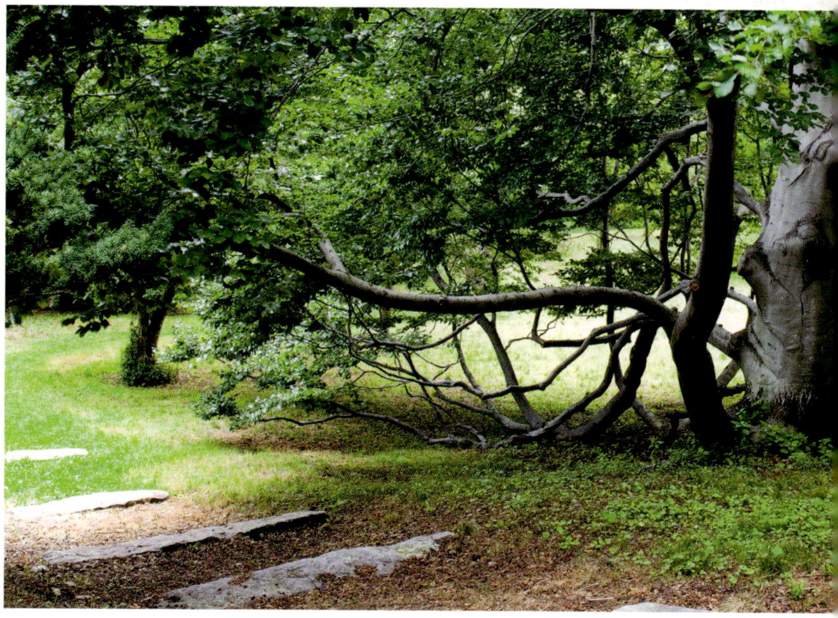

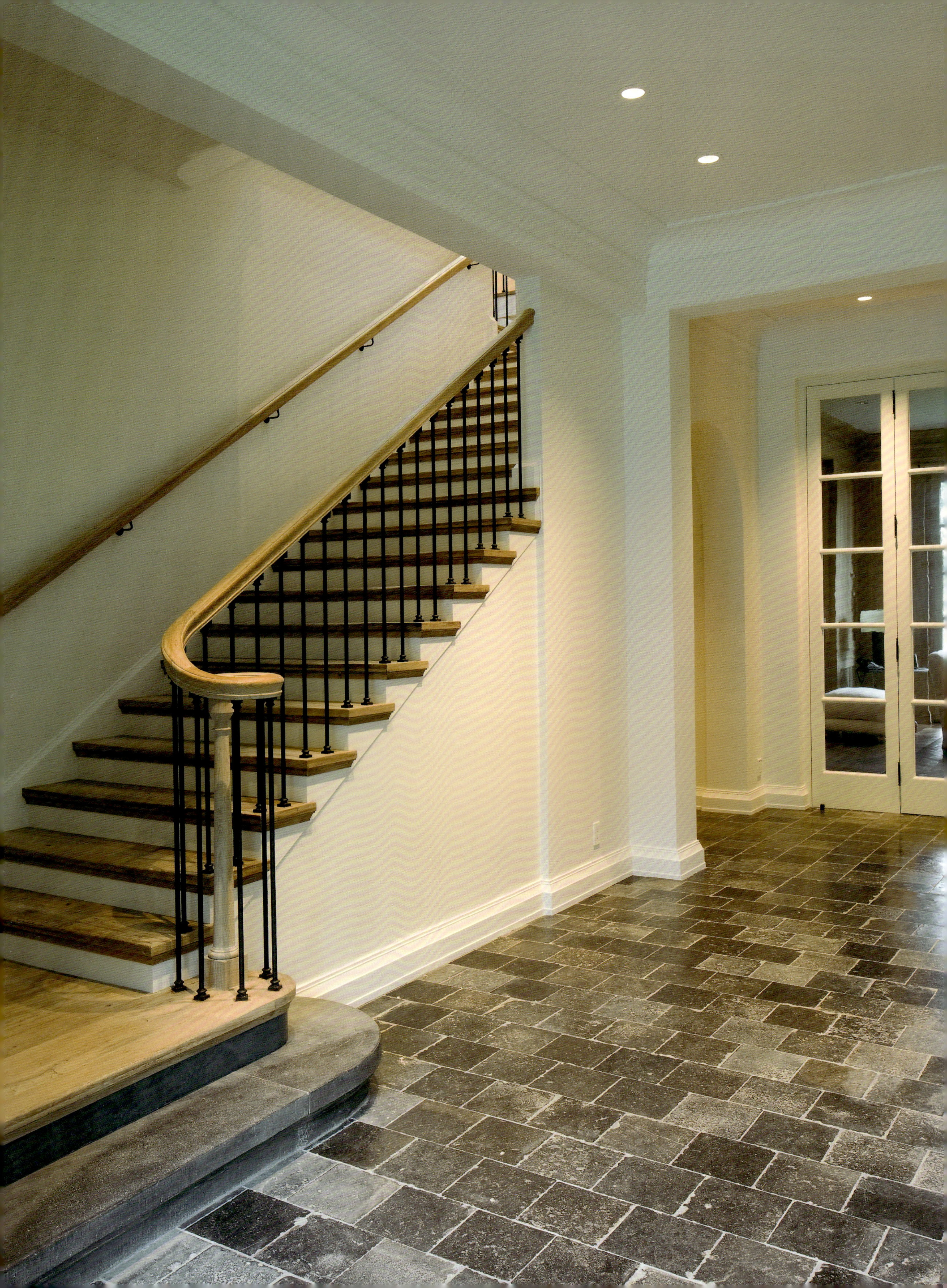

A mix of cultures: American design with architectural antiques from western Europe.

101

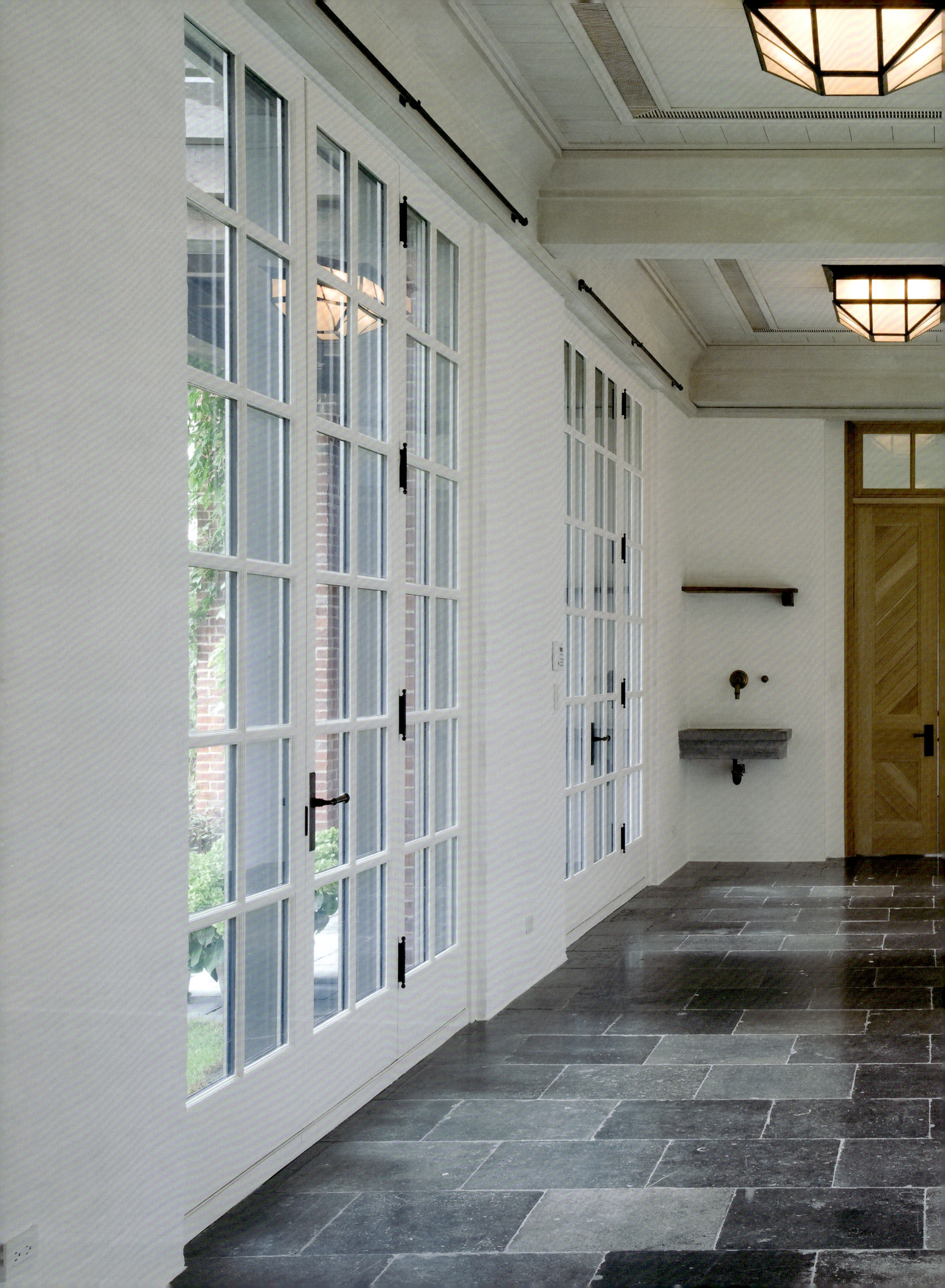

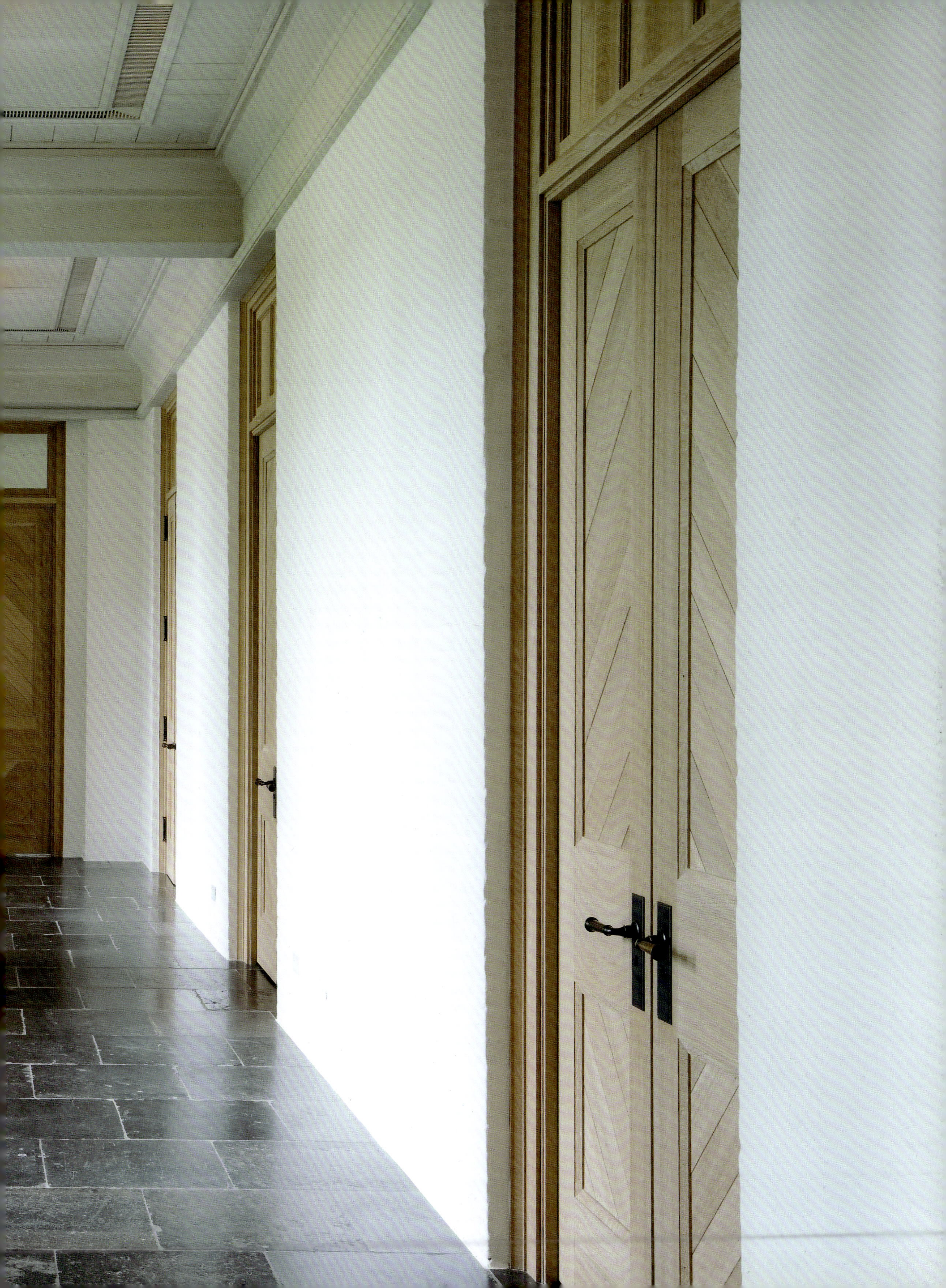

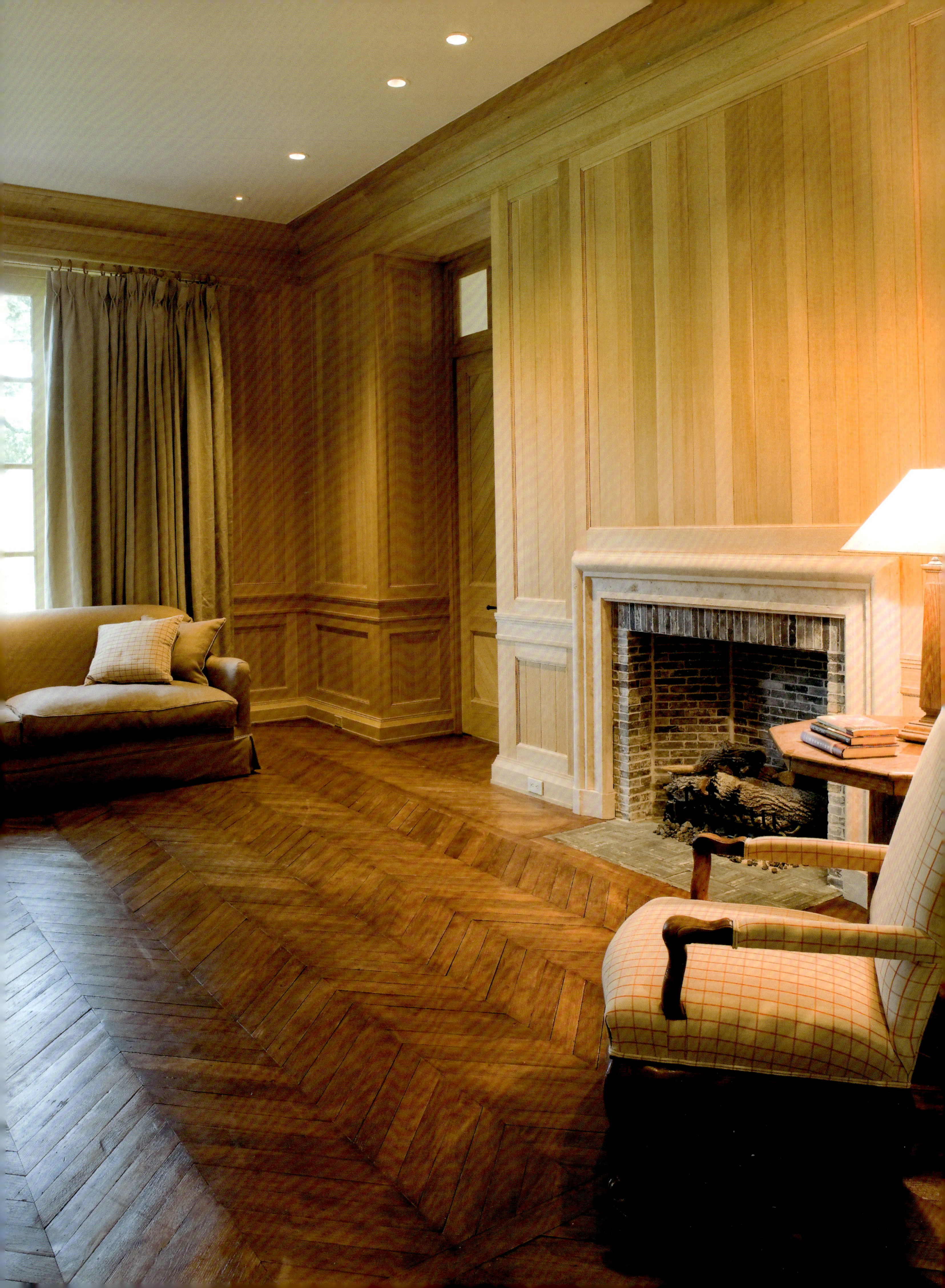

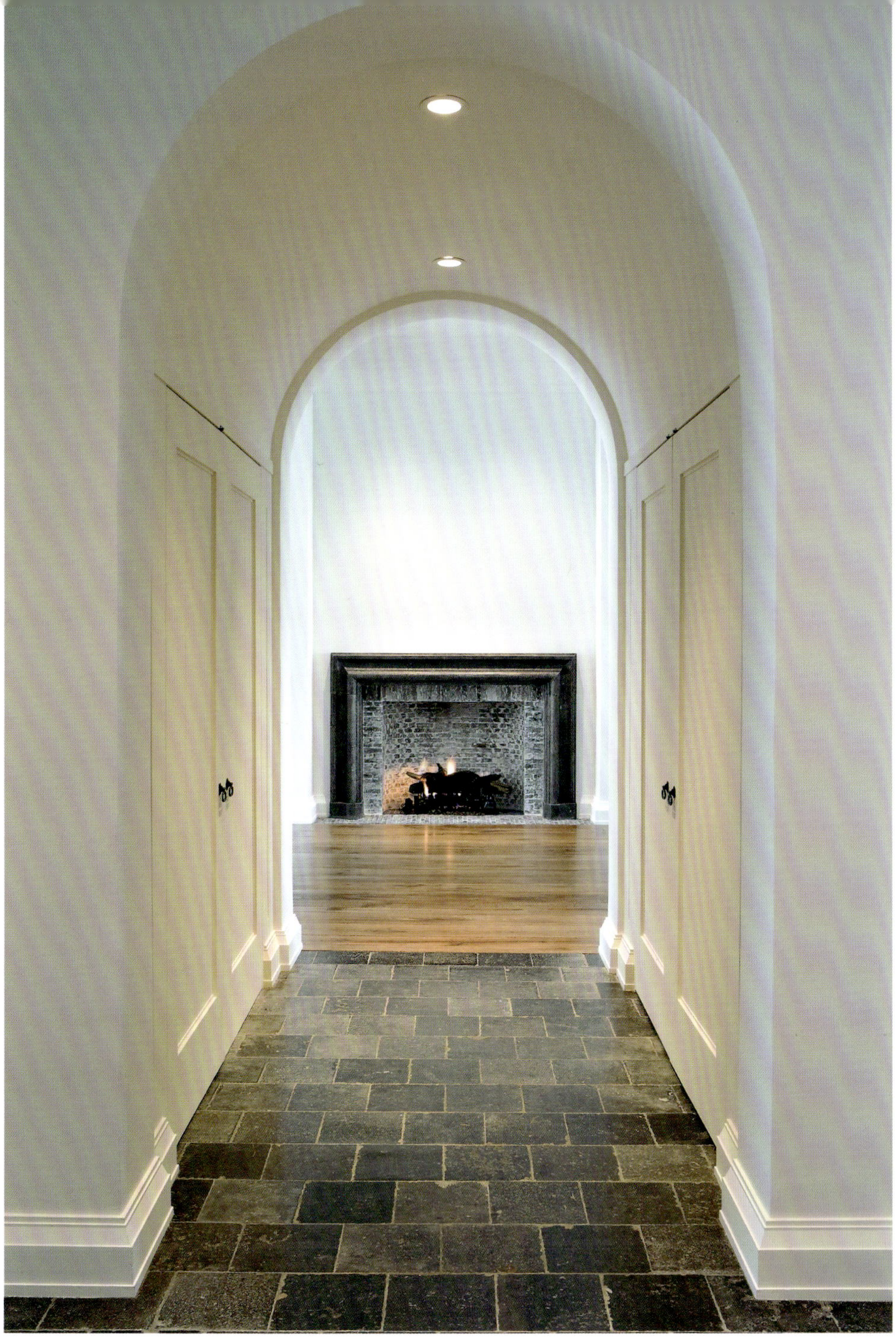

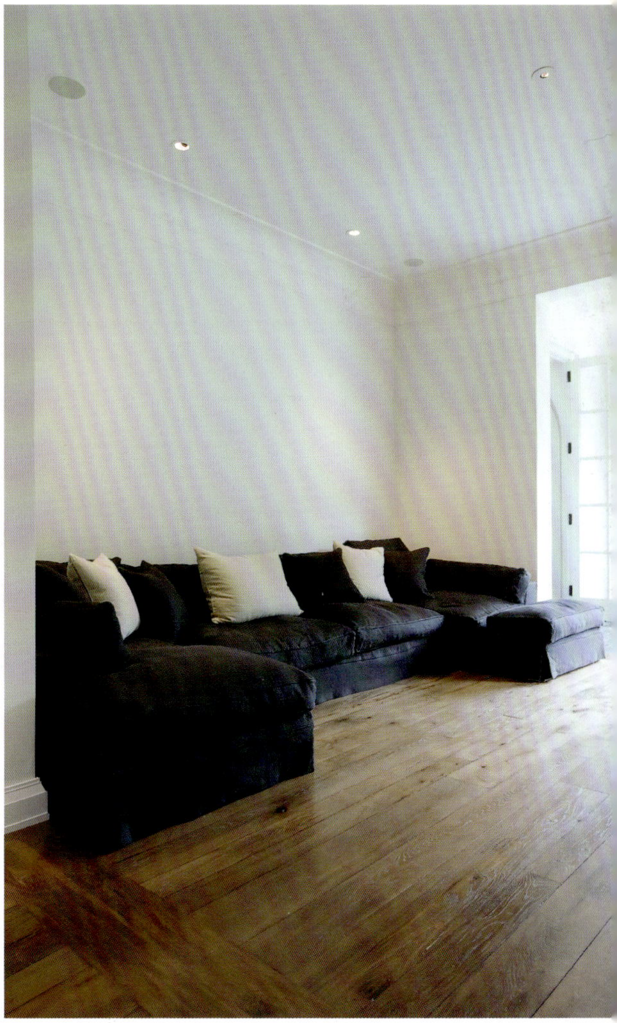

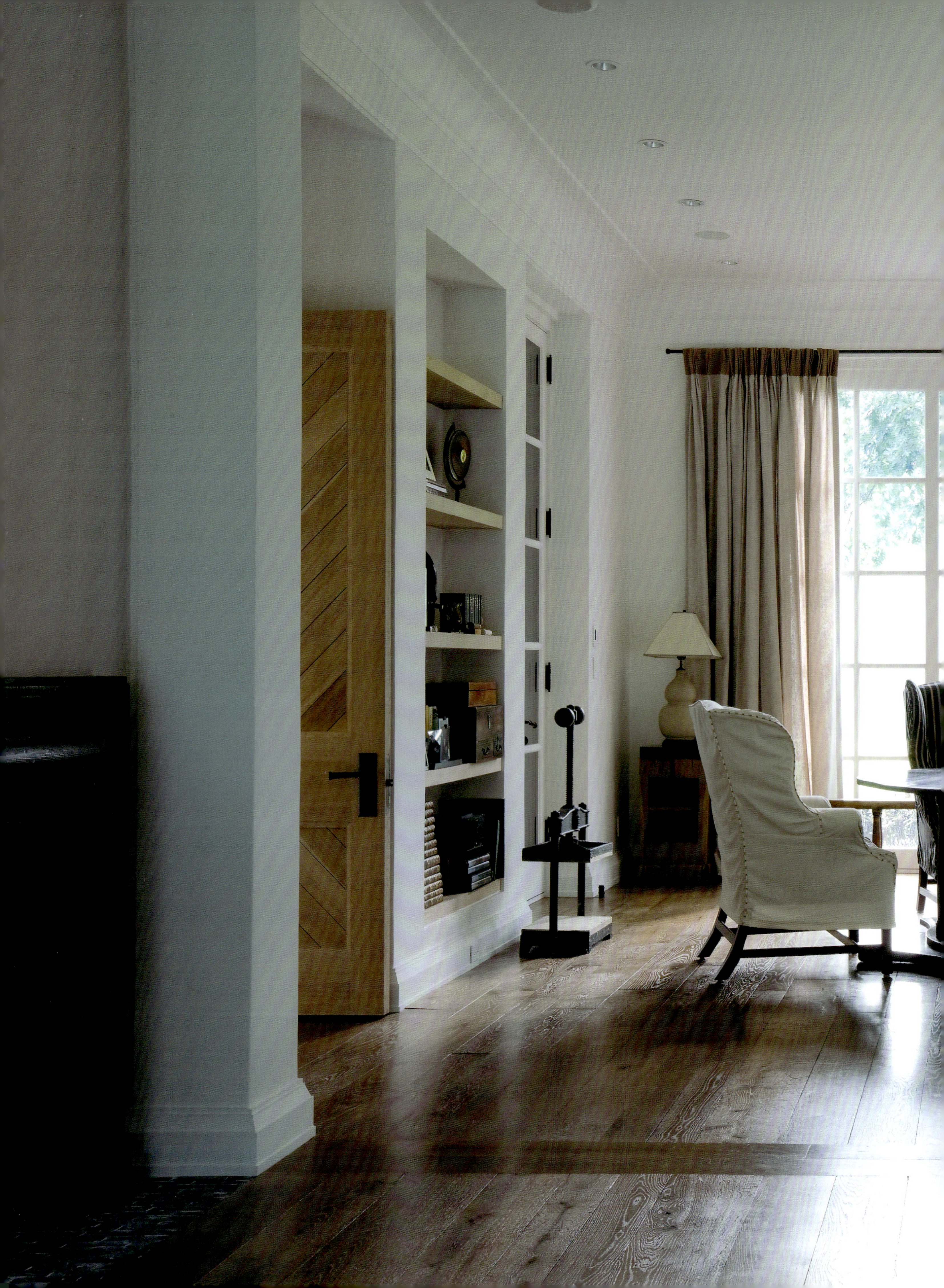

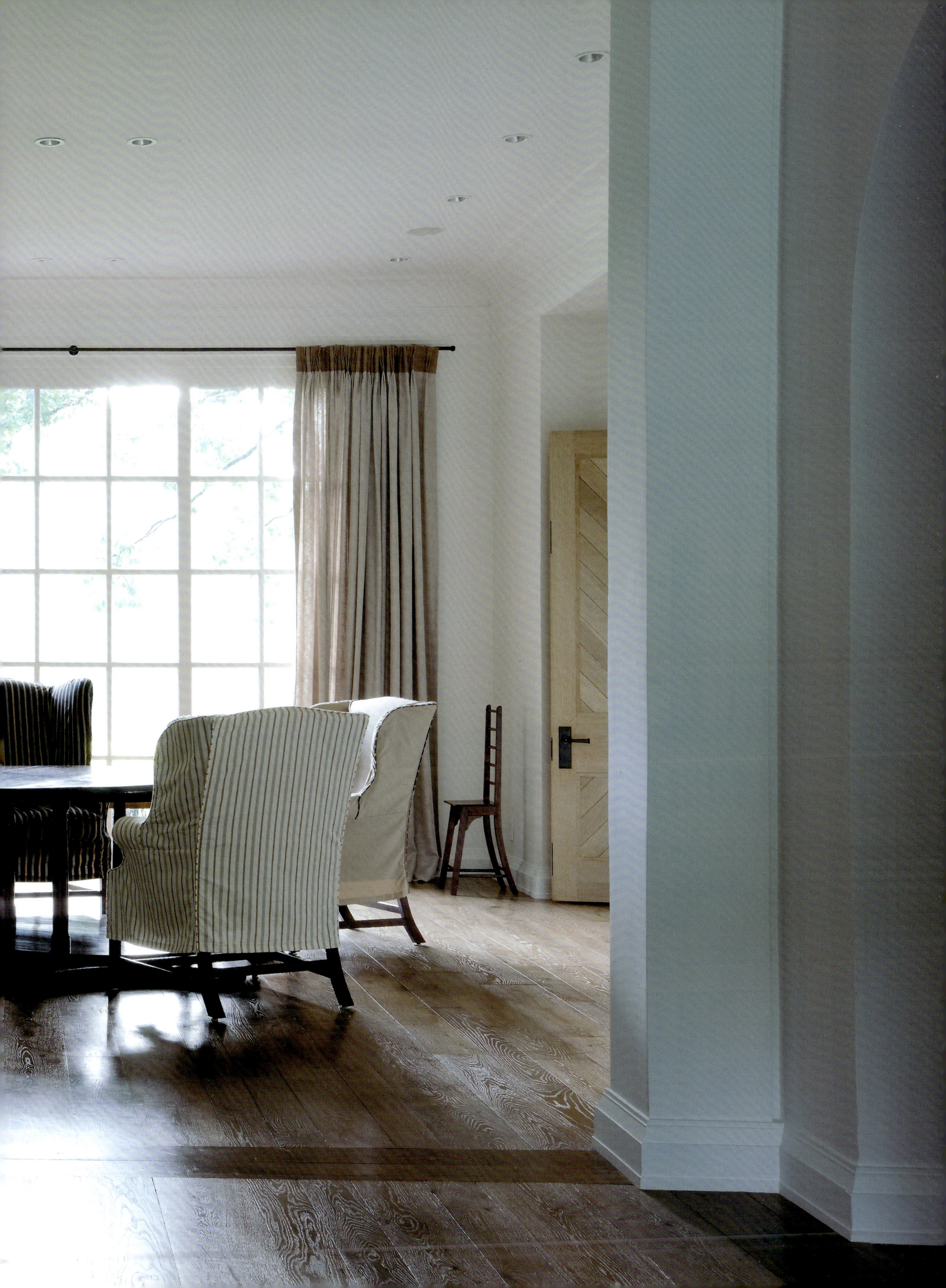

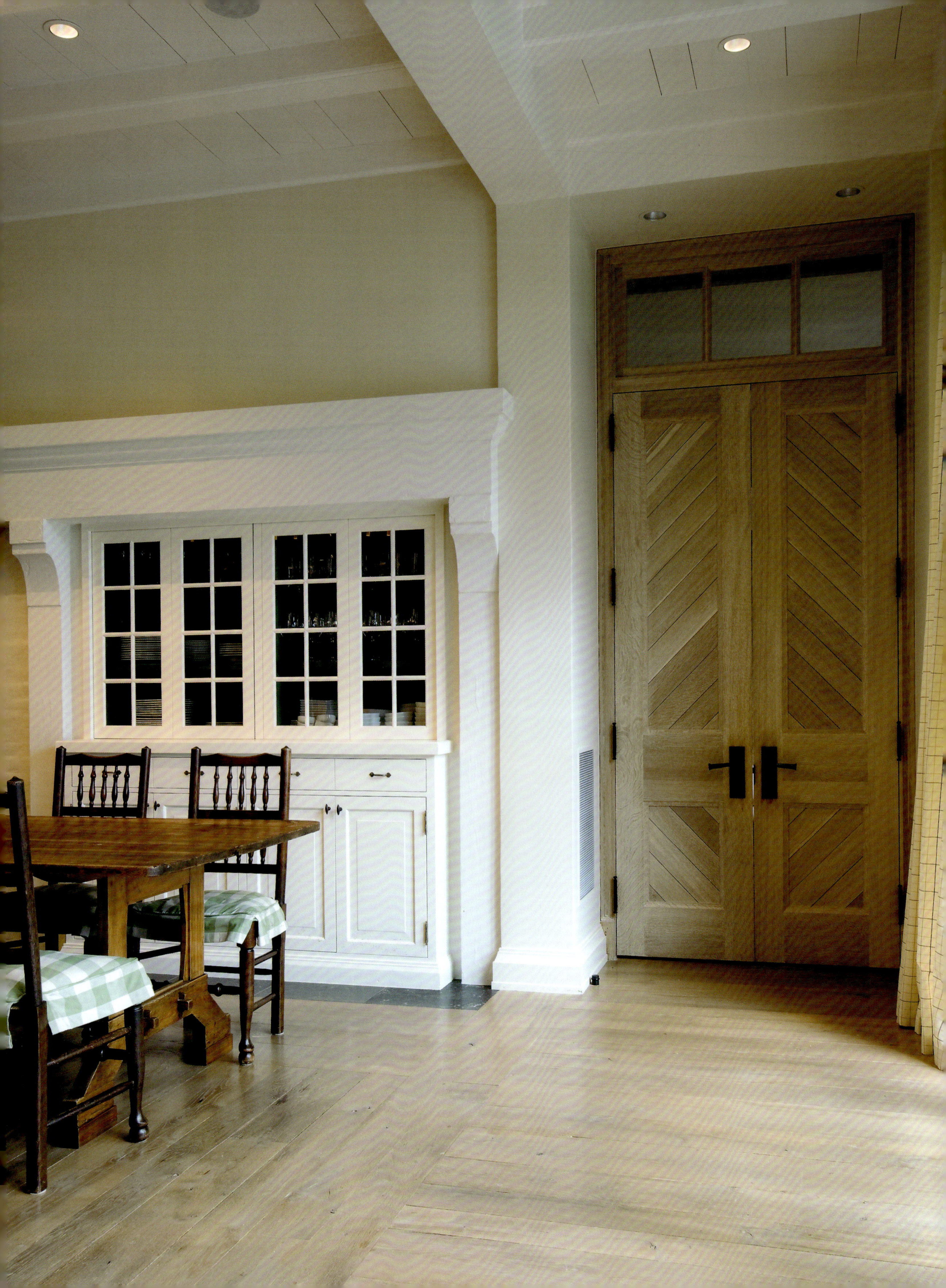

BRUCE BANANTO
    145 W. 28th ST.
    Suite 803
    New York, NY 10001
    T +1 212 563 1750
    F +1 646 416 6218

EA2
European Architectural Antiques
    26 Heistgoorstraat
    B – 2220 Antwerp / Heist op den Berg
    T +1 617 894 04 95
    info@ea2.be

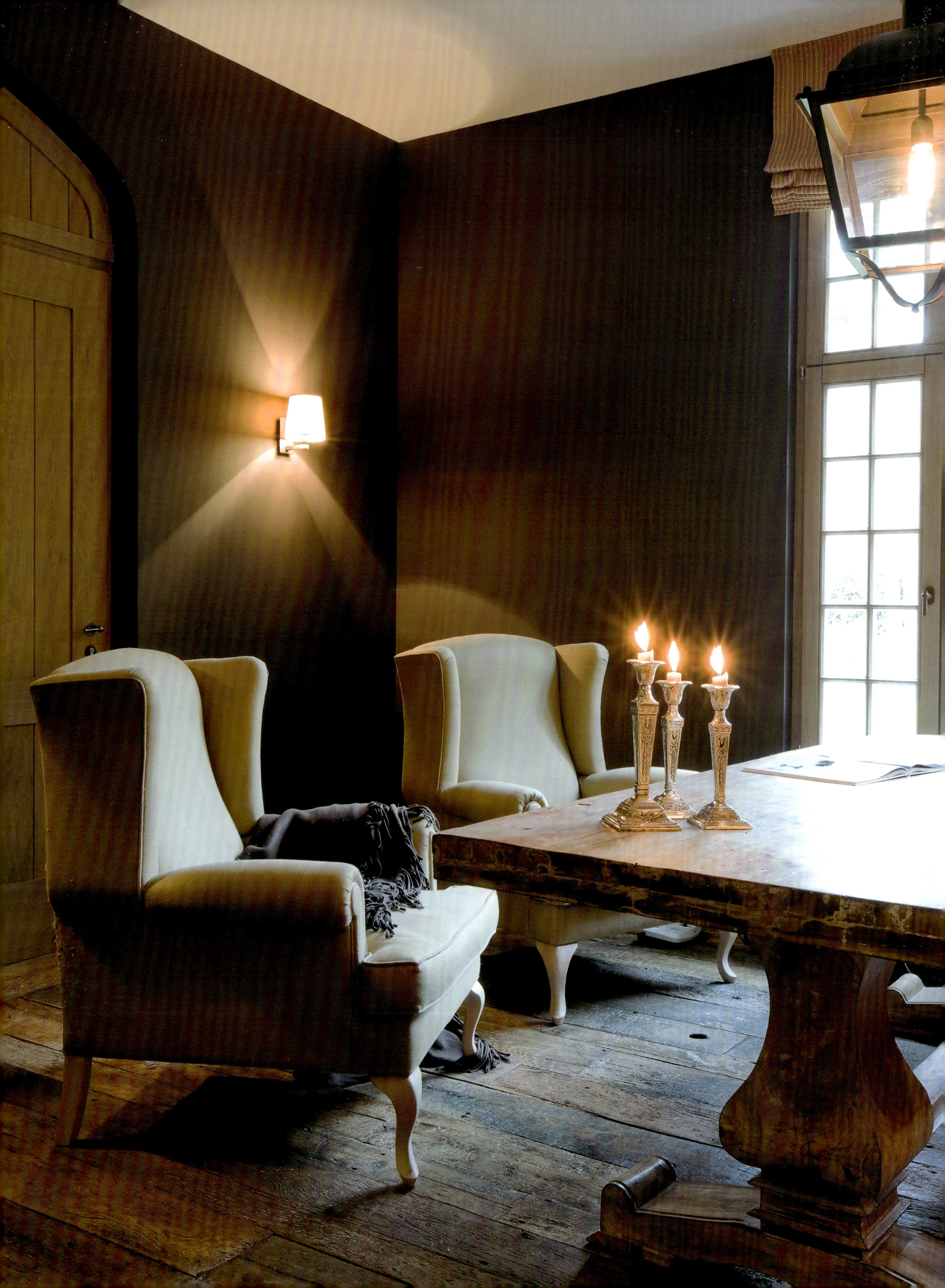

AN INTIMATE ATMOSPHERE

Costermans built this classic country house in the green countryside surrounding Antwerp.

Historic building materials were used consistently throughout the project, lending the house a timeless and intimate atmosphere.

An antique table now used as a desk. The floor is in antique planks of solid French oak.

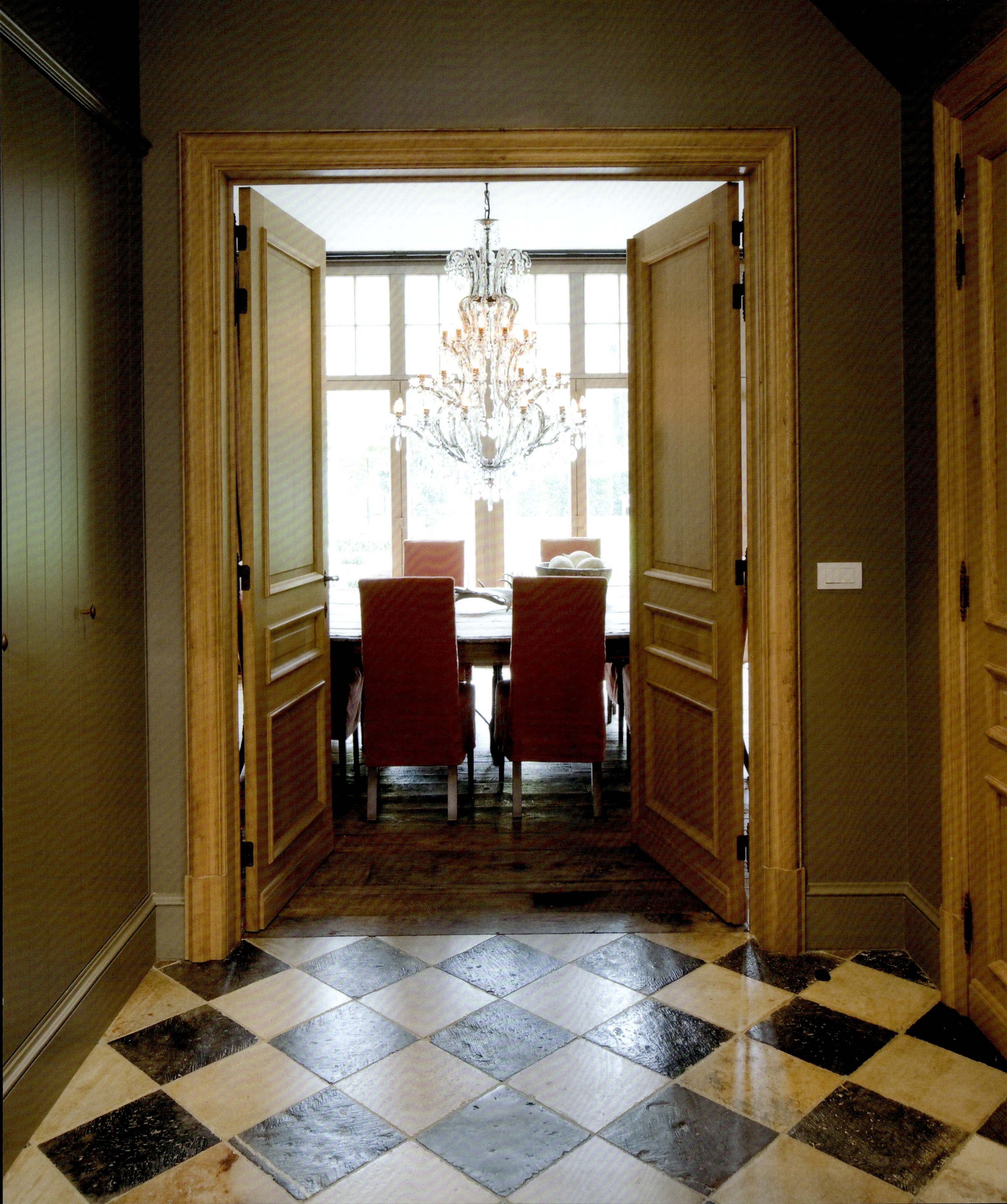

The entrance hall is in an antique chessboard pattern made up of slate and Burgundy white stone. Doors in French oak made to an old model. An oak staircase in English style with wrought-iron balusters fastened to the wall with rose-shaped ornaments. Sanitary room with an antique white-stone washbasin, wall in thick French oak veneer and lighting by Stéphane Davidts. Stairs to the cellar in French oak with a simple wrought-iron rail.

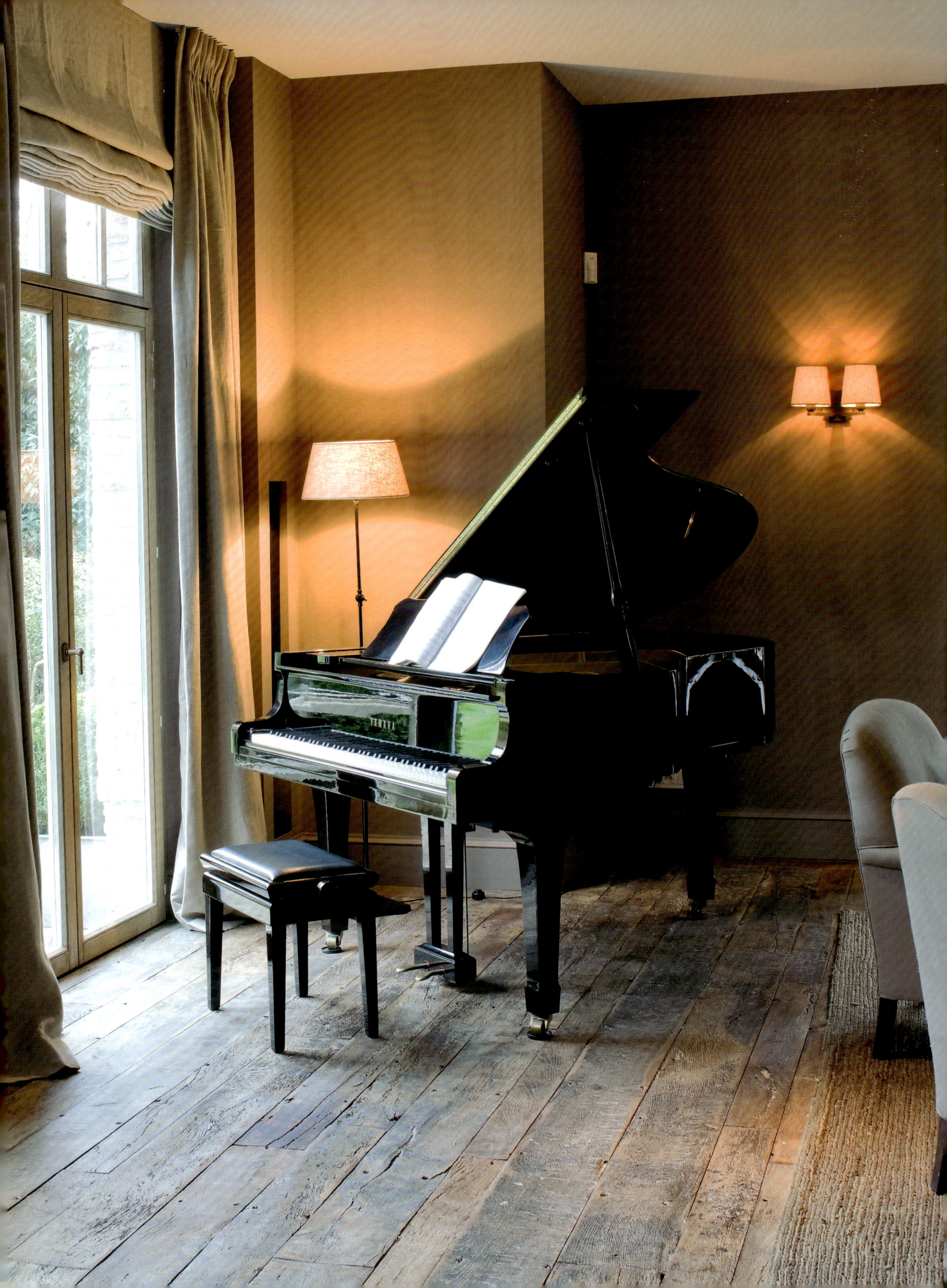

The living room with an old French solid-oak floor and a historic Louis XIII fireplace with authentic wood basket and hearth plate.

p. 116-117
An old oriental door on a simple metal base has been transformed into a coffee table.

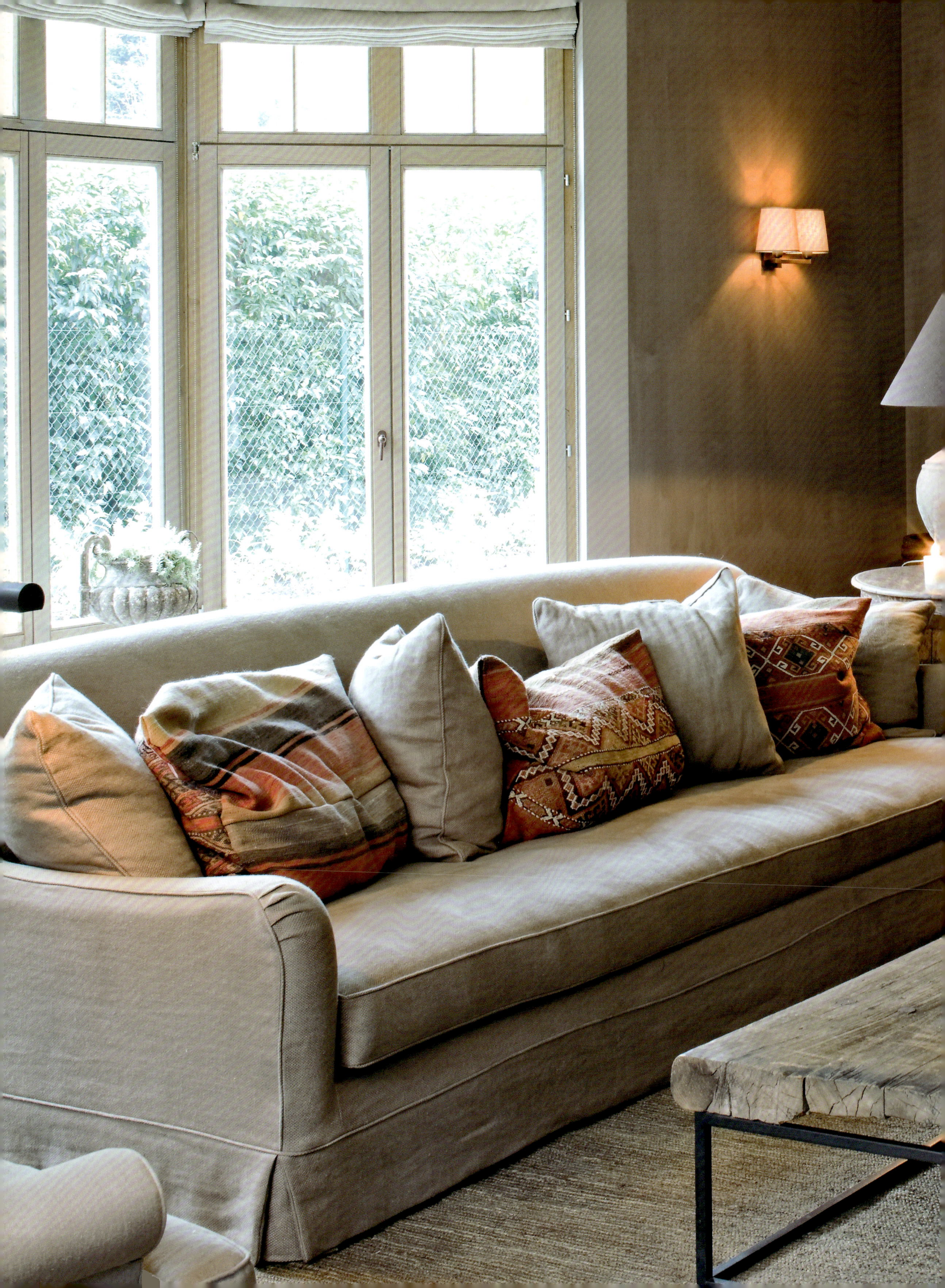

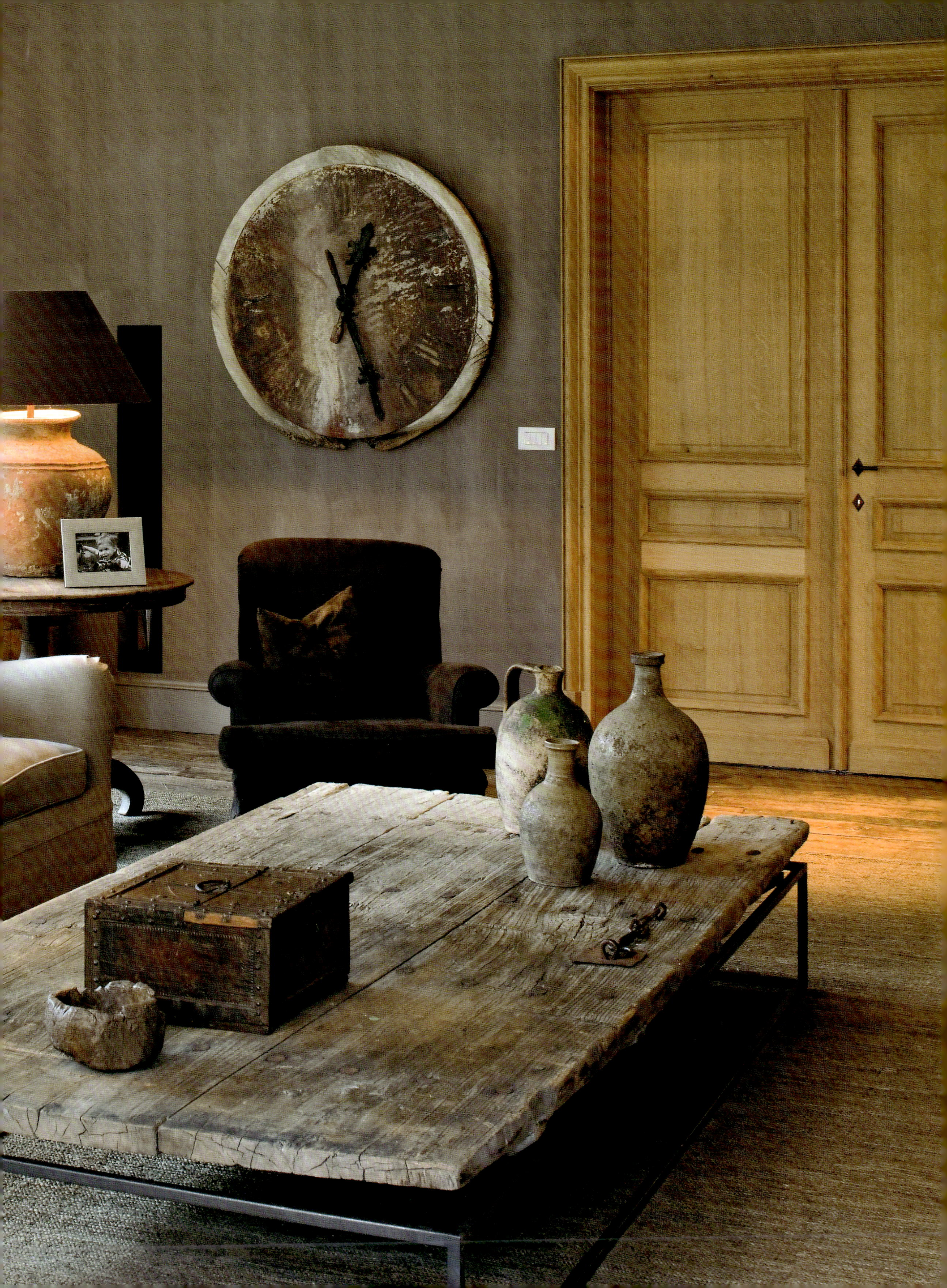

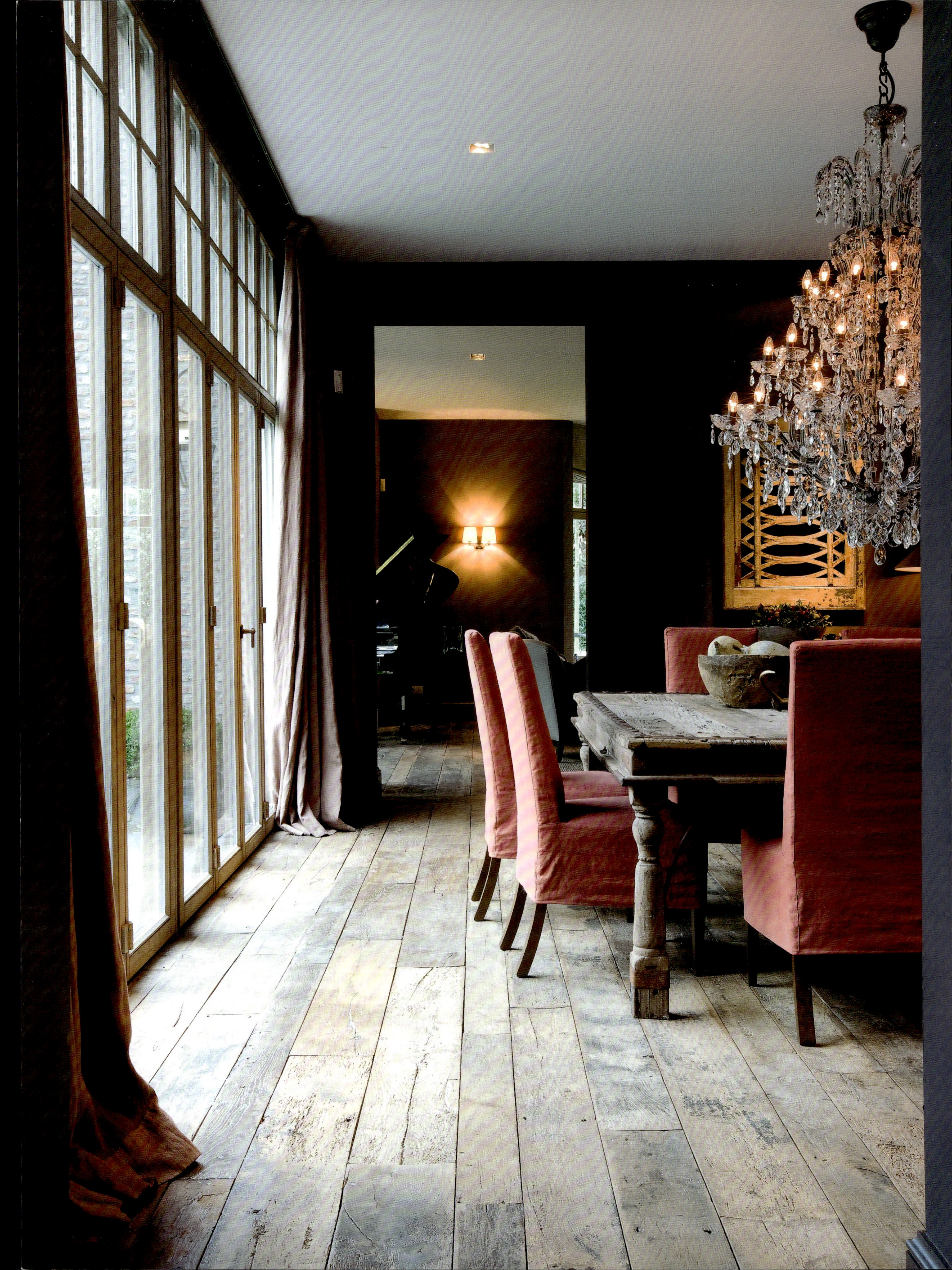

The dining room has the same warm and intimate atmosphere. The eye-catching piece in this room is the impressive crystal chandelier.

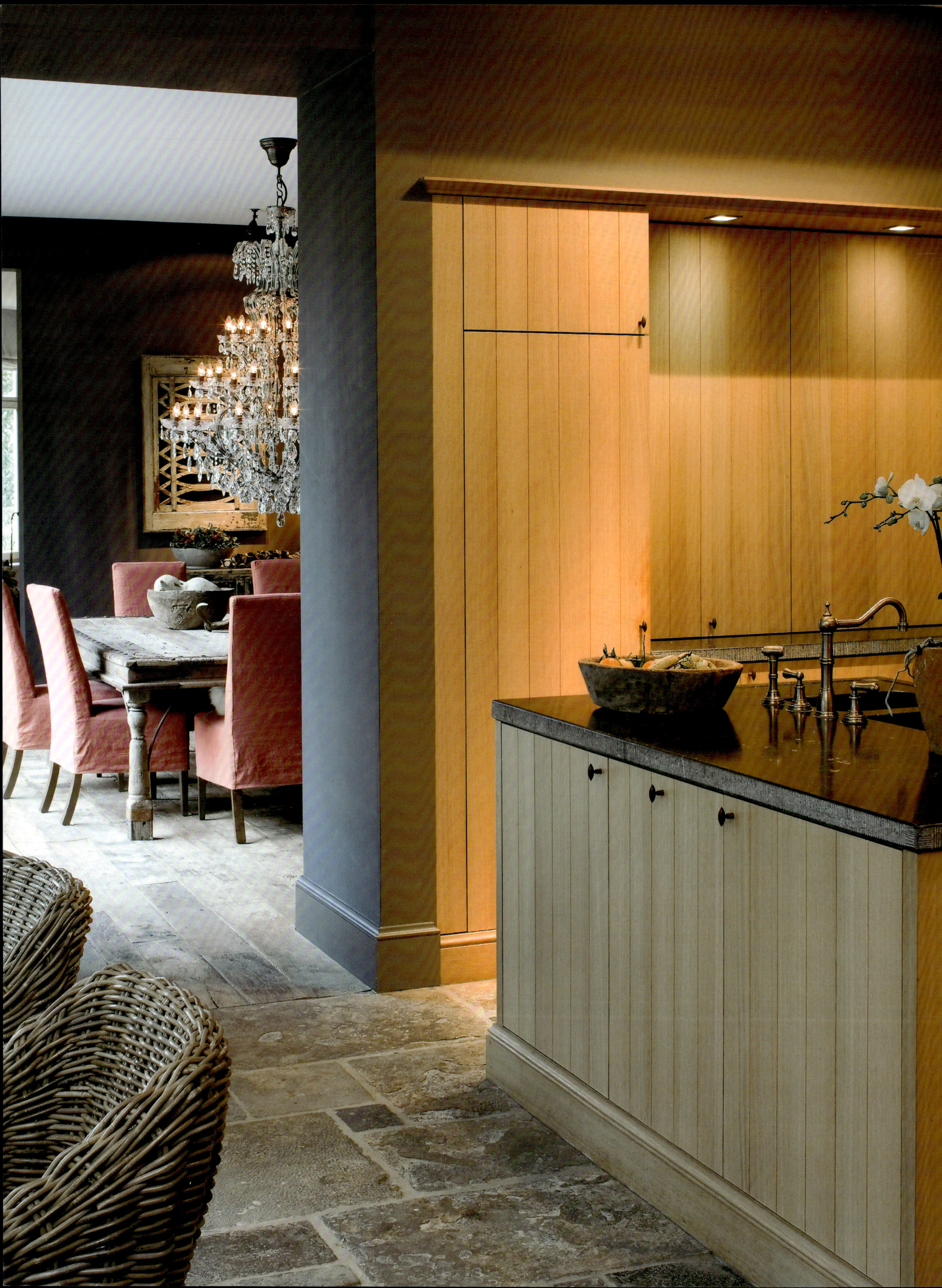

p. 120-123

The spacious kitchen with its sleek units in thick French oak veneer. Floor in bluestone laid in broken bond. The stove is by Delaubrac; the work surface is in smoothed bluestone. Taps by Perrin & Rowe.

The scullery is in French oak, with an antique Louis XV washbasin in white stone and taps by RVB.

The sinks are in solid stone and the edges of the work surfaces have a hand-cut finish.

The wall above the stove is in handmade Moroccan zeliges.

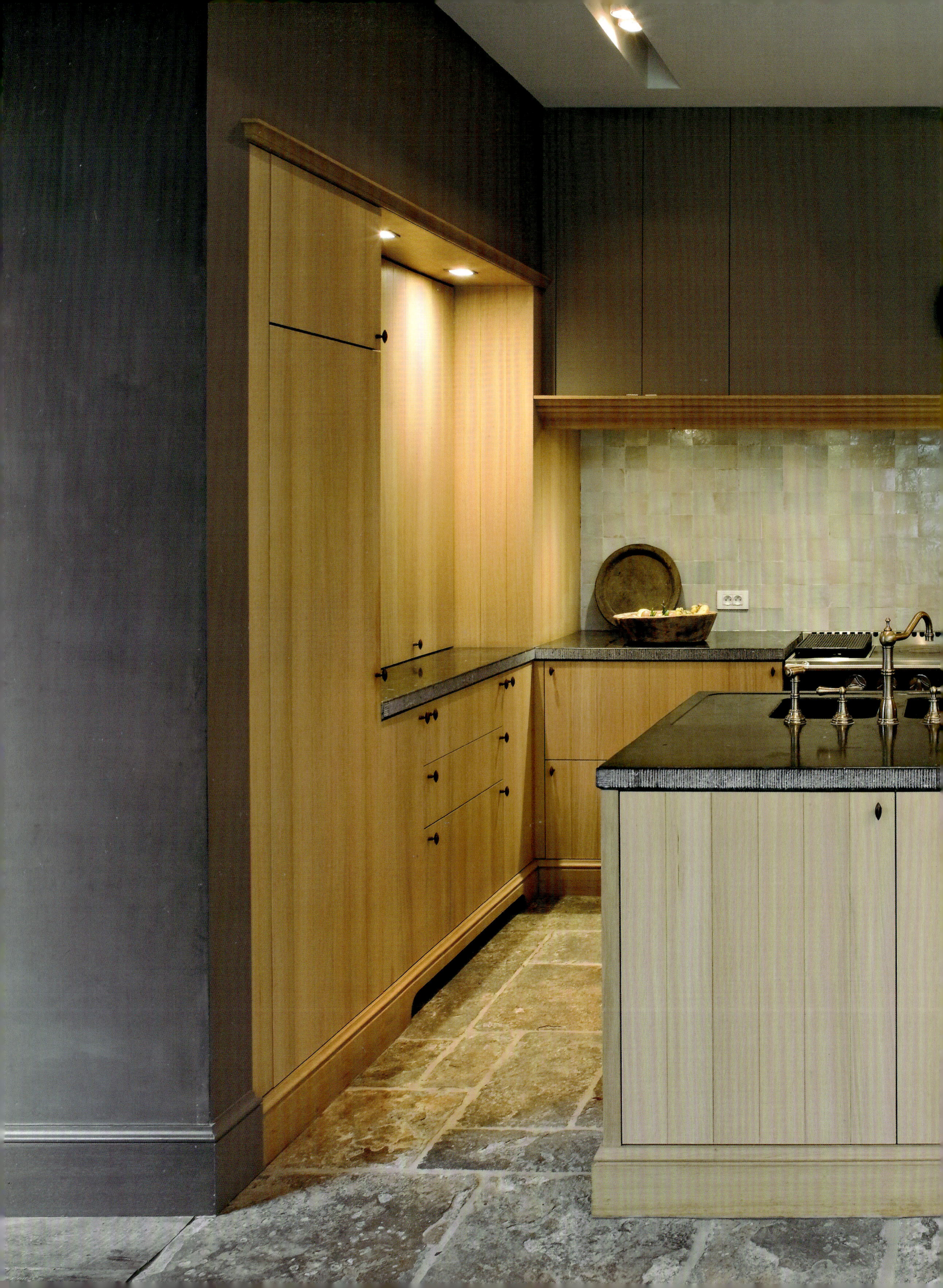

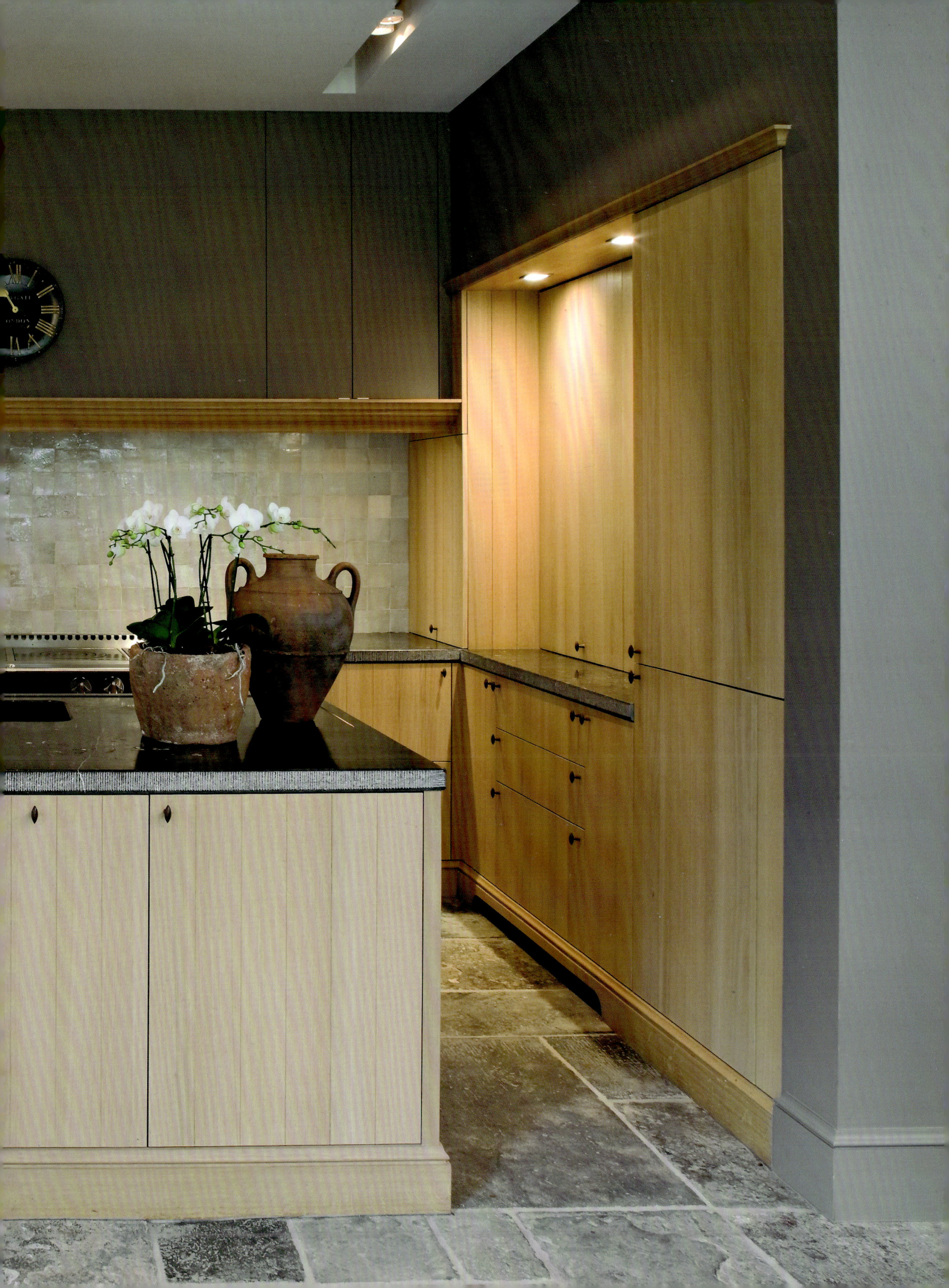

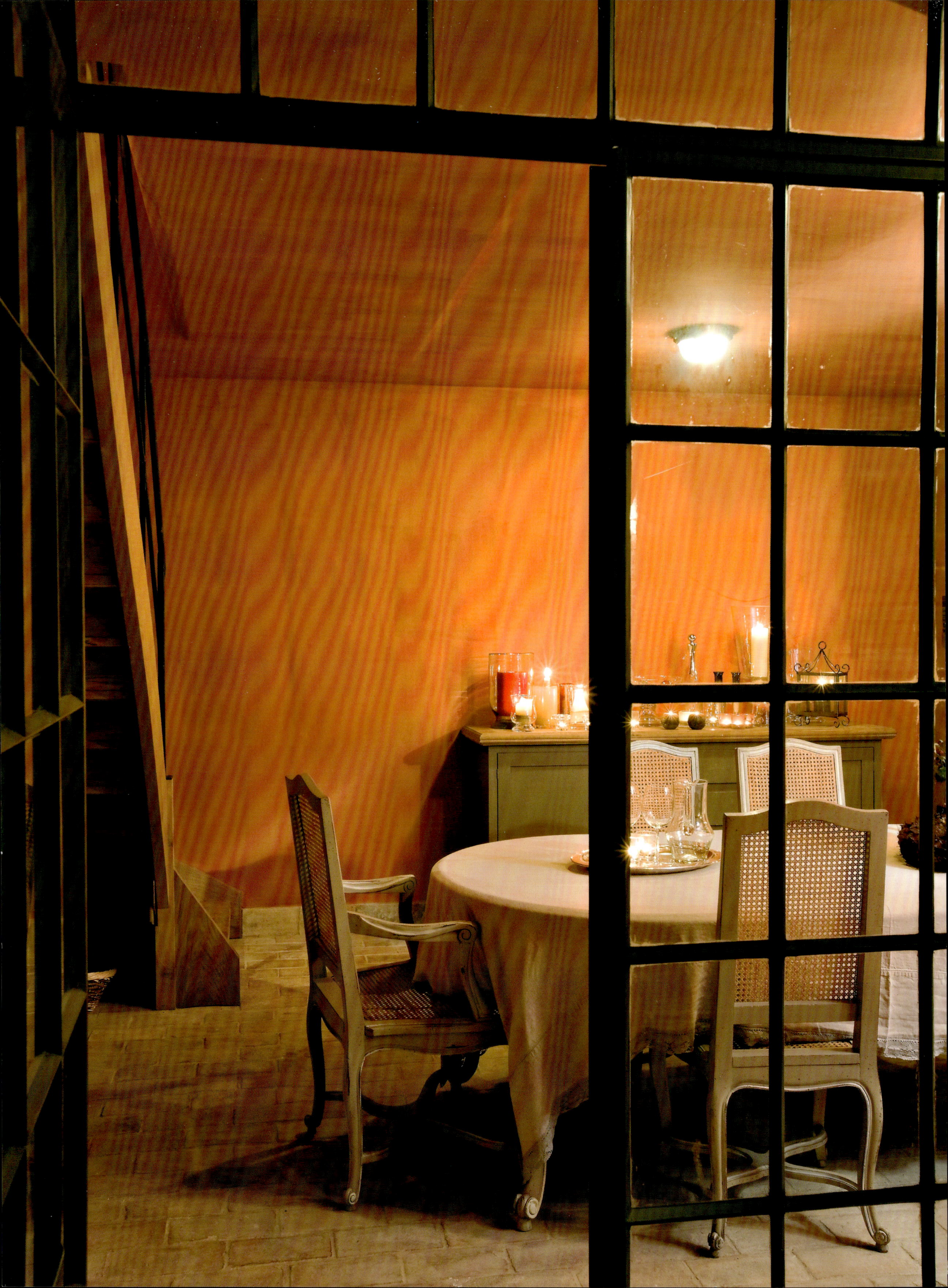

This door in glass and wrought iron leads to the wine cellar and tasting area.

On the floor are antique terracotta flagstones. The wine racks are built in old klampsteen bricks; the ceiling and stairs are in French oak.

COSTERMANS
    Dwarsdreef 52
    B – 2970 Schilde
    T +32 (0)3 385 02 44
    F +32 (0)3 384 29 66
    www.costermans-projecten.be
    info@costermans-projecten.be

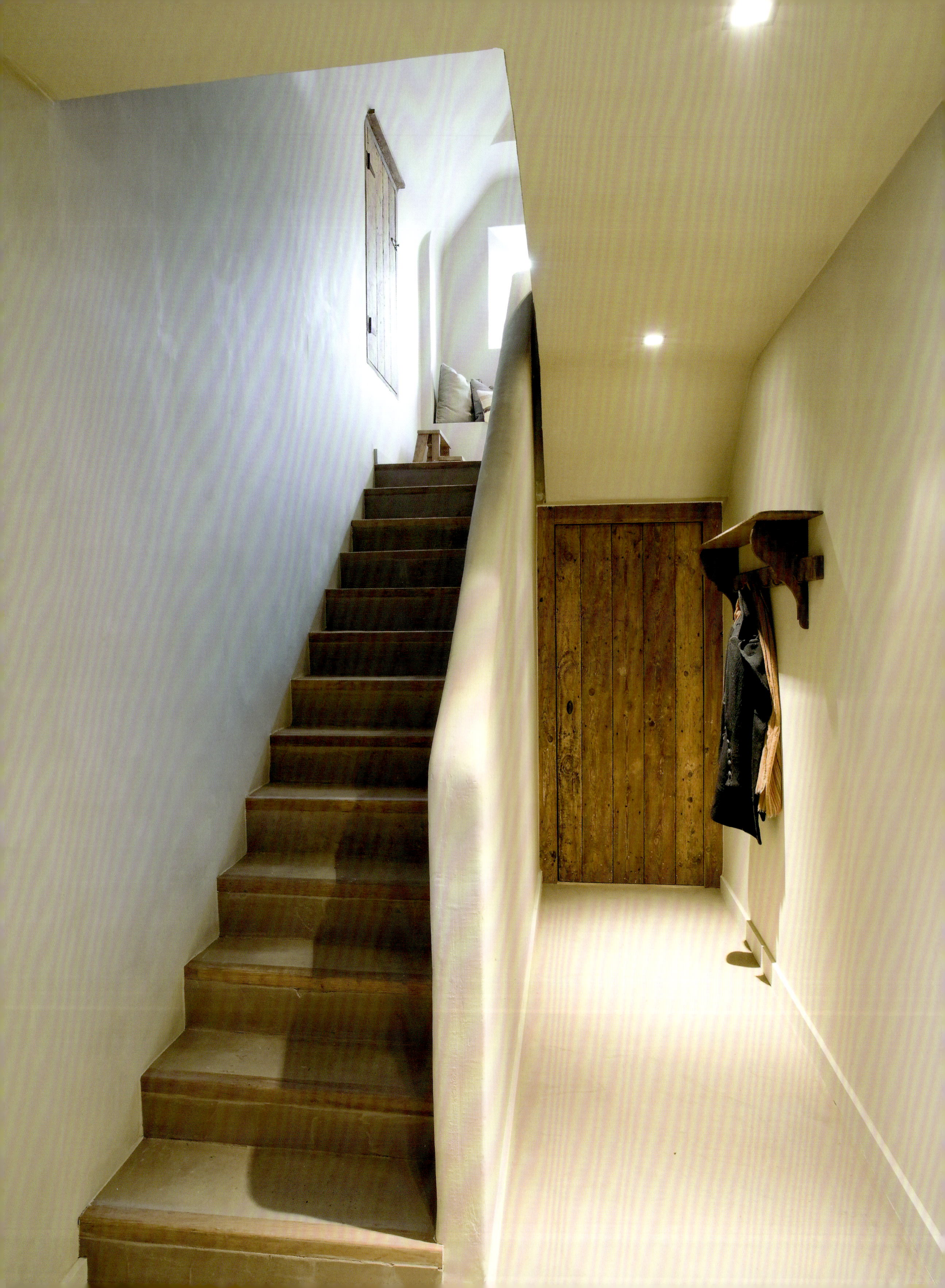

AN ODE TO COUNTRY LIVING

This beautiful country house with a meadow view is the result of a very close collaboration between Porte Bonheur and Natalie Haegeman Interiors.

Ingrid Segers and Annemie Coppens, the founders of Porte Bonheur, had this house built in a rustic style with an emphasis on the use of old materials.

The house was then furnished by NH-Interiors, with an atmosphere of warmth and cosiness as the aim.

The entrance hall is pure and simple.
The walls and the banister have been given a rough plaster finish. The stair nosing is in oak.
The doors and the hatch (which leads to the attic) were made in old pine.
The floor is also very plain, with a cement finish.

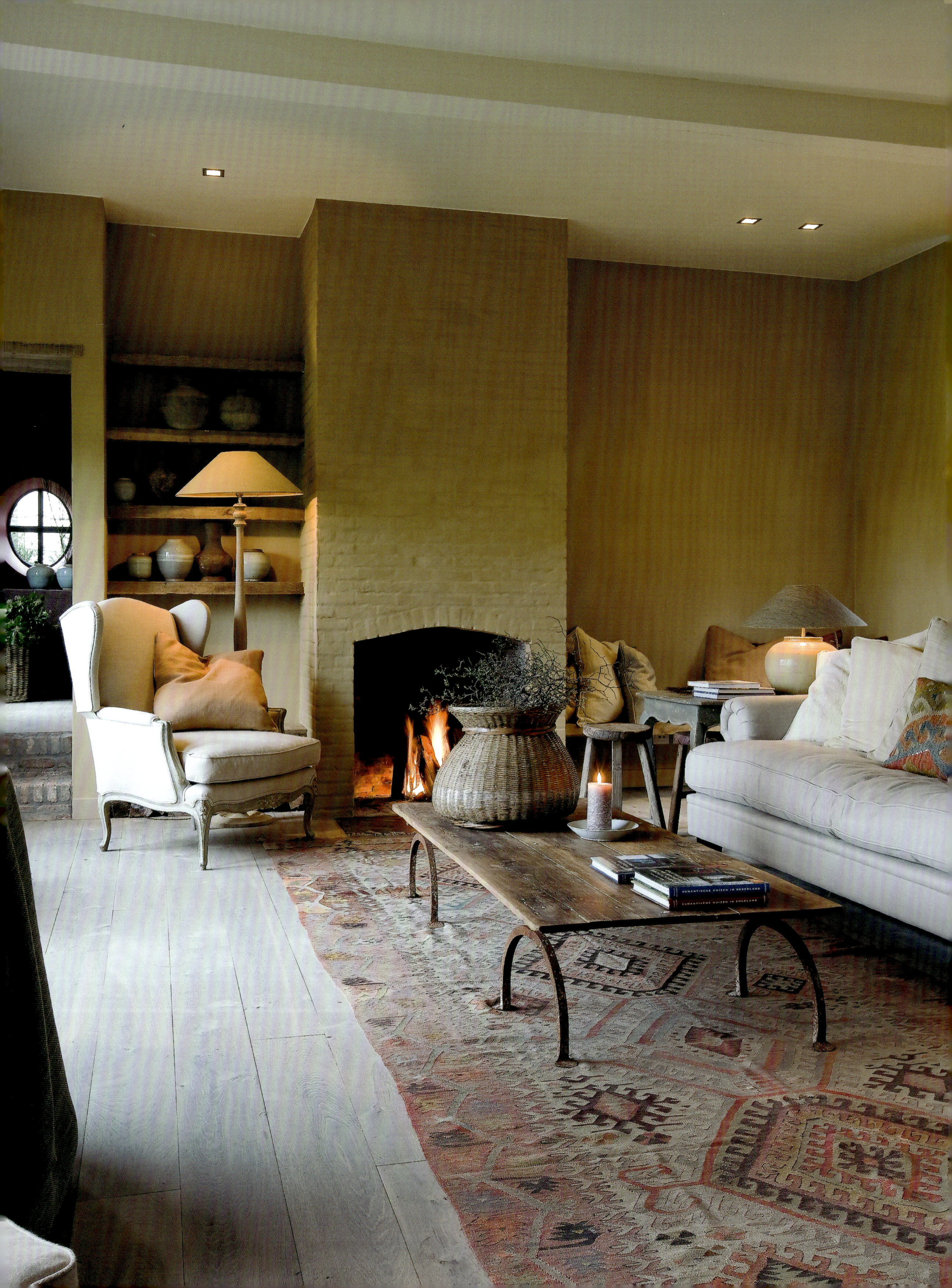

Oak floors and an old-oak beamed ceiling, which was subsequently painted, were chosen for the living room. Steps in old "paepesteen" bricks.
The coffee table is made from an 18th-century door with a wrought-iron base from Venice.
Antique kelims from Turkey are scattered throughout the house.
The open fireplaces have been rendered in lime.

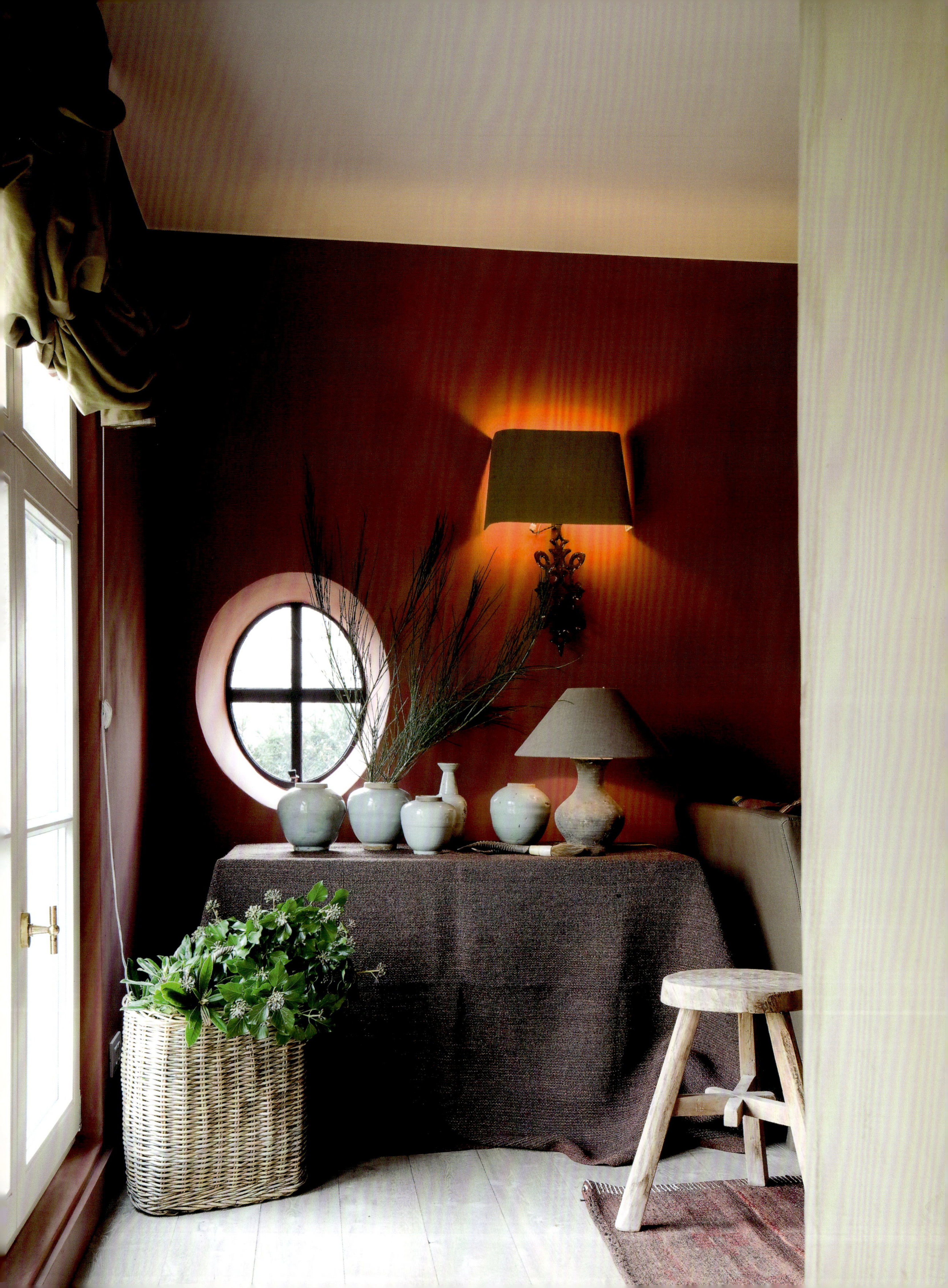

The walls in the TV room also have a lime finish. As throughout the rest of the house, the colours were chosen on the spot.

Coffee table in 19th-century oak; wall light made from old ironwork.

In the centre of the wall on this page, two symmetrical steel windows.

In the dining room, as throughout, old pine doors with authentic handles have been used. The desk in old pinewood with an original red patina is from Hungary.

Old terracotta floors (a mixture of red and black tiles) have been used in the scullery and washing area. Made-to-measure doors in old pinewood. The small washbasin in Belgian bluestone is operated with a foot-pump.

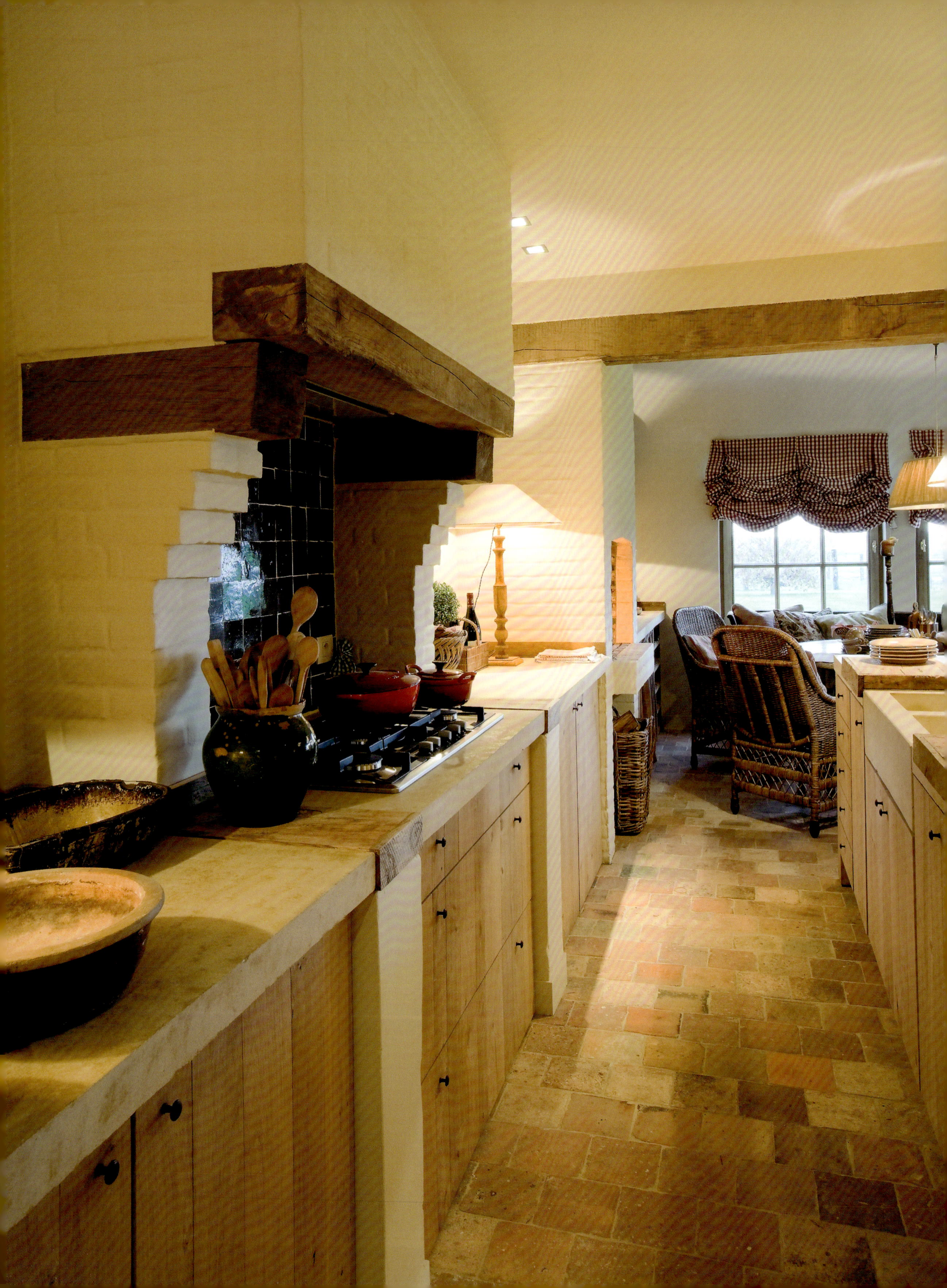

The kitchen units are in oak; the floors are in old terracotta tiles.
The concrete work surface was given a special treatment and made to tone with the oak.

A raised open fireplace in a wall with a lime finish.

The old pinewood bench painted in "faux bois" effect and the table are from Hungary.

Kelim cushions made from old kelim rugs.

Old oak shutters in the corridor leading to the dining room. Custom-made lampshades in beautiful linen fabrics have been used throughout the house.

135

The upstairs corridor is also very simple and pure.

Oak floors and oak beds that have been fully restored and covered with velvet. An old-oak workbench as a sidetable. A kelim rug on the floor.

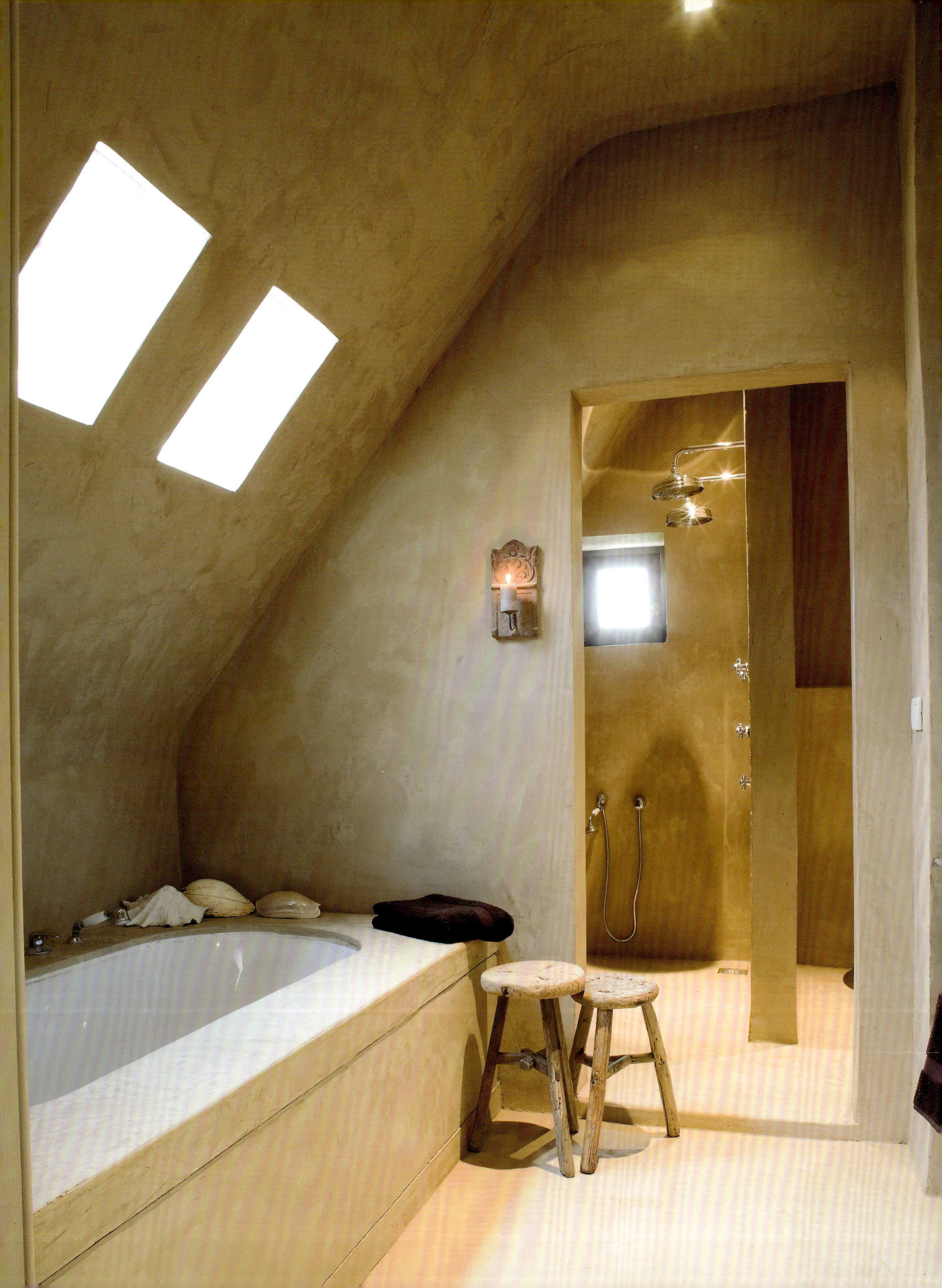

NATALIE HAEGEMAN

    Anthracite bvba
    www.nataliehaegeman-interiors.be
    +32 (0)477 24 24 45
    +32 (0)3 226 76 06

PORTE BONHEUR

    www.portebonheur.be
    Annemie Coppens +32 (0)479 02 99 66

The bathroom and shower are in tadelakt. The concrete washbasin has been given a special finish.

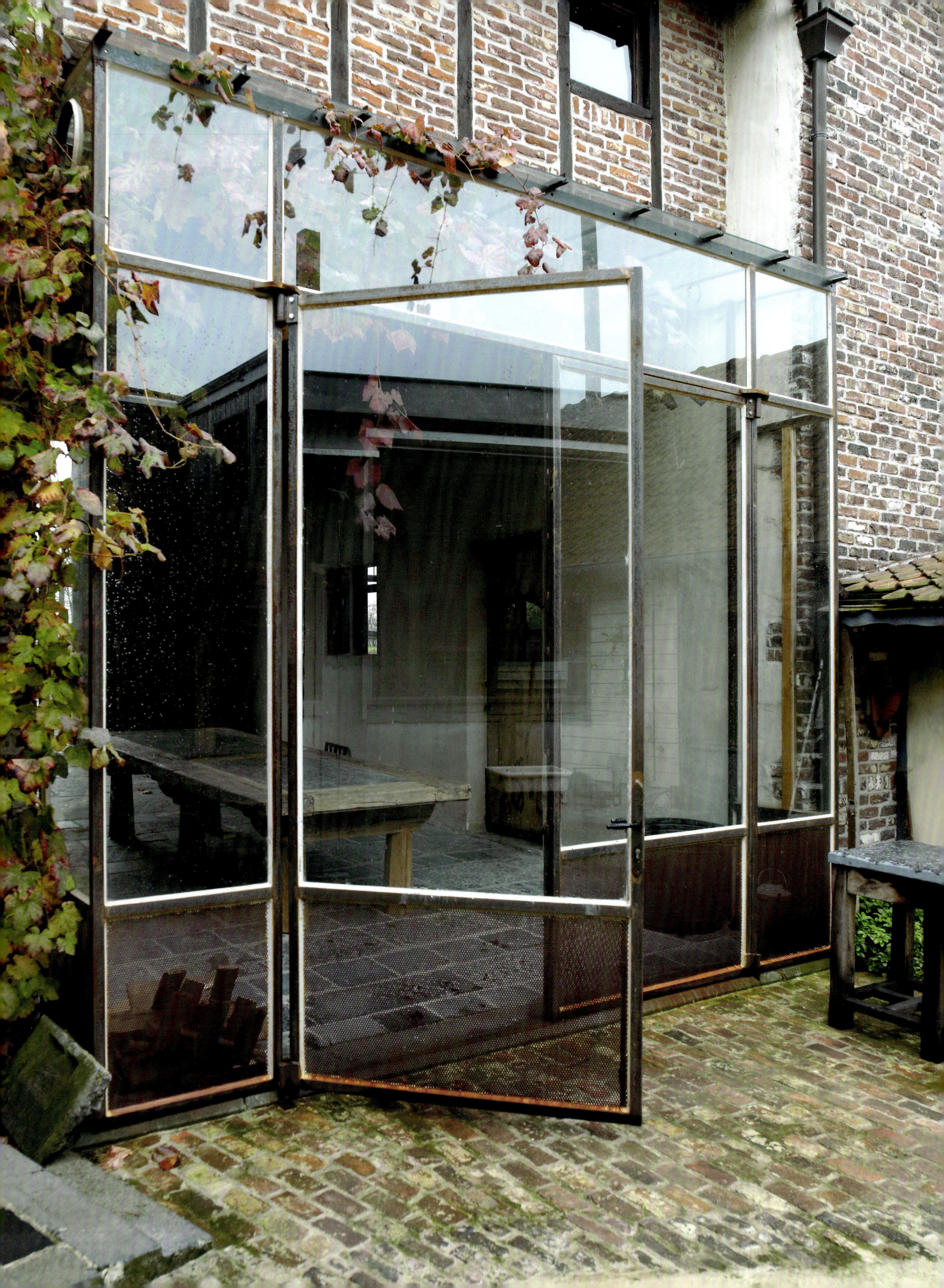

PASSIONATE AND REBELLIOUS, TRADITIONAL AND INNOVATIVE

Cousaert-Van der Donckt create individual tables and cupboards, as well as complete bathrooms and kitchens, doors and stairs, and many other features, both for home and garden. Wood is a strong presence in most of the designs, but iron, stone and other materials are also incorporated into the company's projects.

The staff at Cousaert-Van der Donckt certainly know their job, and this includes both traditional craftsmanship and innovative techniques. All of the staff members, whether they are product developers, carpenters, or antiquarians, have great professional expertise and a feeling for materials, such as wood, iron and stone. They ensure that these materials retain their original quality, whilst putting them to a new use. They are careful in their work: they work with machines and with their hands and their heads. And with their hearts. This is how Cousaert-Van der Donckt develop hard-wearing products with such a personal and artistic cachet.

A random selection of the materials used by Cousaert-Van der Donckt: oak beams, posts from a harbour jetty, larch-wood planking, iron window frames from a demolition, oak floors, clay plasterwork, old natural stone, limewash, reclaimed cast-iron supports and old iron frames.

Cousaert-Van der Donckt's tables are robust and dynamic: they are a powerful presence within the overall design.

A passion for traditional techniques and time-worn materials that have been adapted in line with modern home comforts.

The Dirk Cousaert team see poetry in raw materials that are often neglected, weather-beaten and battered. They recycle and reclaim. They draw strength from simple concepts and streamlined designs. They think around norms, preconceptions and trends to create unconventional and inspired designs for top-quality furniture and other pieces.

COUSAERT – VAN DER DONCKT

Design and creation of furniture

    Stationsstraat 160
    B – 9690 Kluisbergen
    T +32 (0)55 38 70 53
    www.cousaert-vanderdonckt.be
    www.keuken-cuisine.be

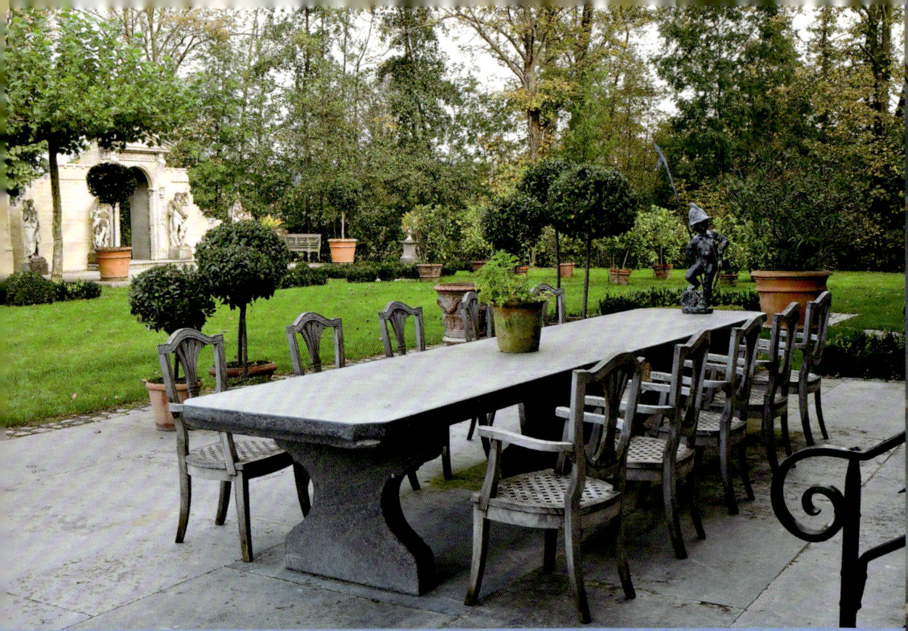
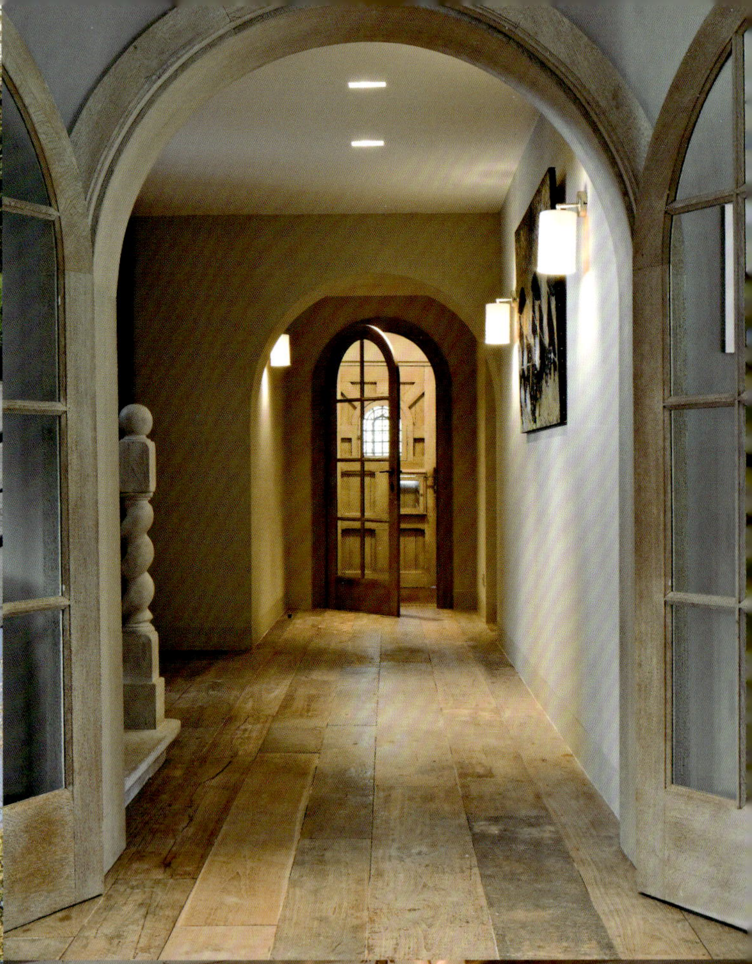
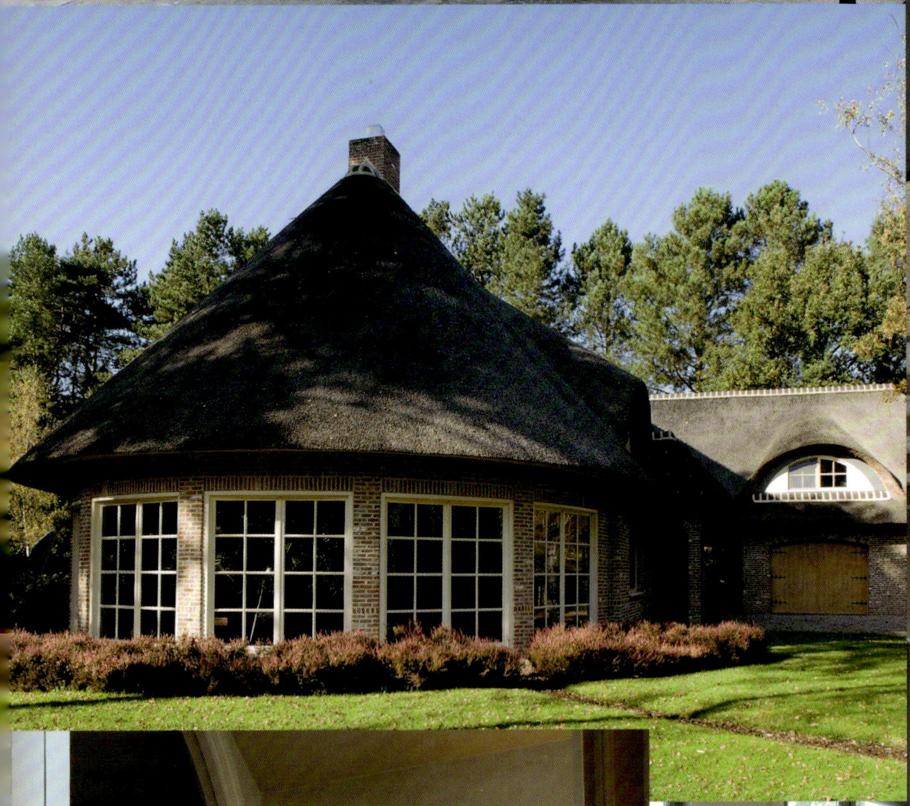
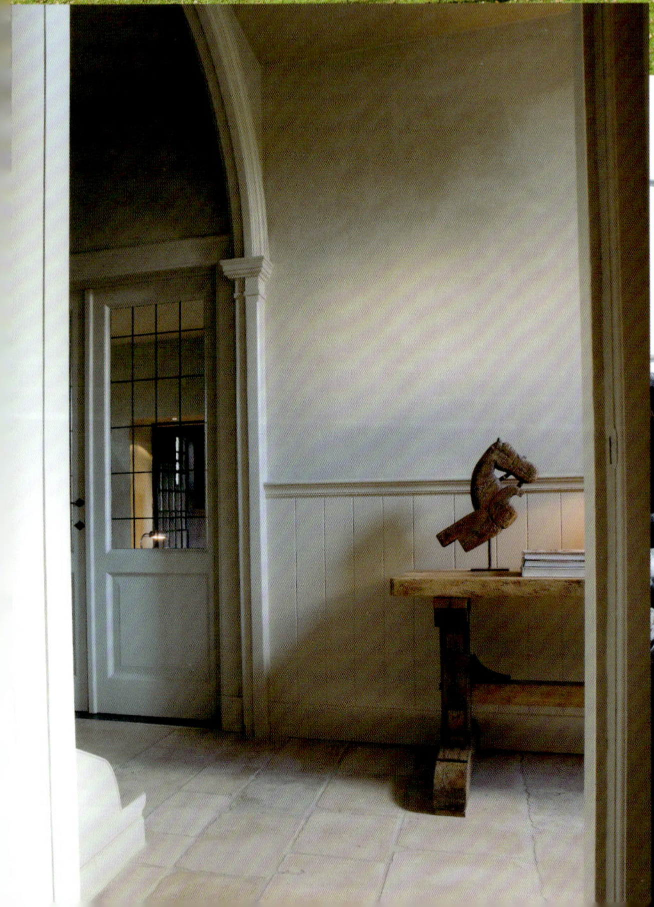
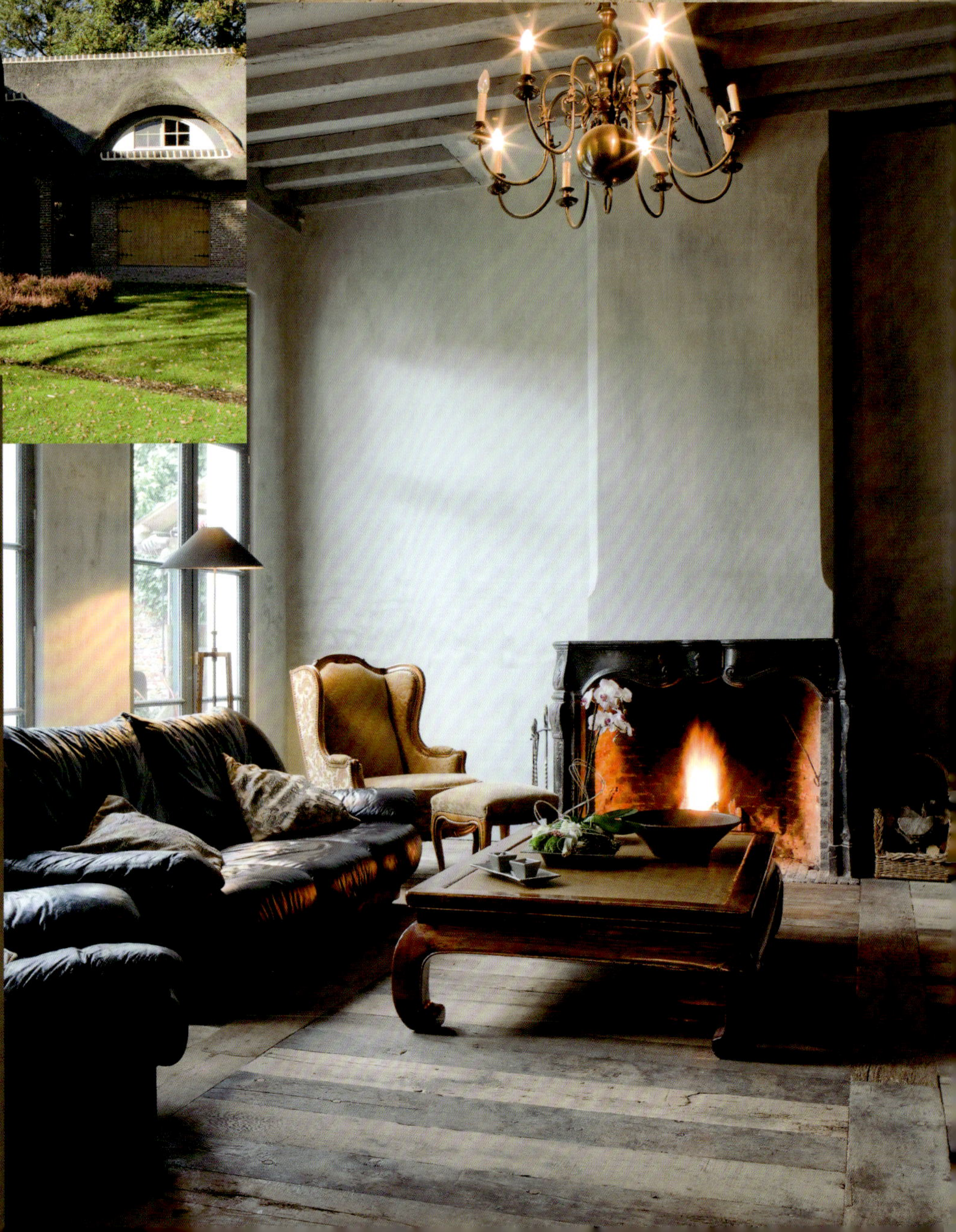

PART II

THE ARCHITECTURAL ANTIQUE DEALERS

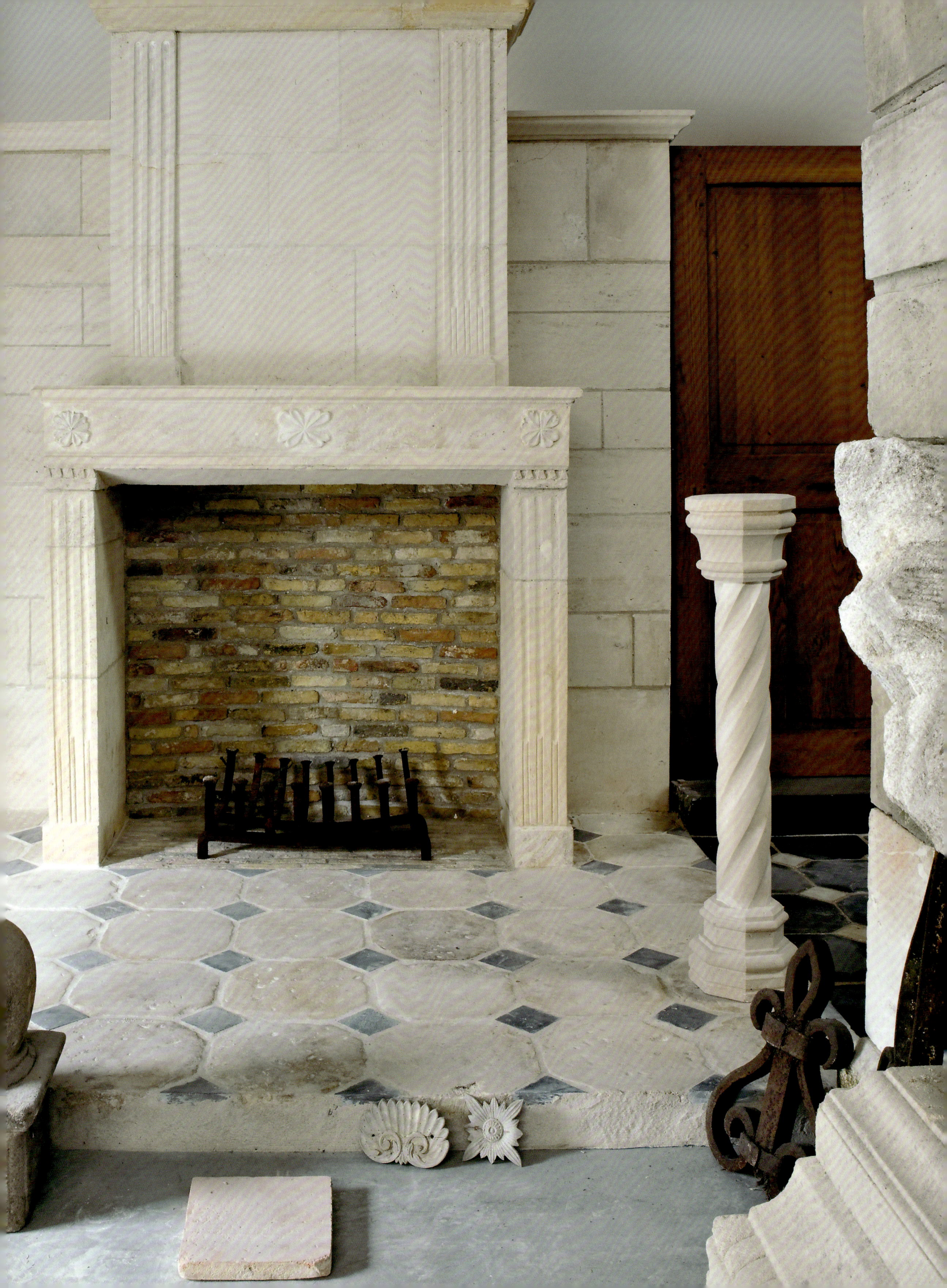

A PIONEER WITH A CAST-IRON REPUTATION

Vanhaelemeesch is one of the oldest Belgian dealers in historic construction materials. Hilaire Vanhaelemeesch started the business back in 1928, concentrating on demolished windmills, with the wood going to furniture manufacturers or being used in restoration work.
After World War II, Vanhaelemeesch bought fireplaces, floors, beams, gates and many other pieces for use in projects throughout the whole of Belgium.

In 2008, this wide selection is still one of the most important features of Vanhaelemeesch. Over the years, the company, now headed by Robert, Katrien and Jan Vanhaelemeesch, has placed increasing emphasis on treating and installing reclaimed materials, such as wooden floors, imposing fireplaces and more rustic-style pieces, antique stairs and window frames.

The collection is also aimed at private individuals: this is an ideal port of call for every lover of antique construction materials.

A Louis XVI fireplace with overmantel. In the foreground, Burgundy tiles with blue cabochons alongside blue Basècles tiles.

150

Some pieces from the wide Vanhaelemeesch selection: white-stone columns and a round 18th-century fountain; two ornamental stone mantelpieces from France; Louis XV double doors in oak; a cast-iron gate and frame; a holy-water stoup in French Bois Jourdan marble; an early-20th-century fountain with two water-spouting cherubs.

VANHAELEMEESCH BVBA
Veldegemstraat 13
B – 8020 Ruddervoorde
T +32 (0)50 27 71 96
F +32 (0)50 27 56 42
www.vanhaelemeesch.be
info@vanhaelemeesch.be

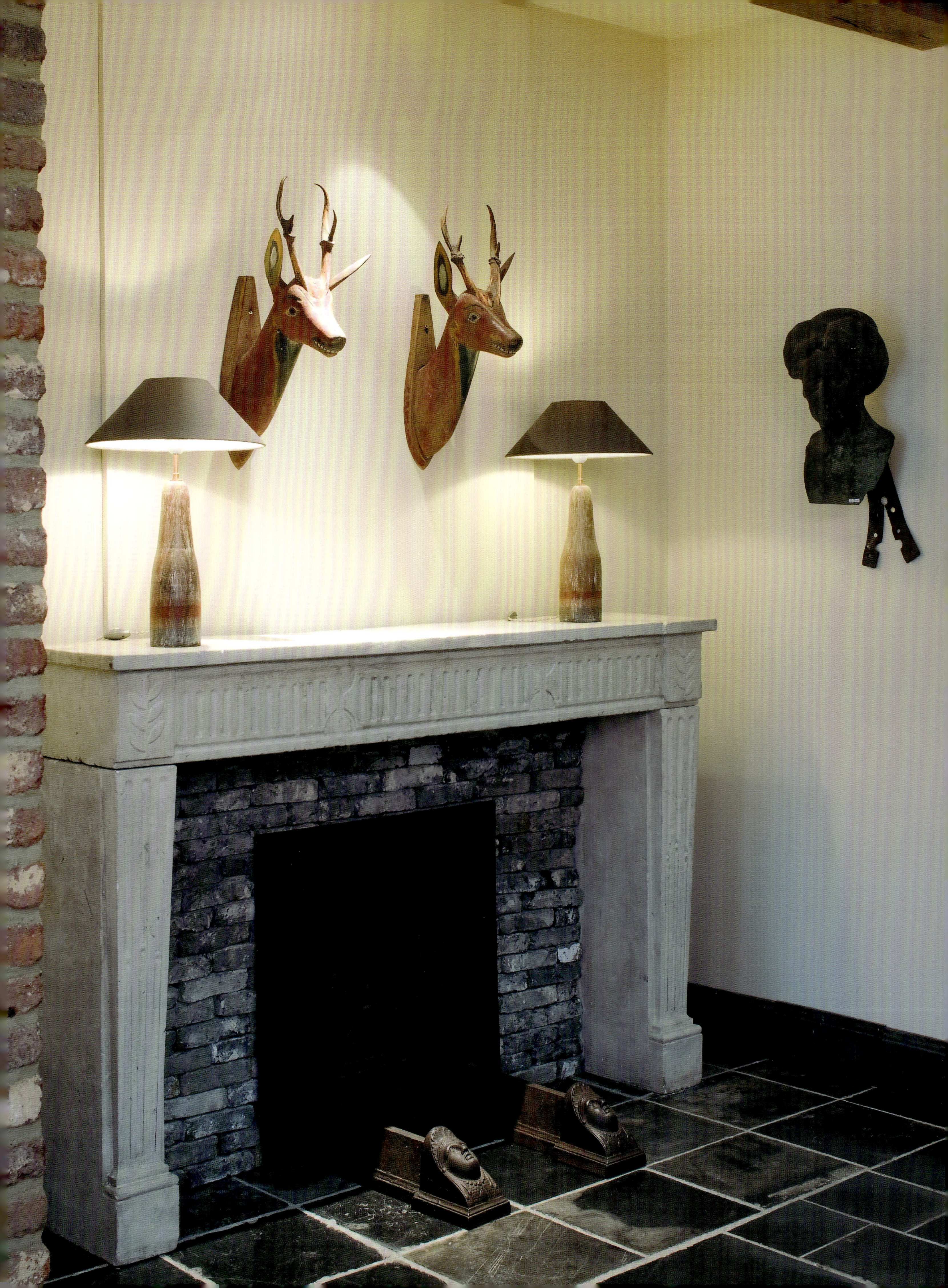

A CREATIVE SYMBIOSIS BETWEEN PAST AND PRESENT

Born out of a passion for saving the most beautiful historic construction materials, Architectural Antiques Theo Evers has expanded to become one of the most important suppliers of historic construction materials for Germany and the Benelux countries.

As dealers in architectural antiques, Theo and Ruth Evers form a unique combination. The strength of their success lies in their personal advice and their practically inexhaustible stocks of historic construction materials and garden features, which can be seen in the company's 3000m² display space and their 4000m² of historic garden designs.

Their inspiring showrooms are also definitely worth a visit, offering a creative symbiosis of past and present, with respect for the historic essence.

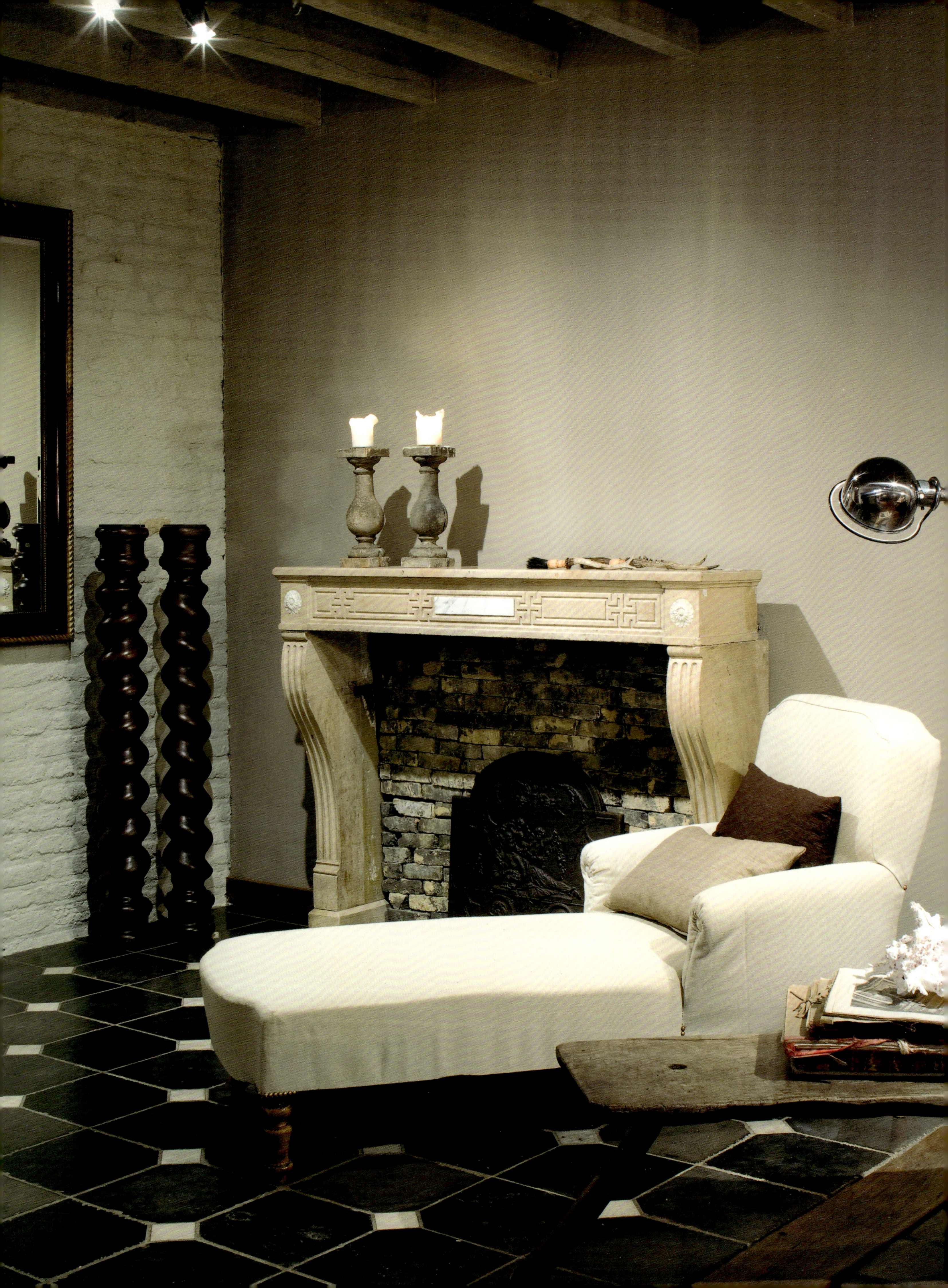

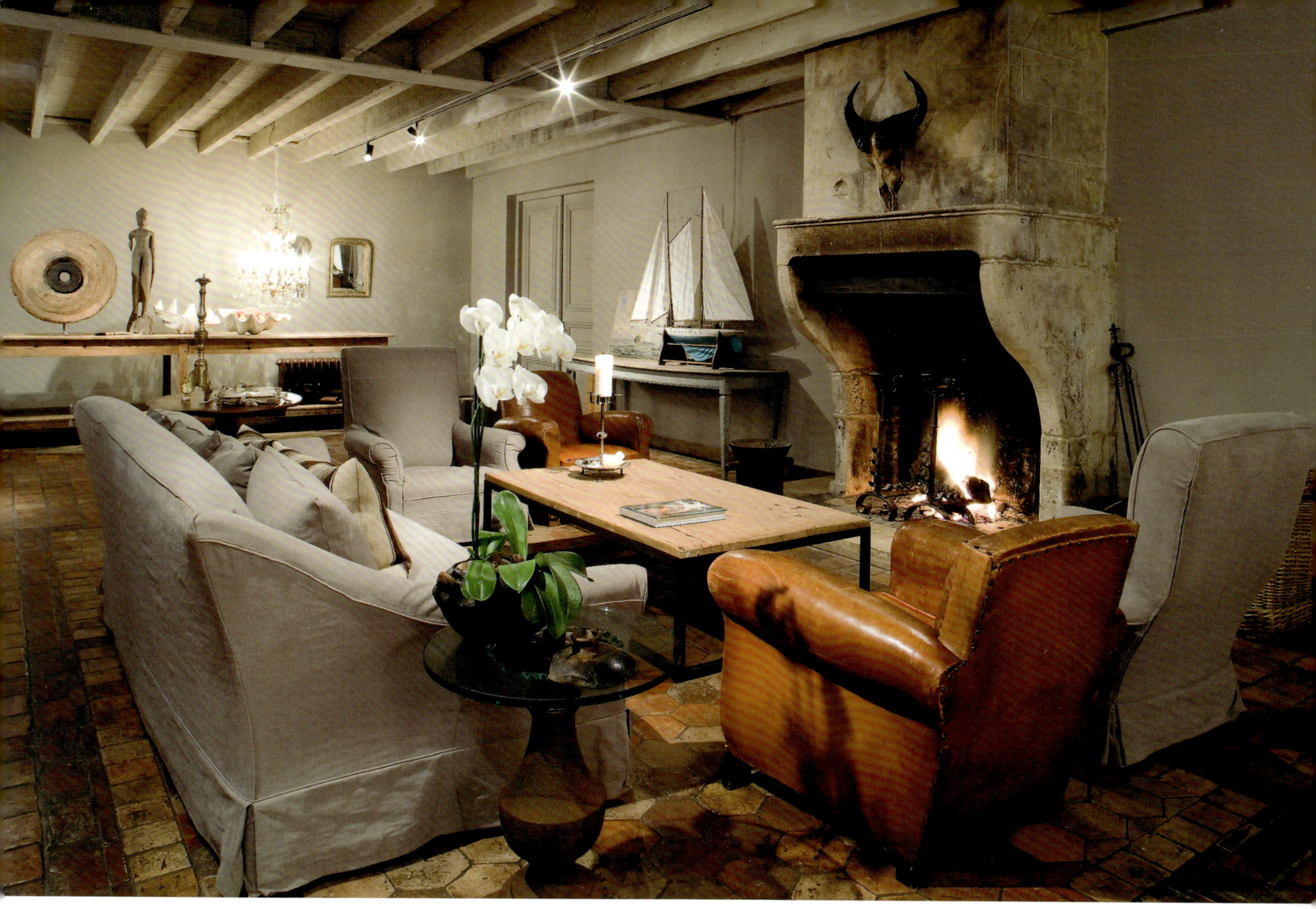

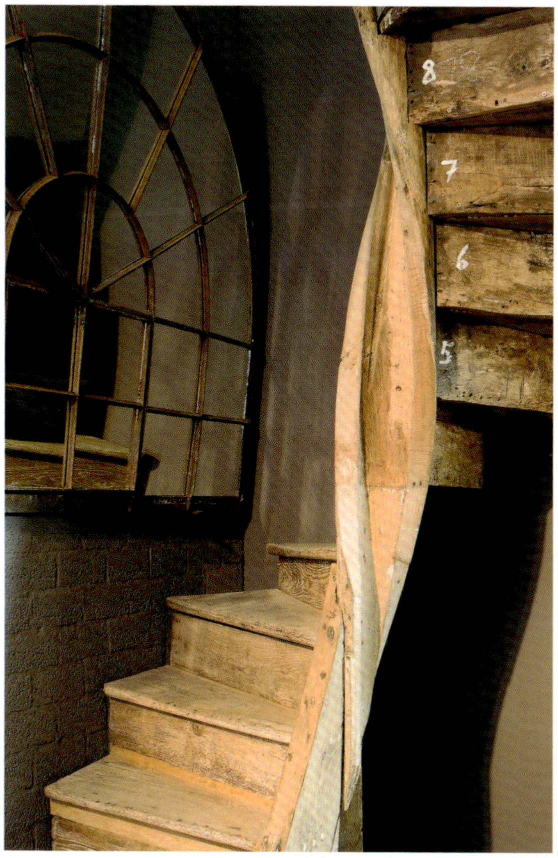
8
7
6
5

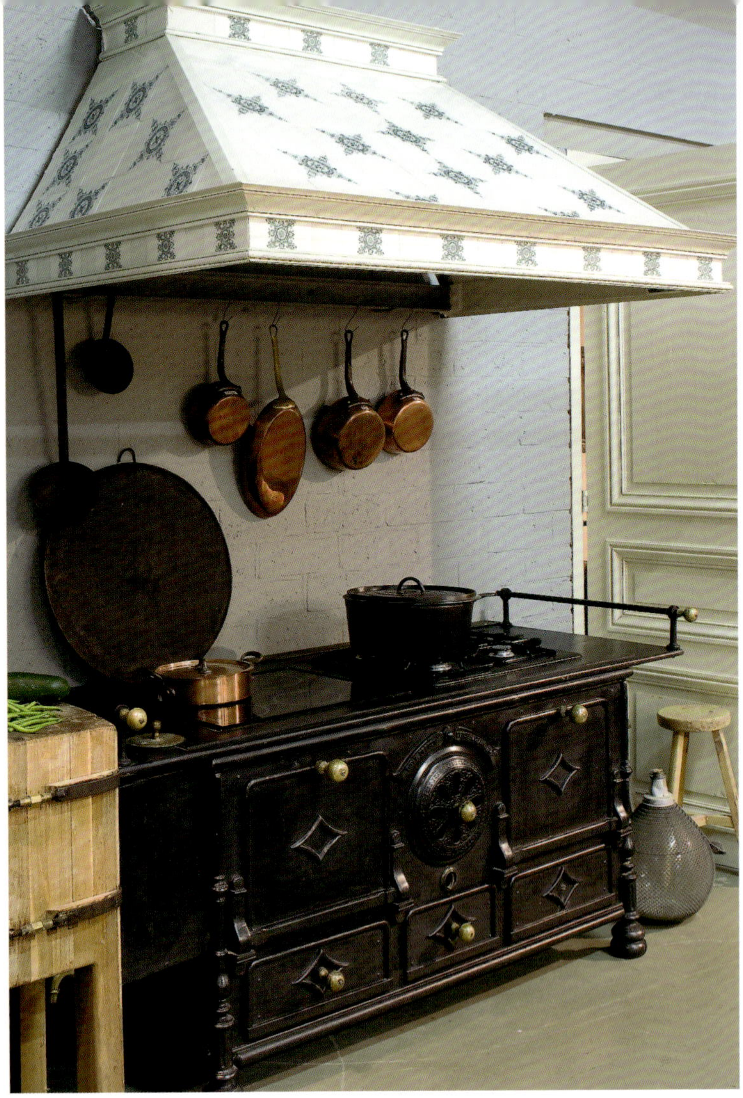

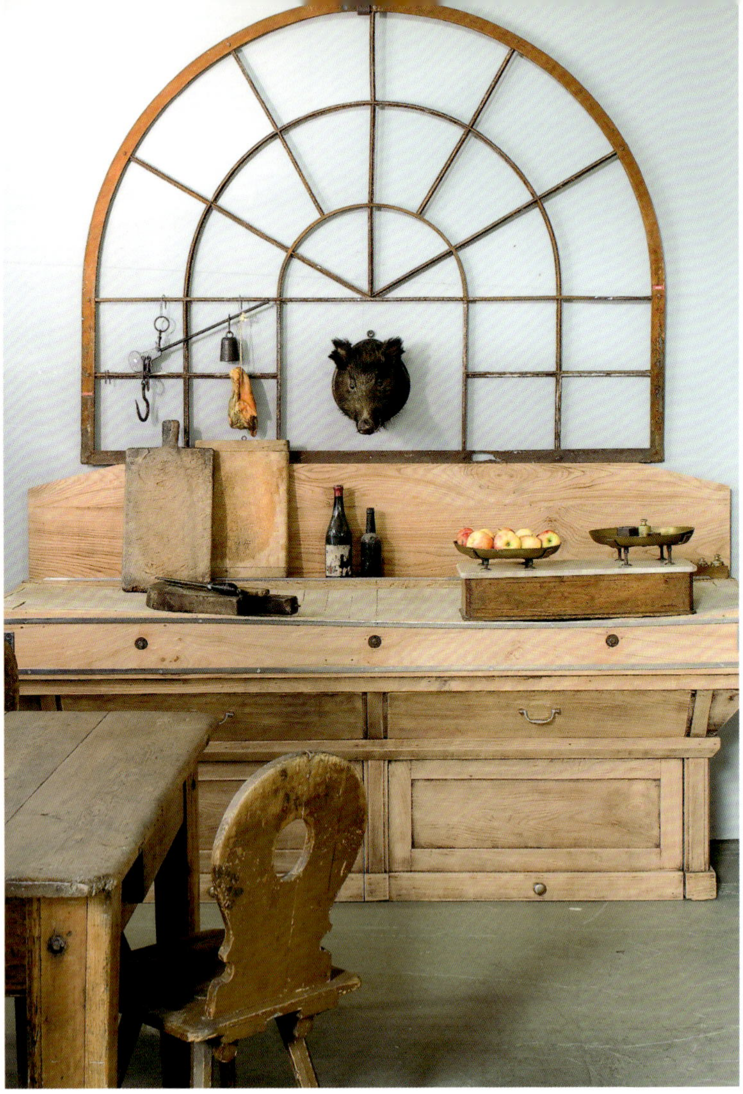

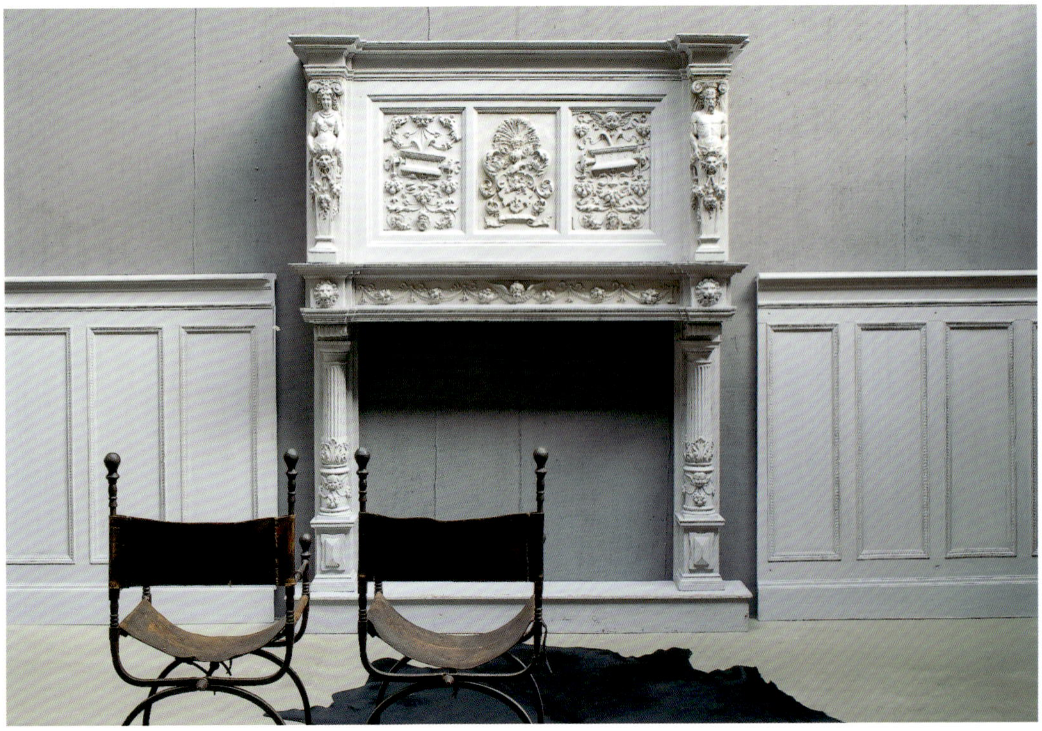

ARCHITECTURAL ANTIQUES THEO EVERS bv
de Koumen 58
NL – 6433 KD Heerlen-Noord
T +31 (0)45 522 33 33
www.theo-evers.com
info@theo-evers.com
Opening hours:
Thursday and Friday from 10.00–5.00.
Saturday from 10.00–4.00.
First Sunday of the month from 11.00–3.00.

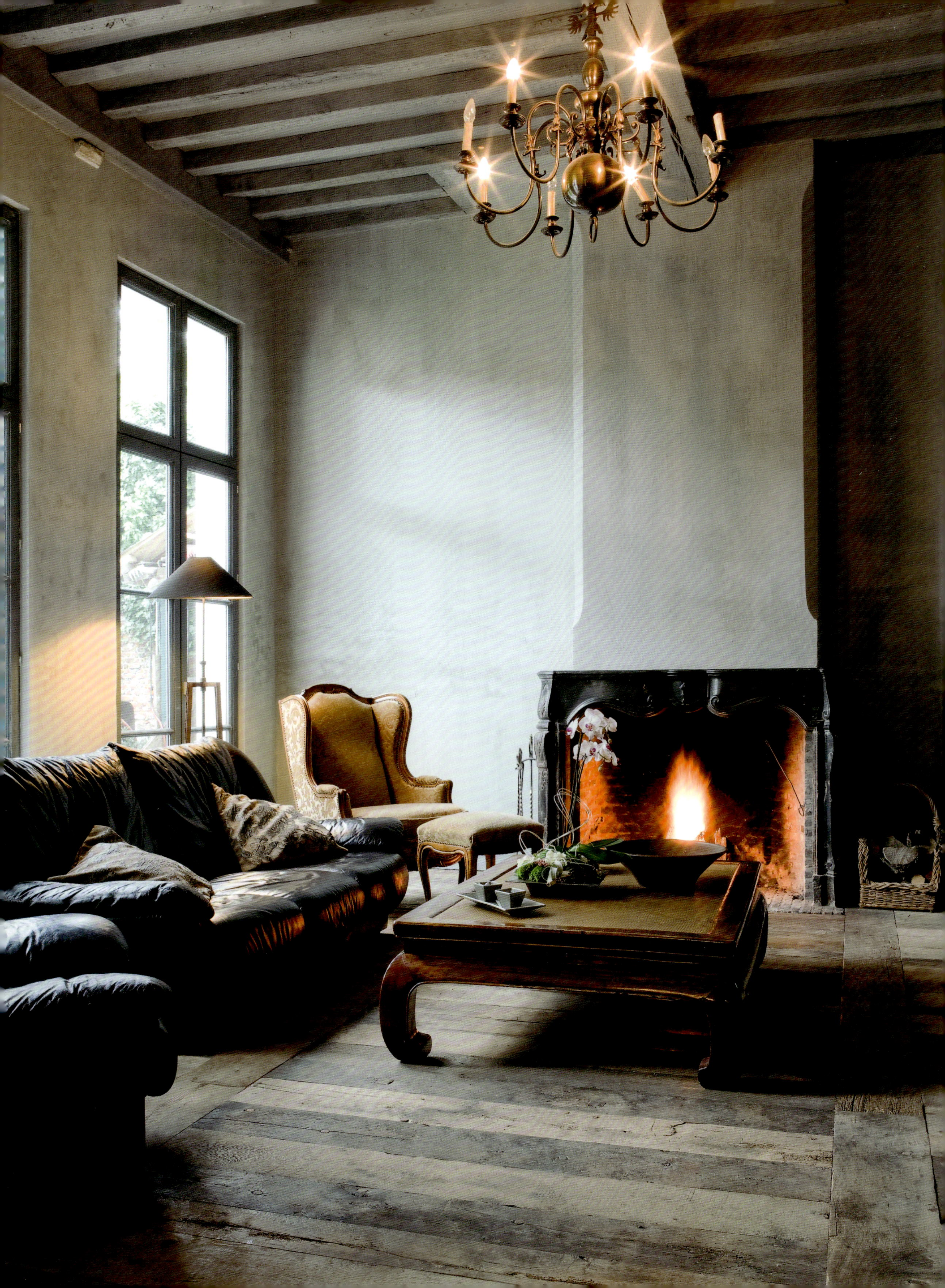

A PASSION FOR HISTORIC WOODEN FLOORS

Filip Redant is an antique dealer and restorer with a particular passion for historic wooden floors.

The most beautiful wooden floors are meticulously restored in the workshops of Passe Partout/Historical Wooden Floors.
The activities of this company from Mechelen also include the installation of authentic (reclaimed) oak floors from the eighteenth century.

In this report, Filip Redant presents a number of examples of his company's outstanding craftsmanship.

This 17th-century oak floor has been laid in three strips, with two long crossbeams in between. These are an allusion to wooden joists beneath, which are in fact not present, as the floor is laid upon a screed base with under-floor heating. However, this look is in keeping with historic examples.
The floor has retained its original patina, including traces of hand-sawing. The surface of the wood has simply been soaped so as to keep its natural appearance.

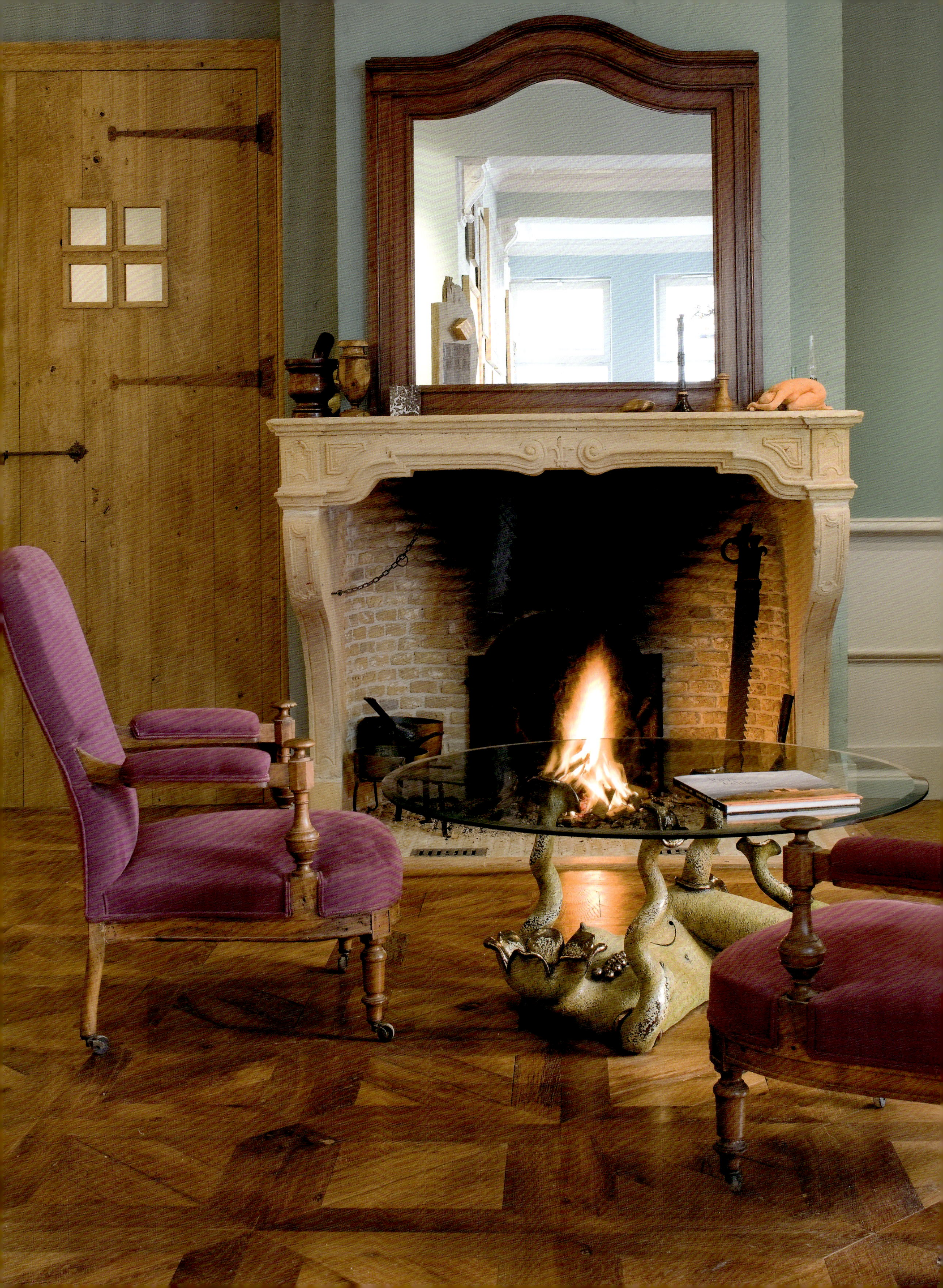

Eighteenth-century Versailles and Chantilly parquet with the original patina, including visible saw marks and hand finish. As in many historic monuments in France, an arrangement of the two contrasting panels was selected here.

A mid-nineteenth-century Hungarian point with its original patina.

p. 160
A 19th-century panel design with panels filled in with diagonal planks (with a mitre-cut frieze section). The panels are arranged in alternation, producing the distinctive pattern. The wood dates from around 1820 and was treated in the company workshop. The surface was planed, then sanded down after installation and finally finished with beeswax.

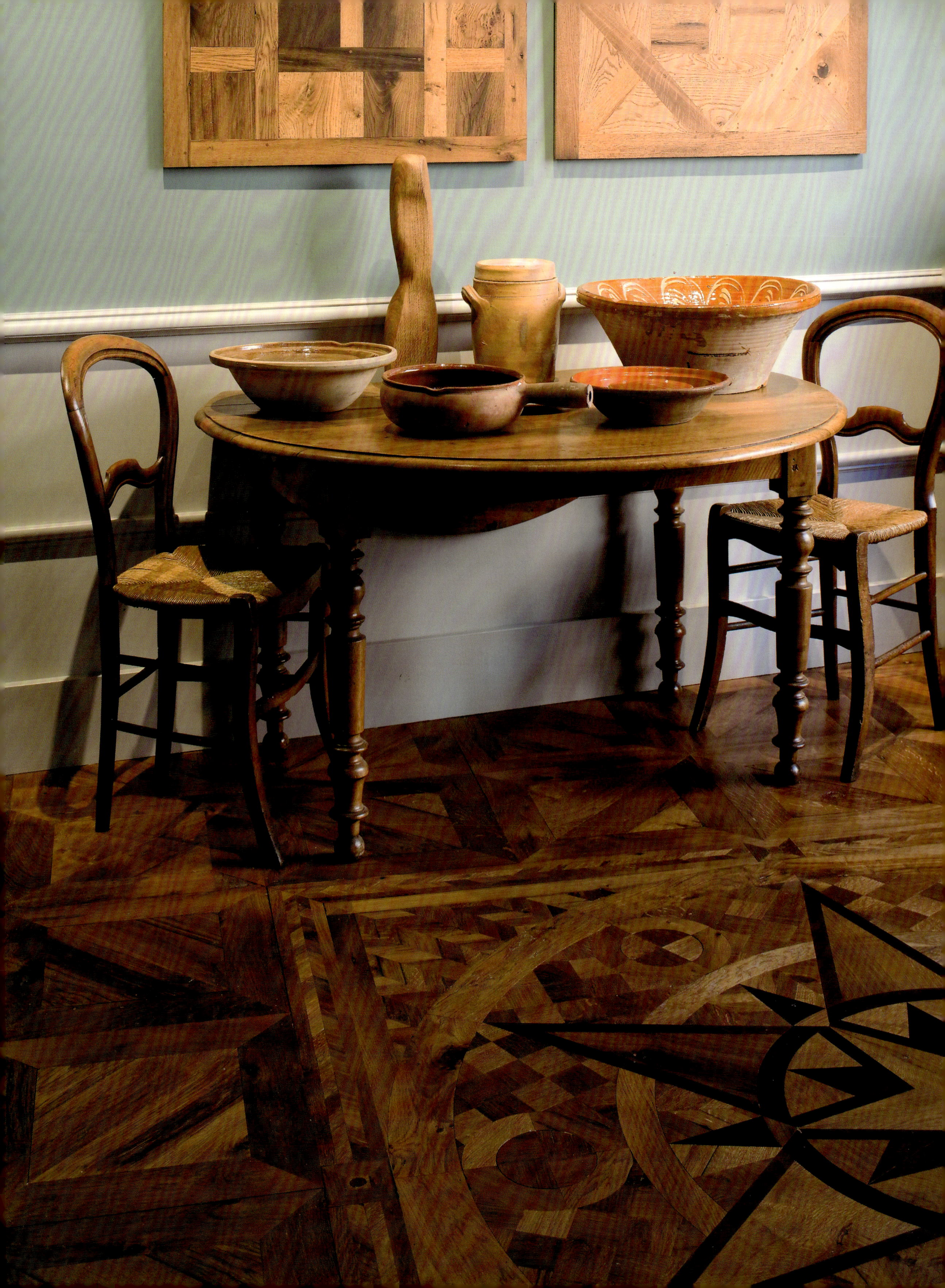

A number of antique parquet floors are on display in the Passe Partout/Historische Houten Vloeren gallery. As an antique dealer and restorer, Filip Redant has many recipes involving different colours and finishes: beeswax, soap and oil. Paints and varnishes are of course absolutely forbidden.

ATELIER PASSE PARTOUT bvba
HISTORICAL WOODEN FLOORS
    Galerij: St.-Katelijnestraat 41, B – 2800 Mechelen
    Postadres: Kazernestraat 15, B – 2801 Mechelen
    MOB.: +32 (0)478 56 49 54
    www.HistorischeHoutenVloeren.be

Marquetry in all kinds of geometric shapes. An interplay of colours is created by grading the old oak before constructing the individual sections. The more complex the task, the greater the challenge.

The star at the front of the photograph is a company design in 19th-century style, in keeping with the surrounding parquet. This star is 180cm in diameter and made up of 1050 separate pieces. A typical period element here is the use of walnut wood as an accent of colour. The furniture and pottery also date from the nineteenth century.

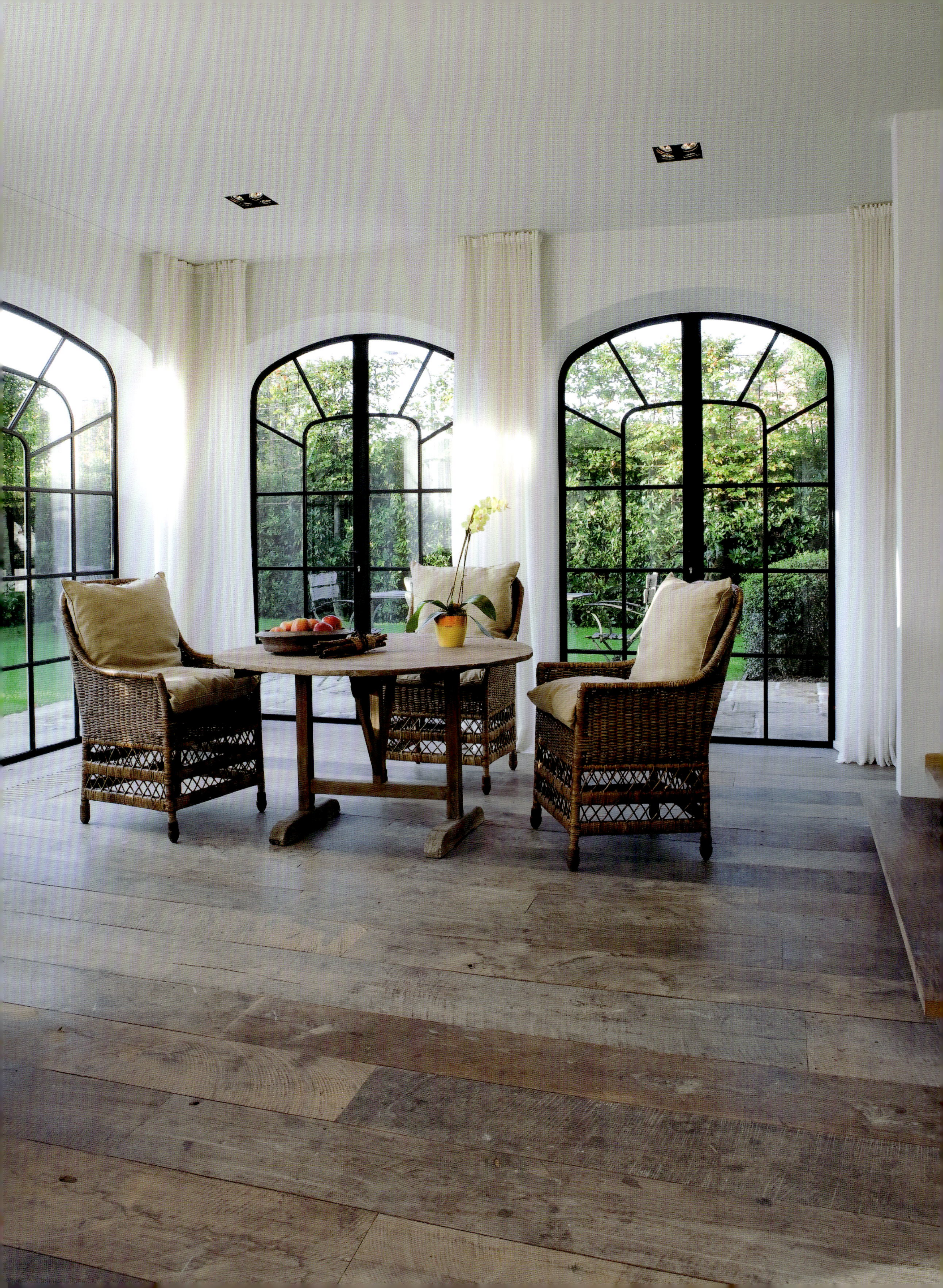

THE TIMELESS CACHET OF UNUSUAL WOODEN FLOORS

The family company Corvelyn is the point of reference for renowned architects, interior designers and private individuals who are looking for exclusive plank floors and parquets.
This company from Aalter produces plank floors in new and old woods, such as oak, pitch-pine, elm, teak and more exotic varieties.

An expert on historic construction materials, Jan Corvelyn goes in search of unusual lots of wood, such as wide planks in old exotic wood from Sri Lanka, antique parquet from a Bulgarian barracks, wide pine boards from granaries in the Jura, beautiful broad brushed planks from a warehouse in Nancy and antique stairs from Fontainebleau.

People who like unusual floors are sure to find something here to their taste: broad pitch-pine planks up to 28cm wide and 9m long or perhaps an antique Hungarian point parquet. However, Corvelyn can just as easily supply a perfect, top-quality floor for a contemporary apartment.

Lovers of wood are welcome to visit the showroom in Aalter and request a guided tour of the huge selection, which is all stored away in the company's large warehouses.

This report presents a number of recent projects by Corvelyn: they reveal the company's passion for unusual, distinctive wooden floors in exclusive, timeless interiors.

For this orangery in a grand country house, Corvelyn used reclaimed teak planks from old houses in Indonesia. The wooden floor was glued and nailed onto an 18mm sheet of OSB with a joist structure beneath. The nails are almost invisible and serve only to hold the planks in place while the glue dries. Granular insulation has been inserted between the joists. The wooden floor fits perfectly with the wrought-iron windows and is level with the terrace, so that there is no doorstep when the windows are open.

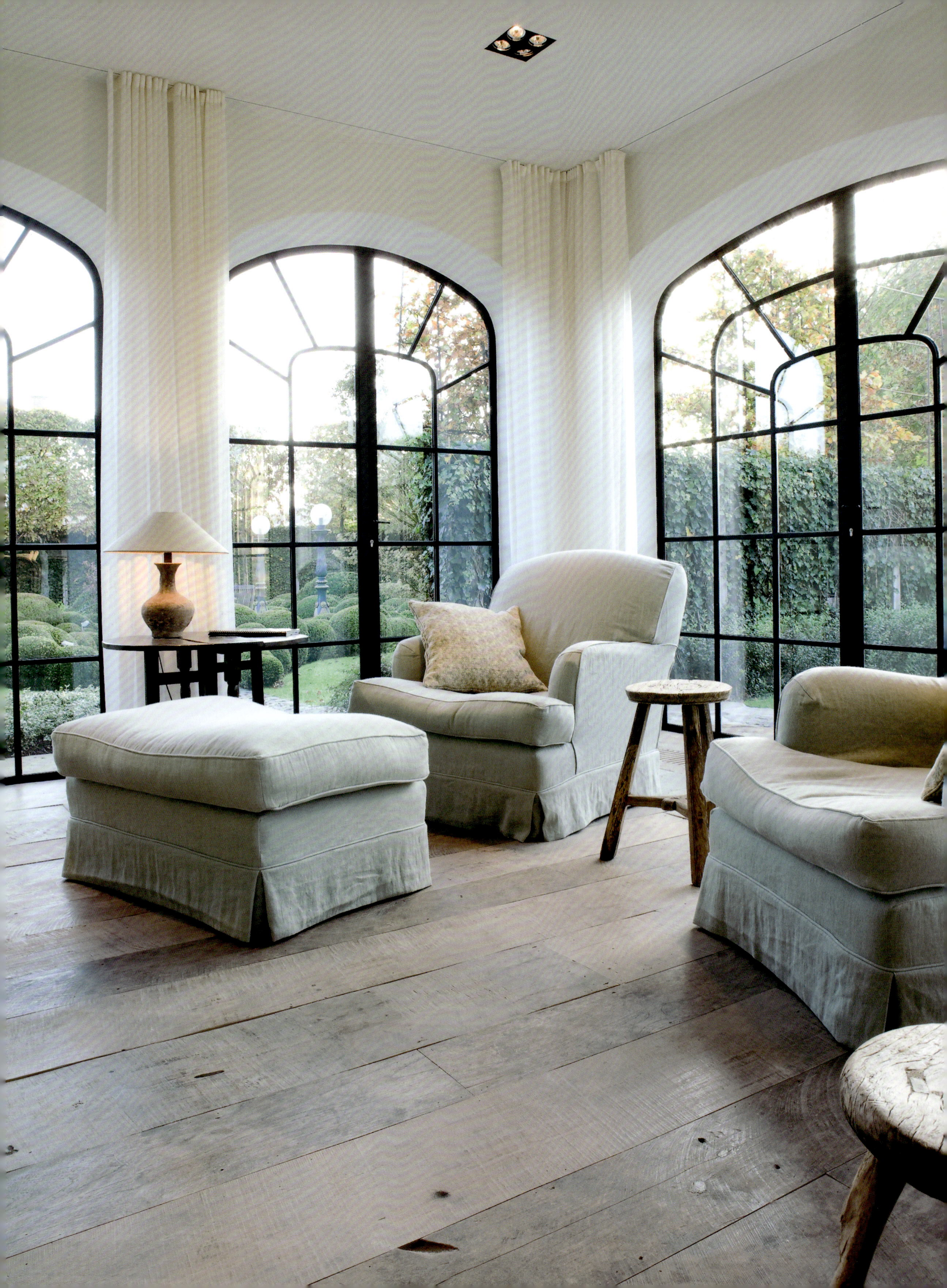

The convector grilles are made with mortise-and-tenon joints from the same reclaimed teakwood as the floor.

Once in Corvelyn's workshops, nails are removed from the planks, which are then sorted and cut to size to prepare them for installation. The cupboard door, bookshelves and stairs are in the same material. The clean lines create an airy atmosphere, with no rough and rustic feeling, completely in harmony with the English garden.

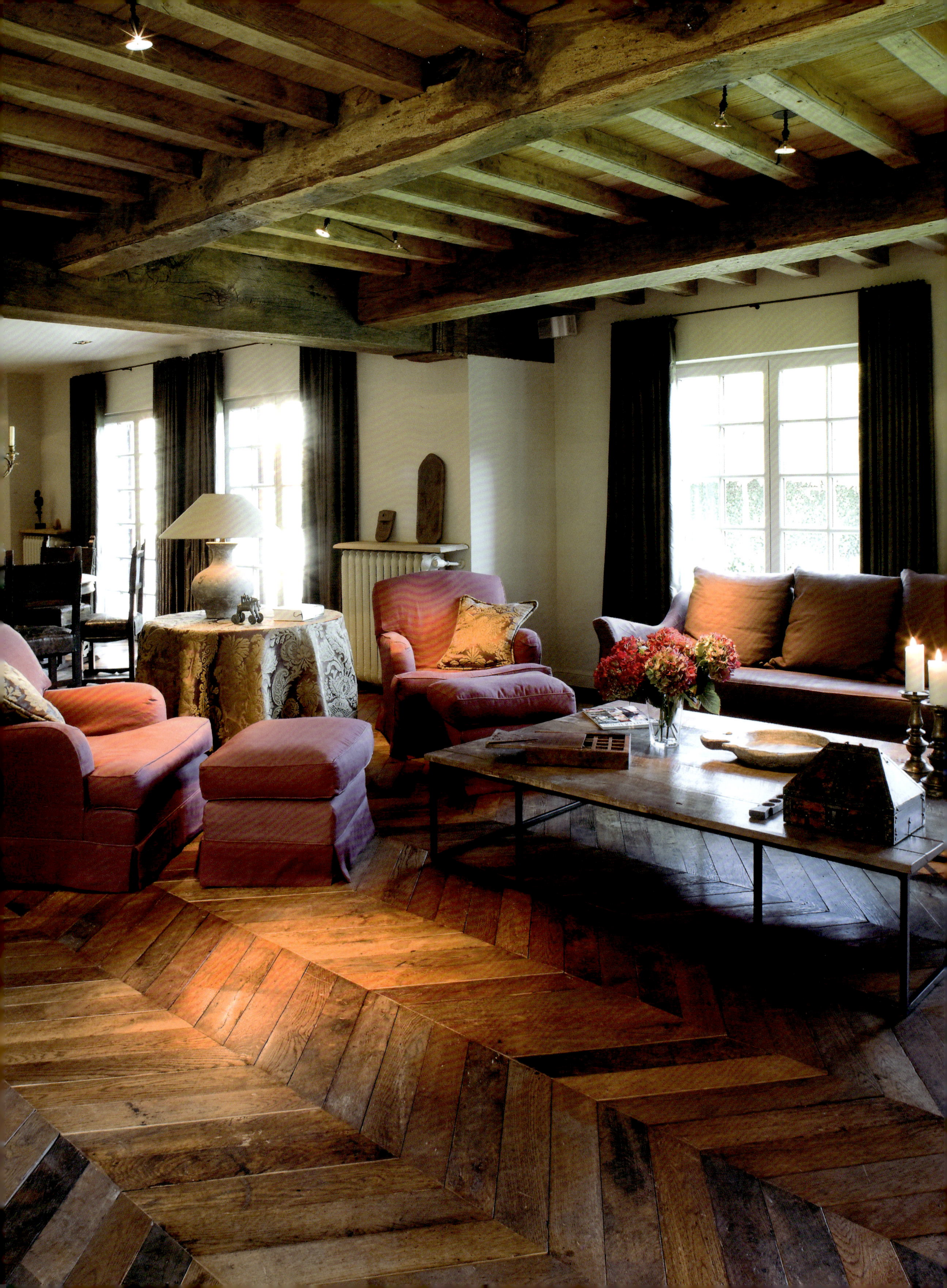

This authentic Hungarian point from 1870 came from the Red Cross headquarters in Avenue George V in Paris, which have now been transformed into a modern office complex. Corvelyn was able to obtain this unique floor of over 3000m² in size.

Owing to its huge surface area, the floor was originally created by a number of craftsmen, and every piece of wood had to be given new, uniform tongue-and-groove joints. The original patina was retained and occasional authentic traces of sealing wax can be seen on the parquet.

No border has been created around the edge of the room, so as not to draw attention away from the Hungarian point. The only finish applied after installation was a new layer of polish.

The oak doors were also created and given a grey finish by Corvelyn.

The double doors here have been placed in a block frame, but Corvelyn also makes simple doors with old planks hinging on two pivots within an iron frame discreetly built into the wall.

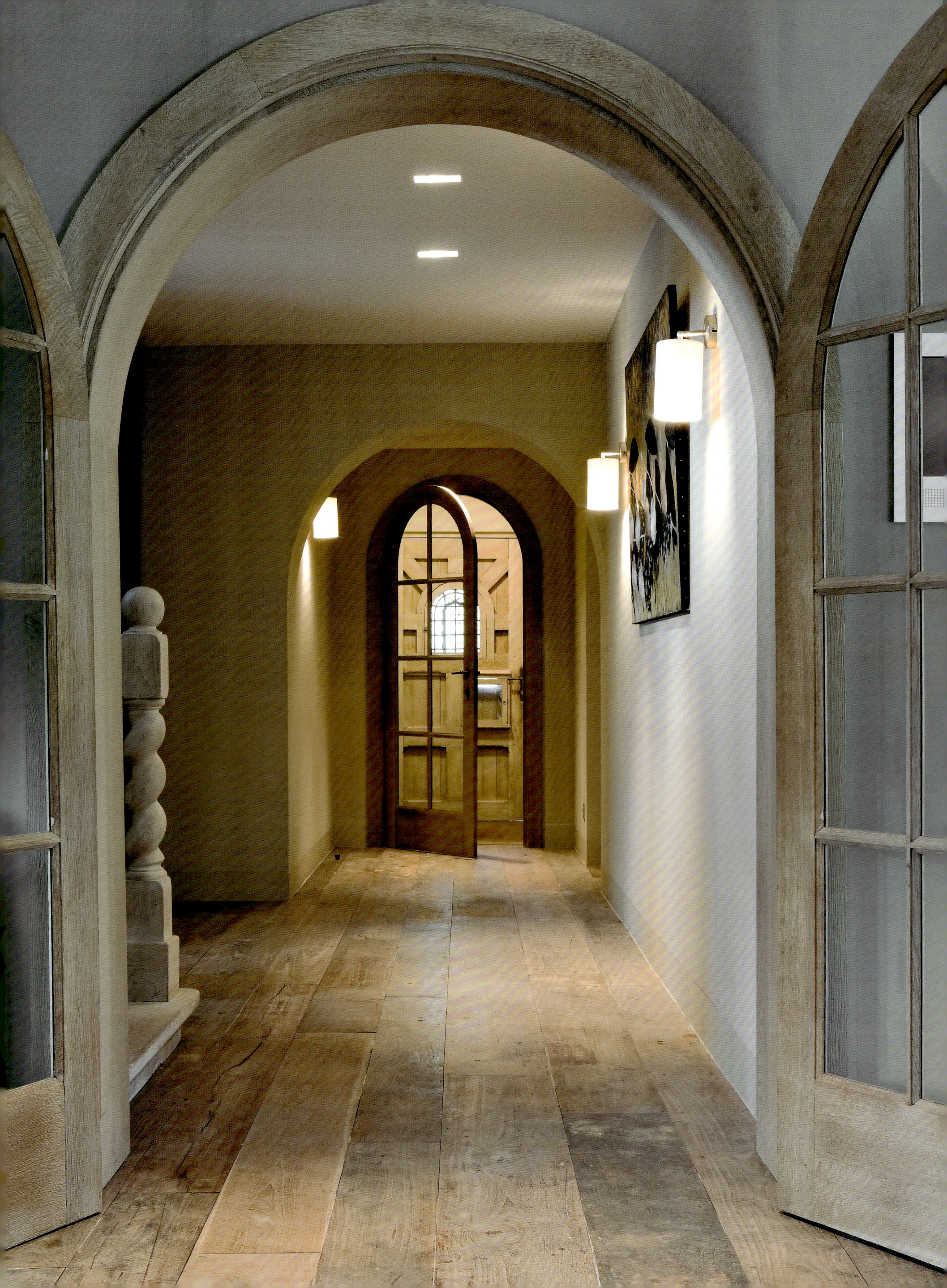

p. 170-179

This holiday home in Knokke has been finished in old teak planks throughout.

The client wanted a wooden floor that was capable of withstanding the scouring effect of the sand and also had a warm and timeless feel.

Under-floor heating was chosen here: old wood lends itself very well to use with this type of heating. The planks, even the reclaimed ones, have to be dried in Corvelyn's special vacuum driers. The company always uses a mosaic oak under-parquet that is given an epoxy coating, then glued together with a top-quality, elastic two-component adhesive. The planks are usually laid in the direction of the light coming from the largest windows or parallel to the shortest wall to make the space appear wider.

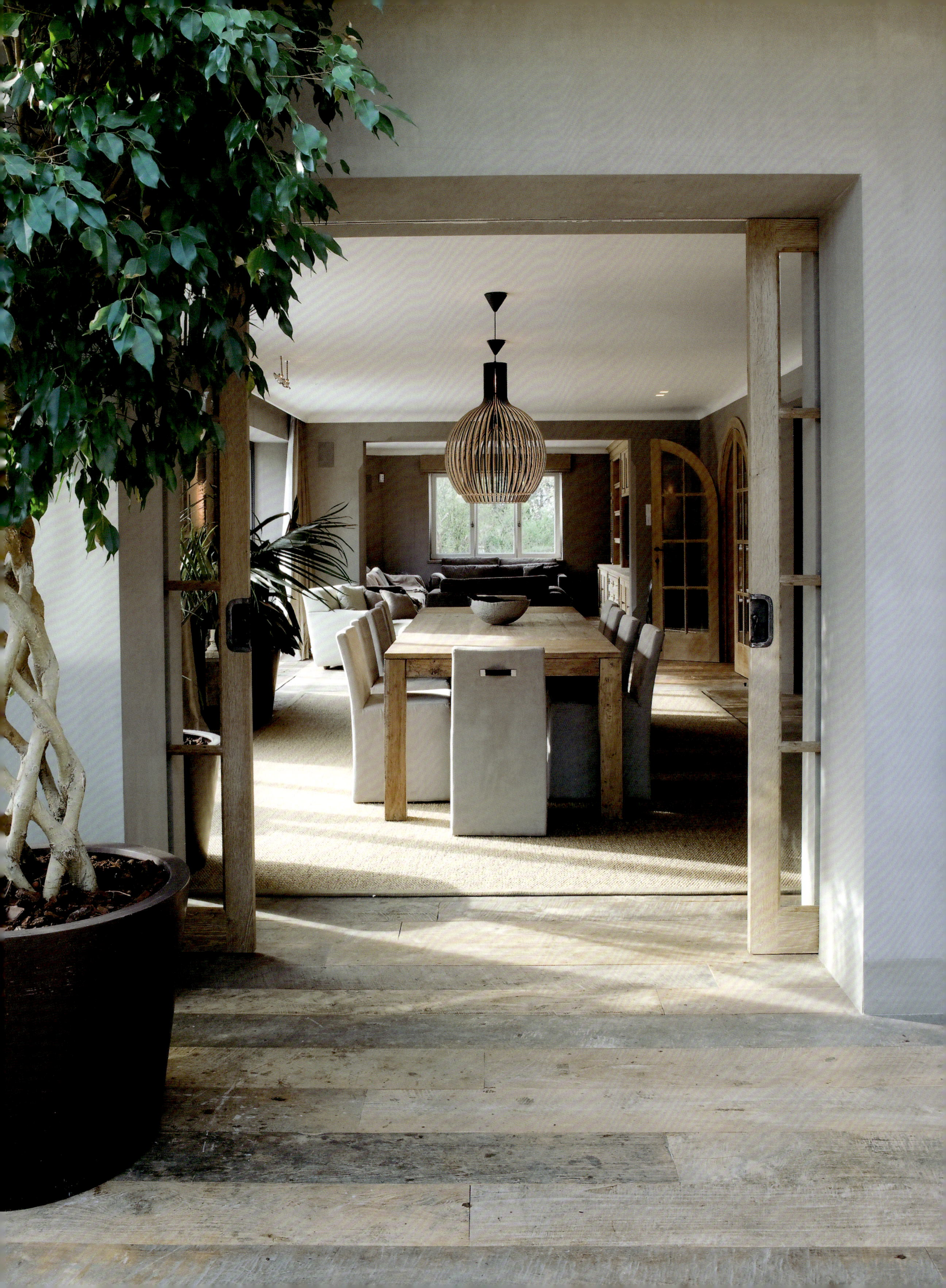

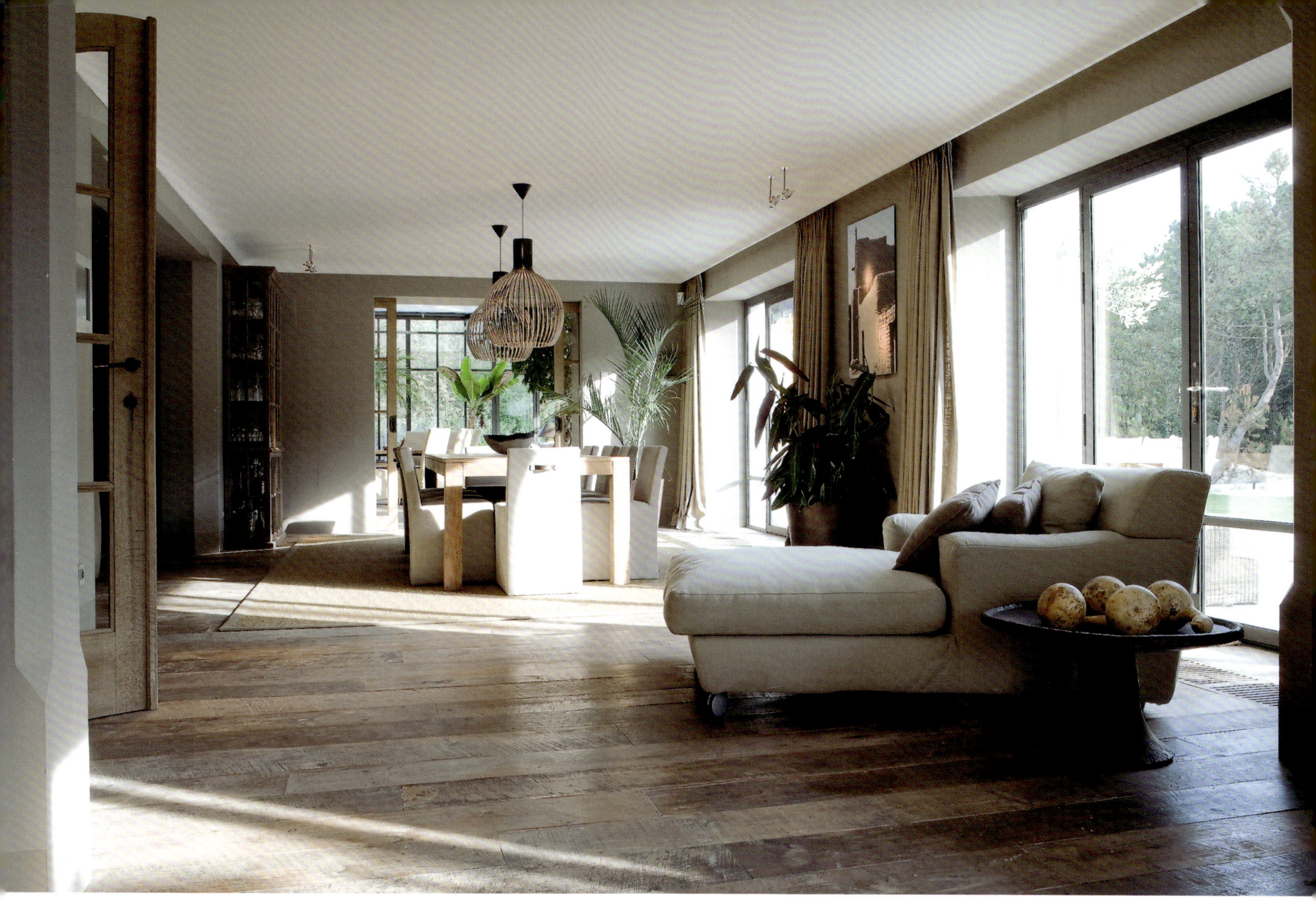

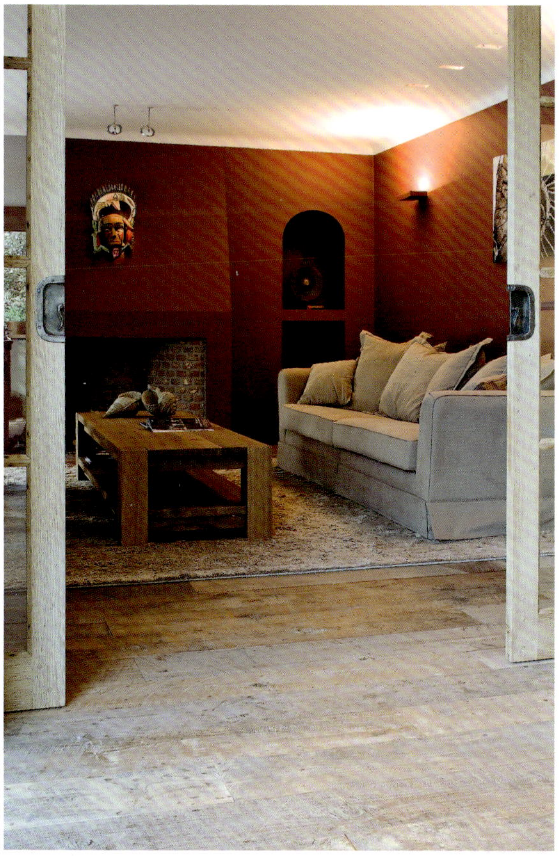

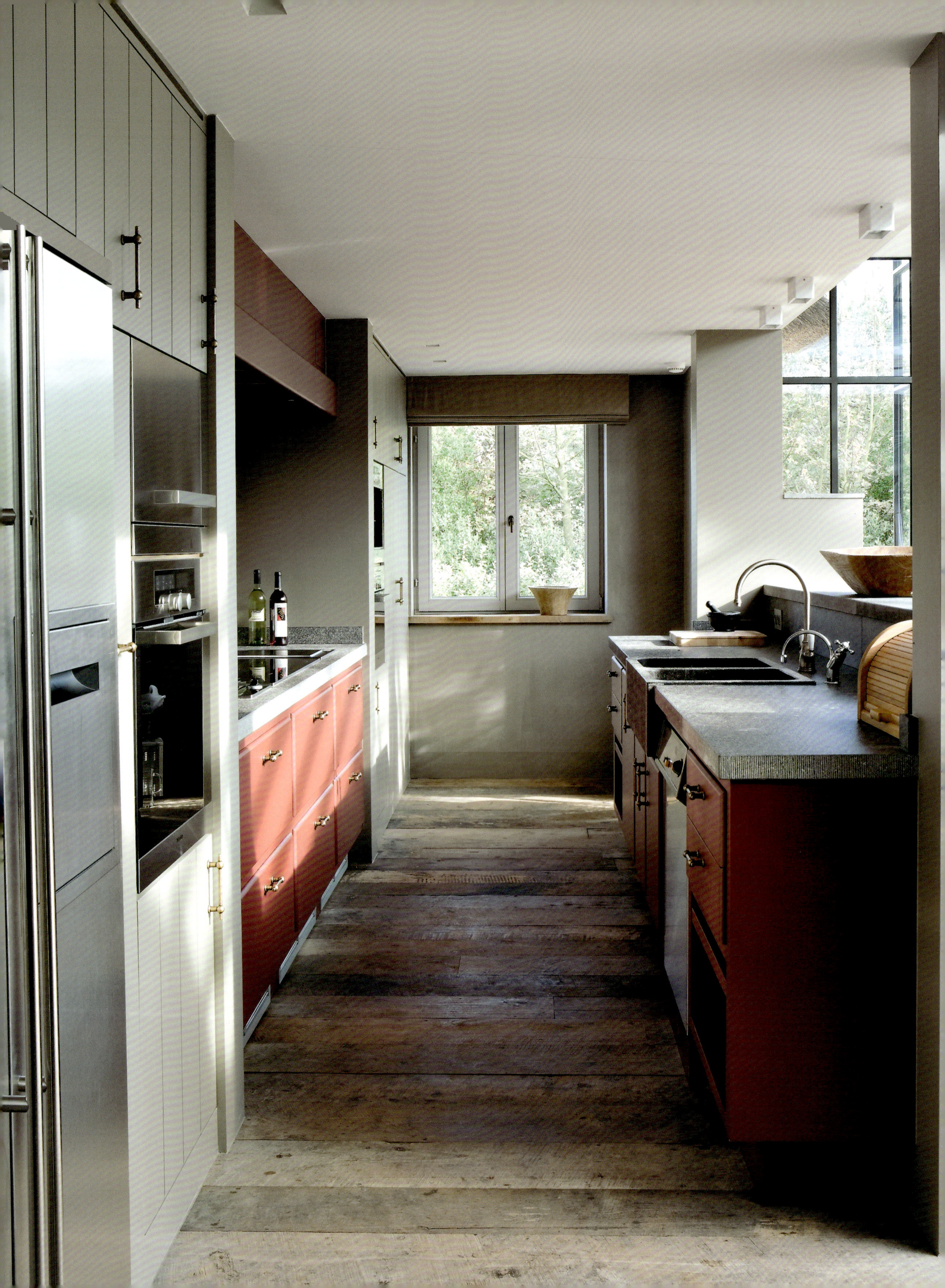

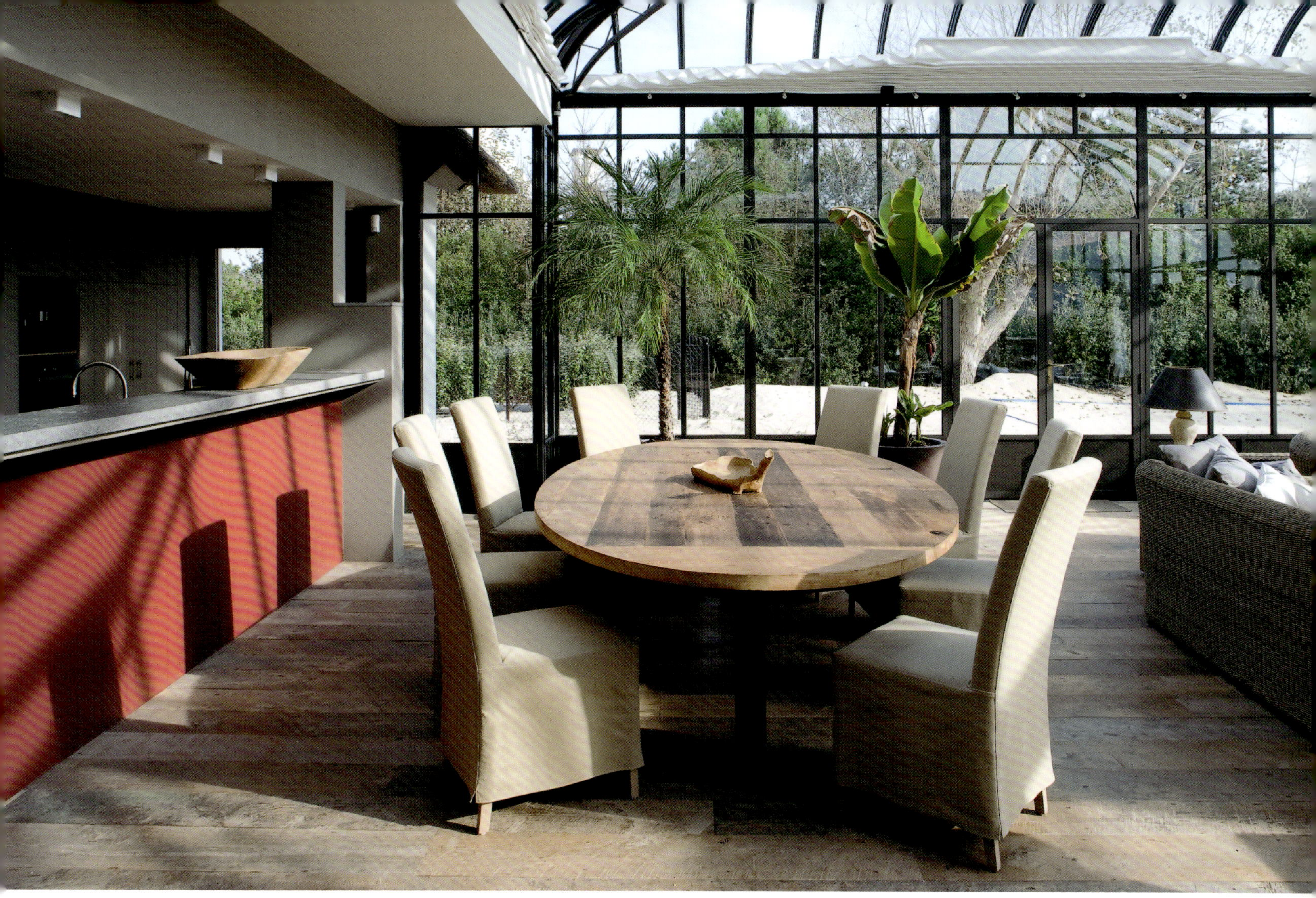

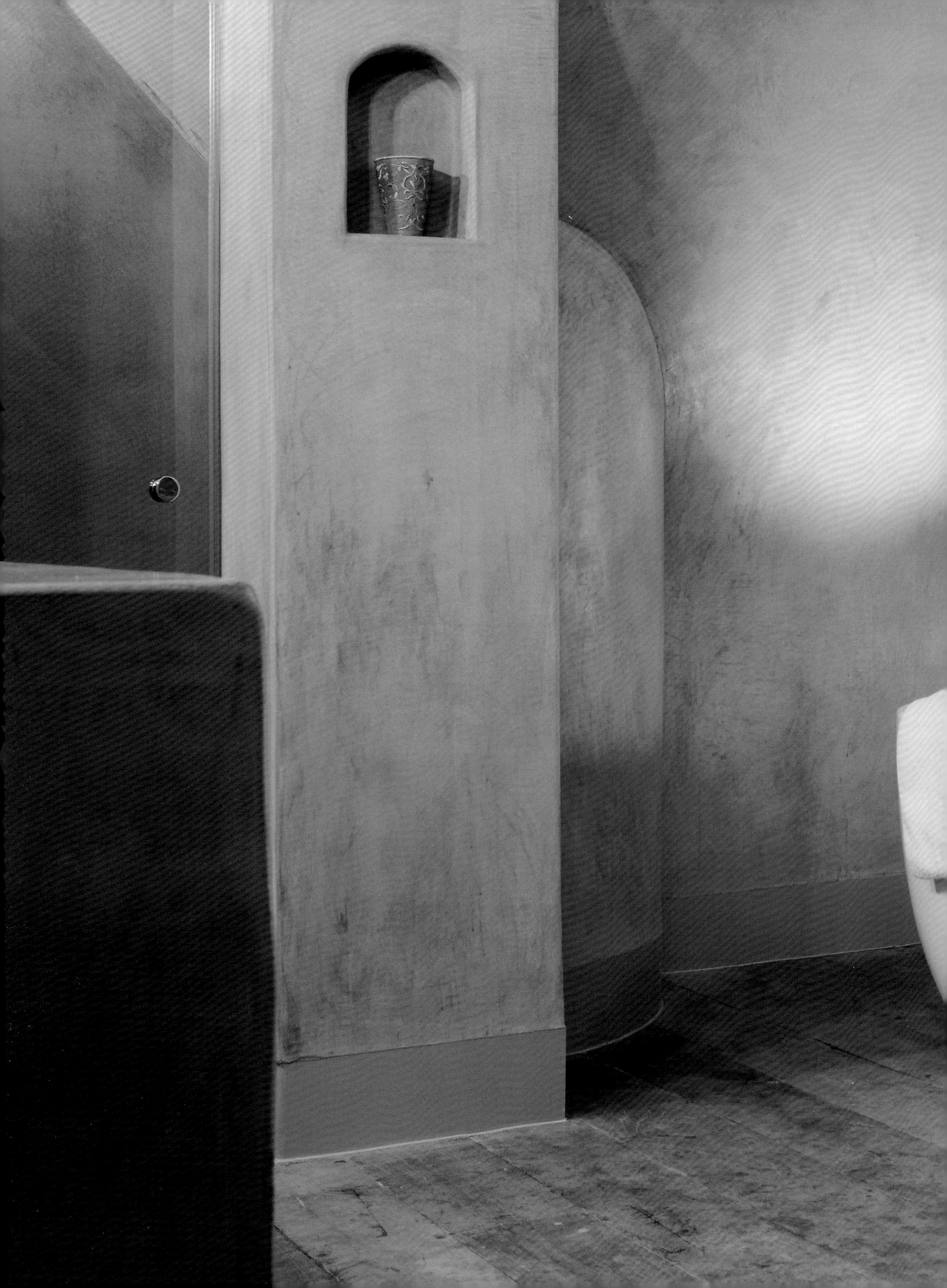

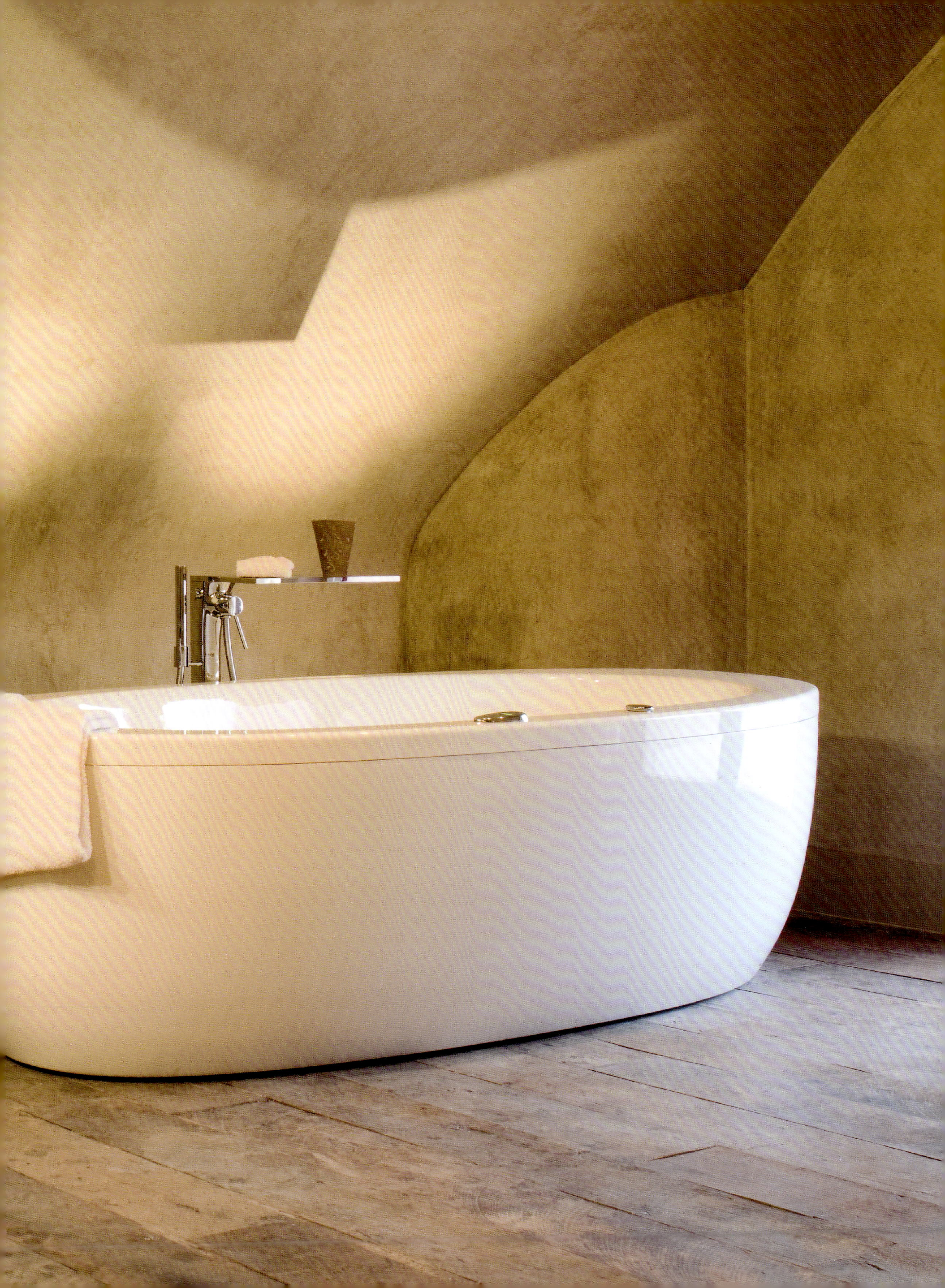

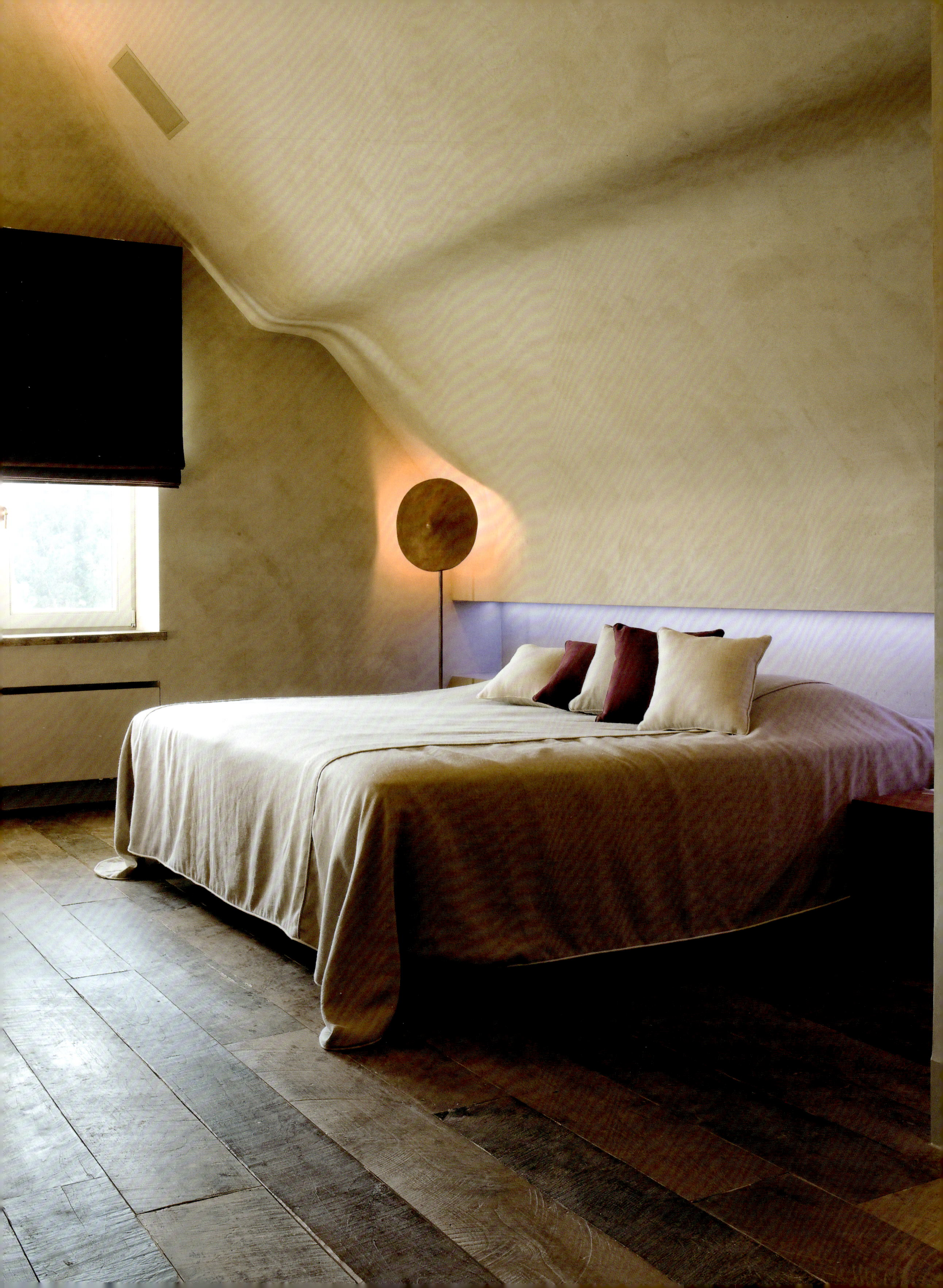

CORVELYN nv
Brugstraat 200
B – 9880 Aalter
T +32 (0)9 325 00 08
F + 32 (0)9 325 00 09
www.corvelyn.be
info@corvelyn.be

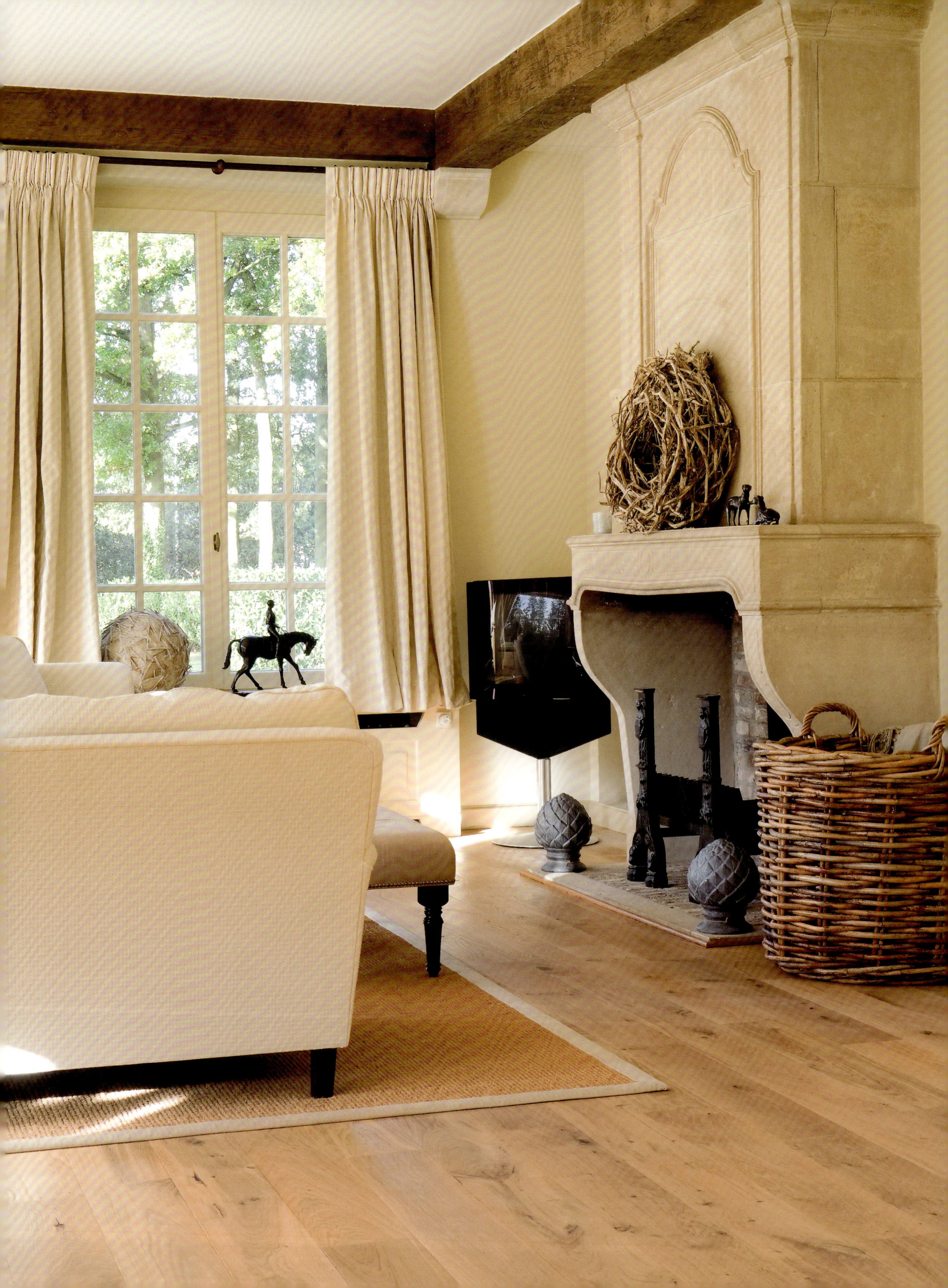

A HUGE STOCK AND A WIDE VARIETY OF OLD CONSTRUCTION MATERIALS

When it comes to old construction materials, Kempische Bouwmaterialen is the undisputed number one in the Benelux countries. Nowhere else has such a large selection: the most beautiful facing bricks, roof tiles, wooden floors, stone floors, wall tiles, doors, sanitary fittings, garden ornaments, fireplaces and many other pieces are all displayed on a site of over ten hectares.

The real speciality is the wide assortment of old bricks: the company always has around sixty types in stock.

This vast choice means that you can find everything you need to fit out an entire house at Kempische Bouwmaterialen. The company's main selling point – along with the wide range – is the immediate availability of stock including facing bricks, old doors, roofing materials, and floors in wood, stone and terracotta, all clearly presented in a beautiful Kempen setting.

An old Burgundy fireplace, old oak railway planks and a beam in old oak.

A bluestone washbasin and authentic Holland withe tiles with decoration.

An old church floor, an old oak staircase and a made-to-measure door in old oak.

An old church floor with a skirting board of Holland white tiles.

Old Leipzig tiles and authentic Holland withe tiles.

Old oak wall units.

Two old fireplaces in Burgundy stone.

This washbasin was specially made by hand in bluestone. On the wall, old handmade bricks.

Old French terracotta tiles, laid in rows.

An oak table and old terracotta tiles.

An old terracotta floor and a custom-built kitchen work surface in aged bluestone.

Wine storage made of old klampsteen bricks. An old bluestone trough and an antique tap.

An old bluestone floor and an open fireplace made out of an old well.

Stairs in old terracotta.

187

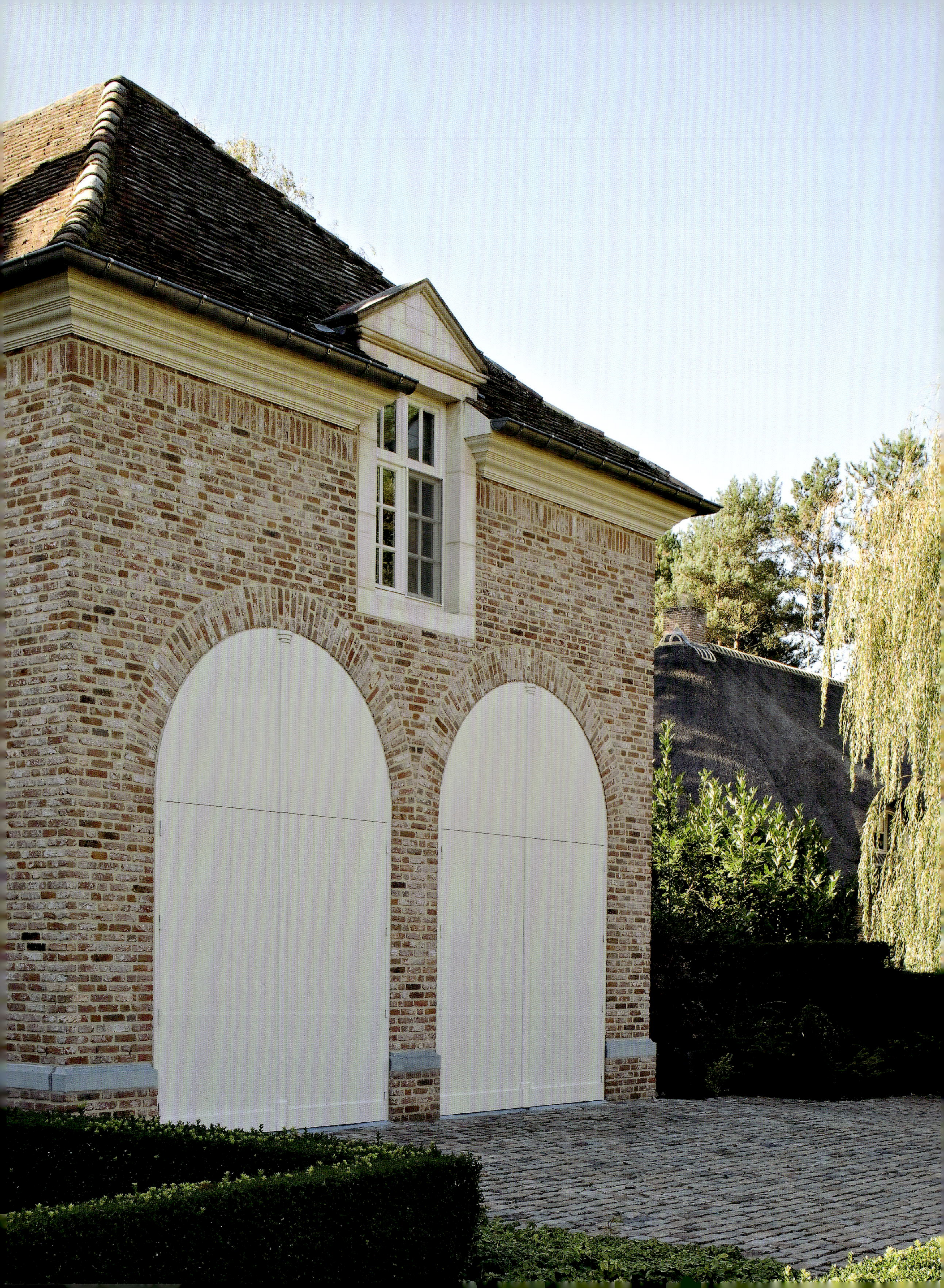

Old klampsteen bricks have been used as facing bricks.

KEMPISCHE BOUWMATERIALEN
Bleukenlaan 20
B – 2300 Turnhout
T +32 (0)14 42 04 01
F +32 (0)14 42 34 37
www.kempischebouwmaterialen.be
info@kempischebouwmaterialen.be
Opening hours:
Show room open from Monday to Friday from 8.30–12.00 and from 1.00–6.00.
Saturdays from 8.30–12.00 and from 1.00–3.00.

Bluestone surface and wall clad in old paapsteen bricks.

New paapsteen bricks with an aged appearance and old Burgundy roof tiles. The fired clay clinkers are also old.

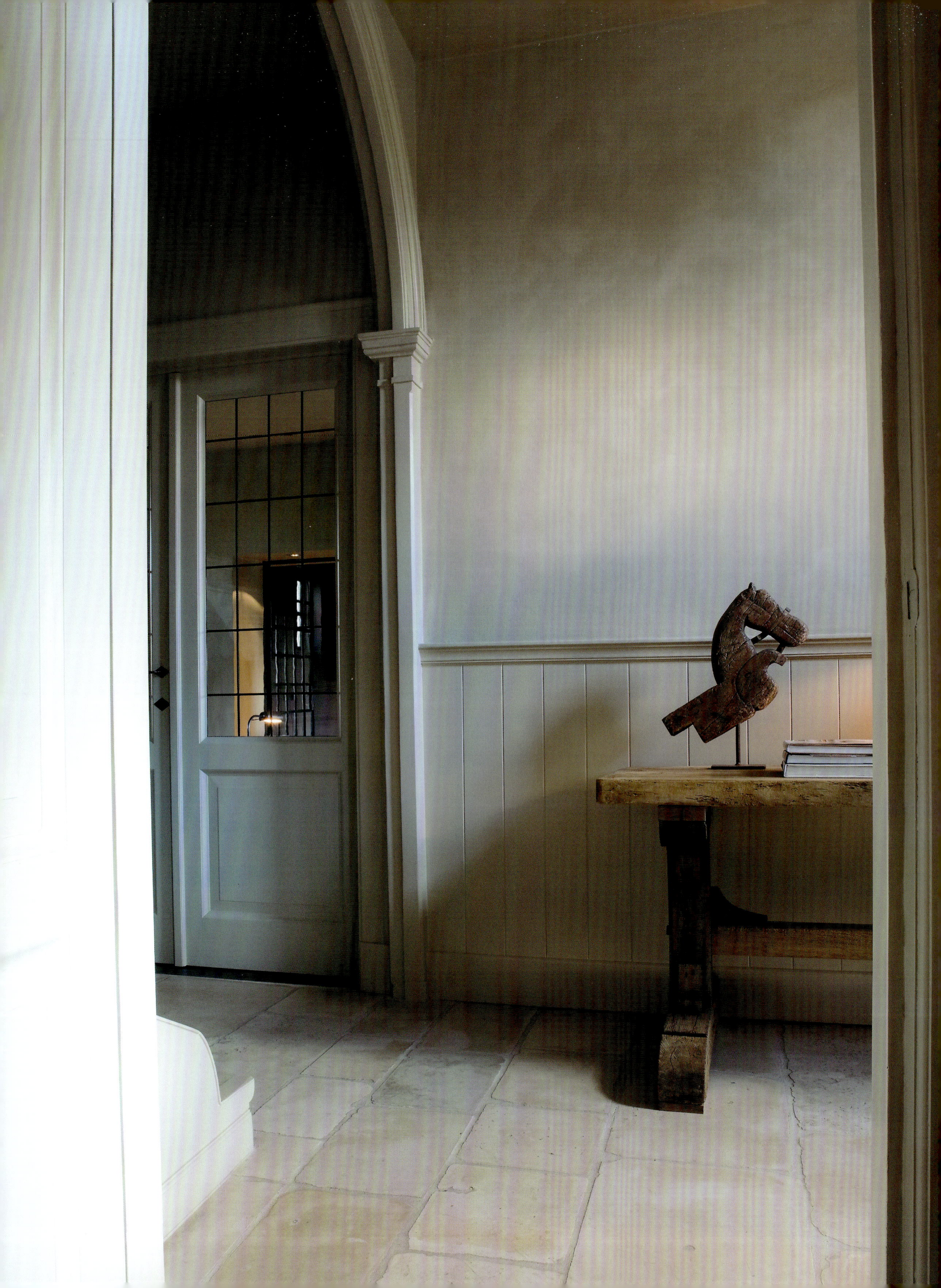

A PASSION FOR ANTIQUE CONSTRUCTION MATERIALS SINCE 1965

In the mid-1960s, Lambert van Alebeek founded a business dealing in old building materials: 't Achterhuis. This company has expanded to become a renowned wholesaler and retail outlet for architectural antiques, partly through the efforts of the second generation.

The outstanding reputation of 't Achterhuis is based on a number of factors:

- The company offers a very good balance of price and quality.
- Excellent service: the customer receives personal advice from the skilled staff of 't Achterhuis.
- A wide range: 't Achterhuis has a most varied selection, with a great choice of all kinds of products.
- All of the work is done in-house: the company has its own sawmill for stone, a smithy, a restoration workshop, transport company, and, if required, can arrange for the installation to be carried out for the client.
- Years of experience: 't Achterhuis has been at the top of its field for over four decades.

Visitors can view a great many model interiors in the inspirational 't Achterhuis showrooms and gain ideas about how to incorporate these historic construction materials into their own homes.

Old Burgundy flagstones laid in rows.

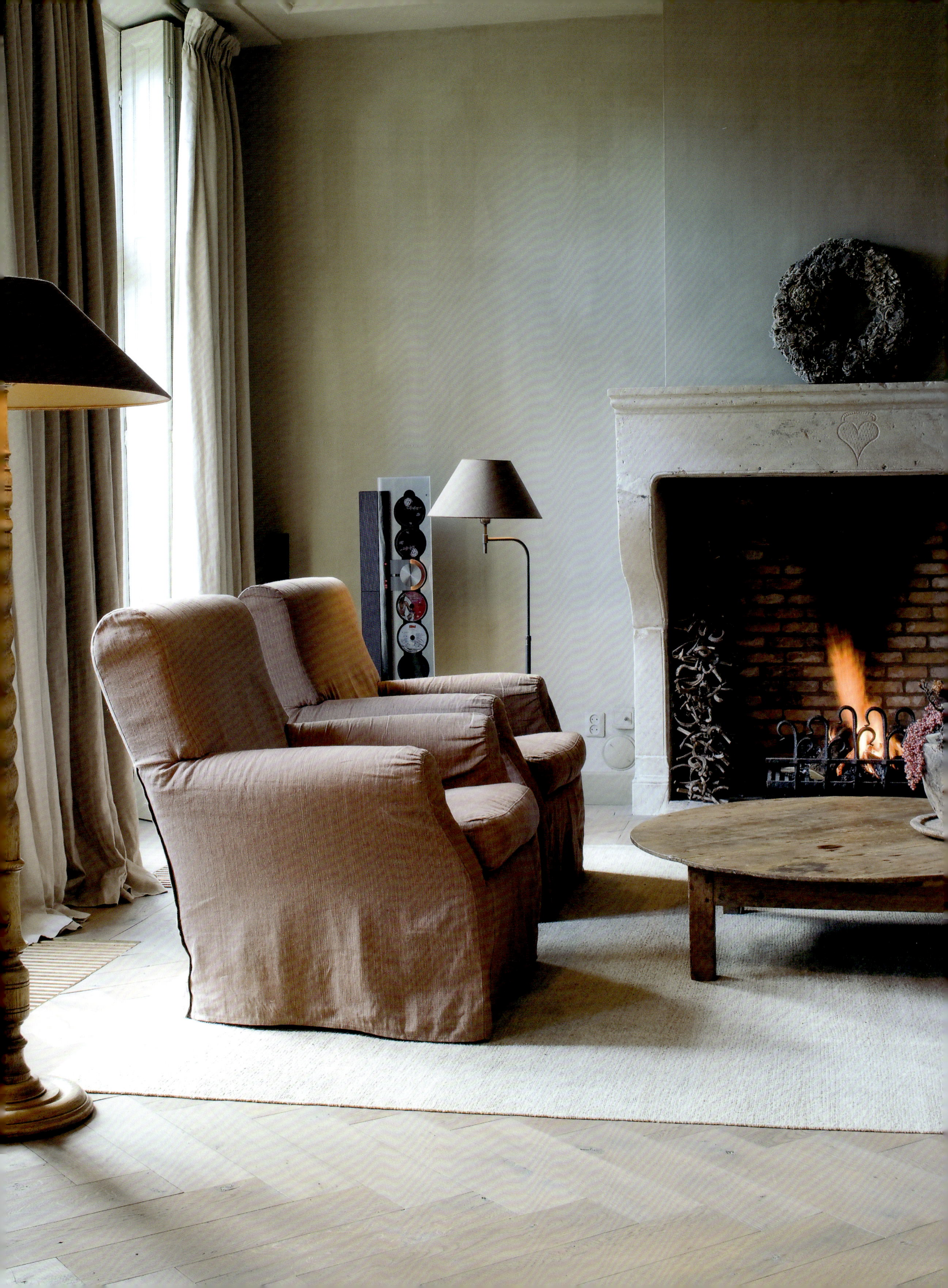

An antique French castle fireplace in sandstone (model: campagnarde) with a back made of old-Dutch yellow ijsselsteentje bricks and a wrought-iron grate. In the foreground, a rustic oak parquet in Hungarian point.
The furniture (chairs, old tables, and other pieces) is also available from 't Achterhuis.

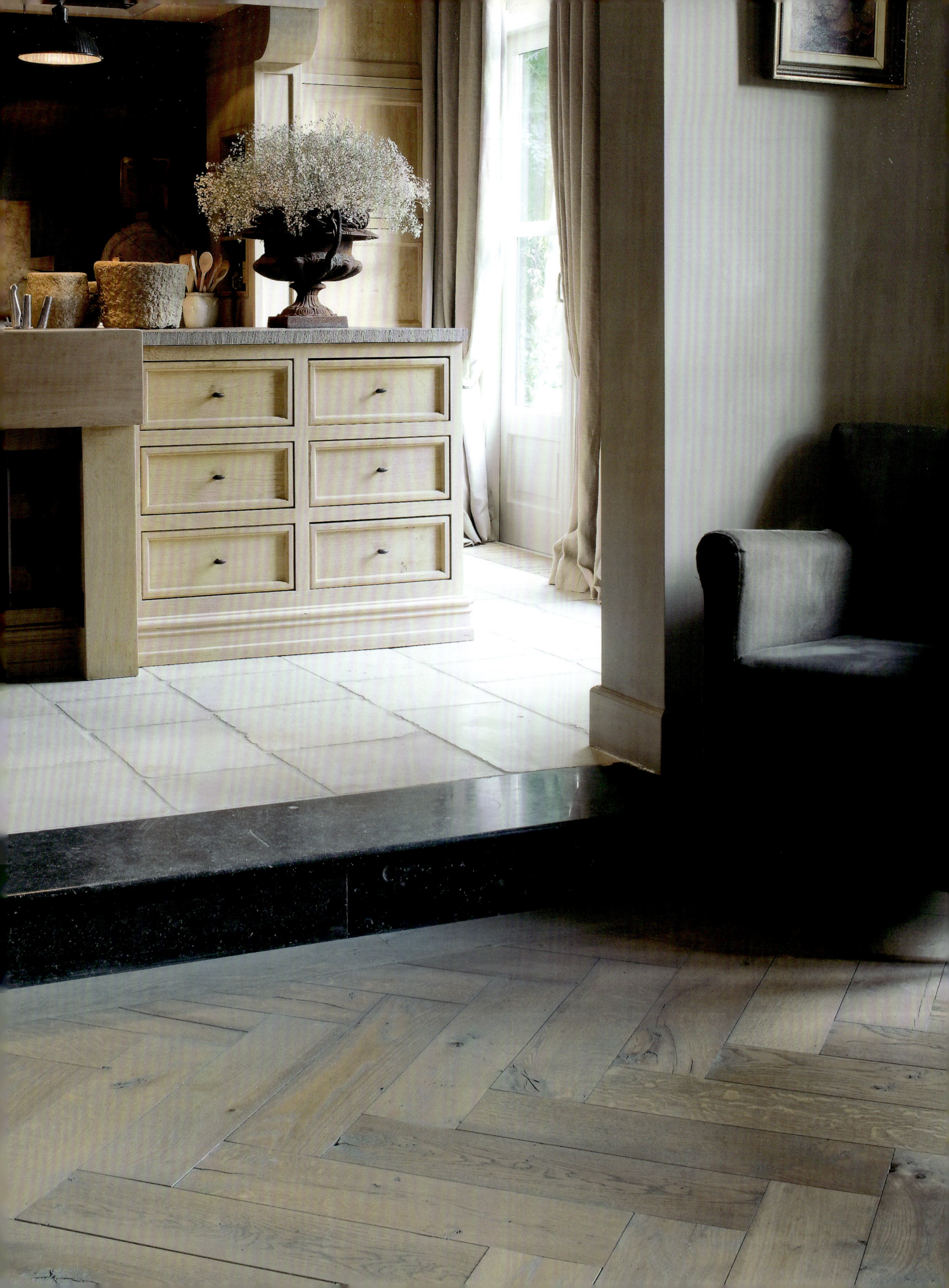

A sandstone pizza-oven with fireplace accessories and a wood store beneath.

In the foreground, a rustic oak parquet floor in Hungarian point; behind is a floor made from old French Burgundy flagstones.

The floor is in tumbled Burgundy slabs (20x20cm).

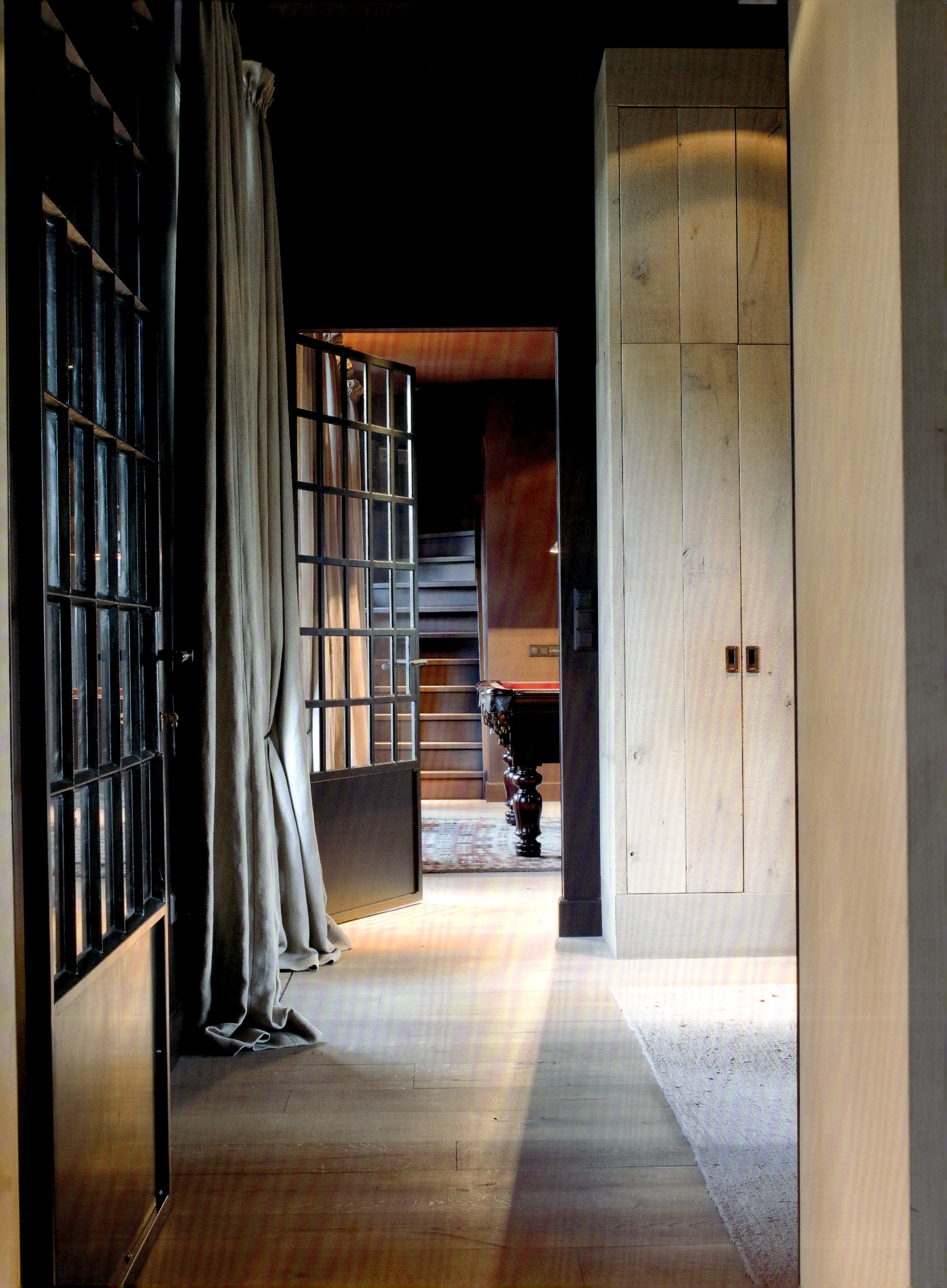

Tumbled bluestone slabs (20x20cm) were chosen for the hall and the bathroom.

Rustic oak planks, extra wide (up to 32cm wide/2.5cm thick).

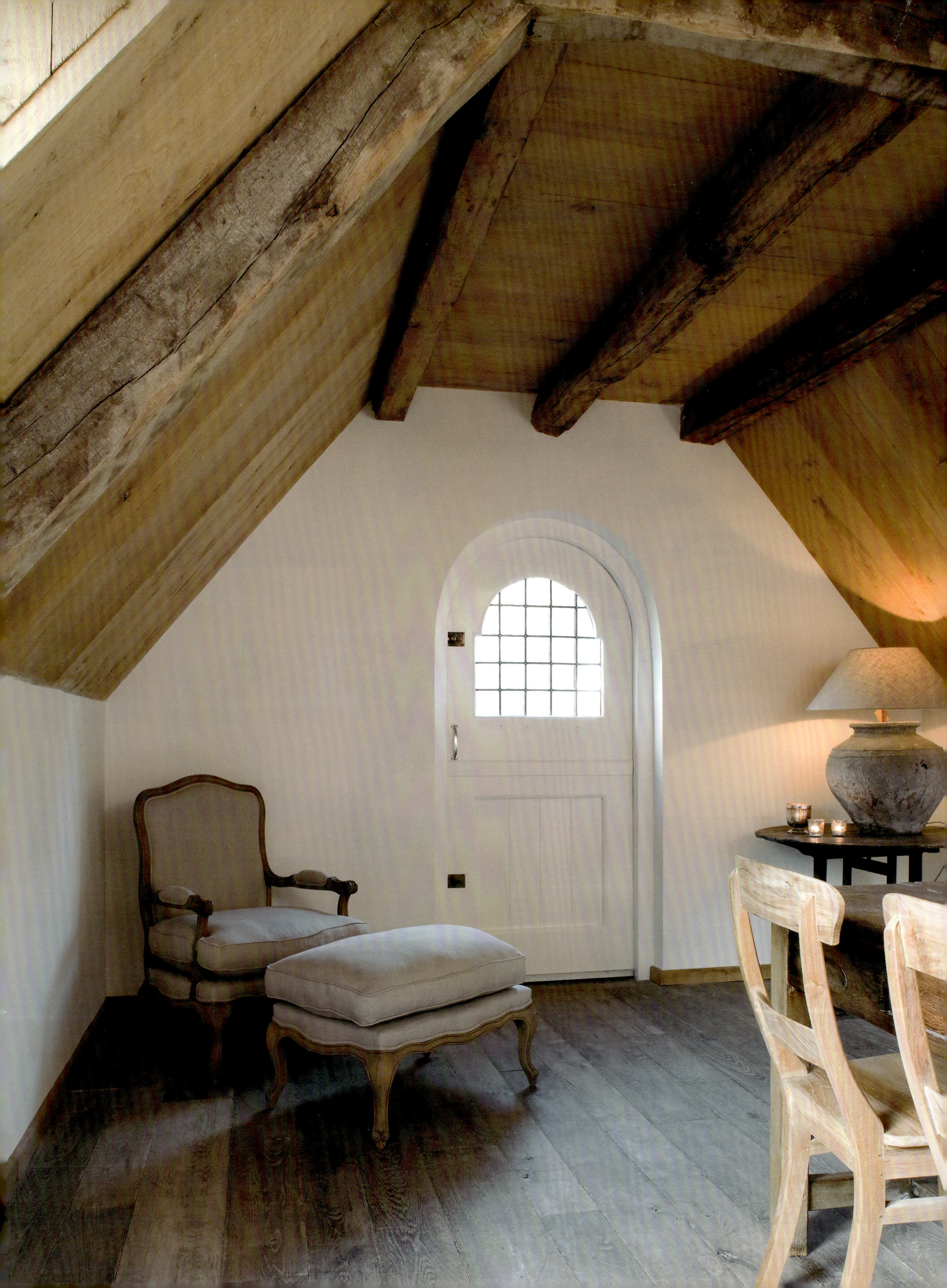

A 19th-century, traditionally aged wooden floor, with a light-brown finish.

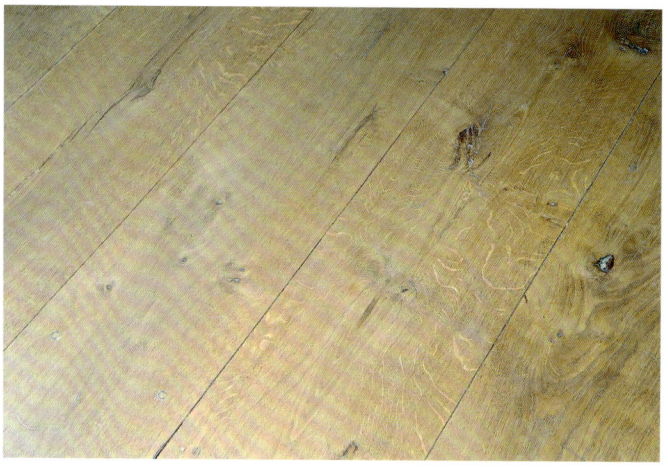

An 18th-century traditionally aged solid-oak floor, with extra-wide boards, an antique oak door and a lamp made from an old sandstone column.

A rustic French oak wooden floor, extra-wide boards, naturally treated.

A 19th-century solid-oak floor with a traditionally aged vieux gris finish.
The ceiling is made of extra-wide solid rustic-oak planks.
Roof in reclaimed oak beams. An old front door with leaded windows. The furniture and the lamp are also available from 't Achterhuis.

A floor in Belgian bluestone, with a smoothed finish, laid in broken bond. An old-fashioned radiator in cast-iron with oak-handled valve, an old iron window, an antique table and child's chair.

Bluestone, with a rough, aged finish, laid in rows, and an antique floor in white Carrara marble.

A replica spiral staircase.

Bluestone, with a rough, aged finish, 40x40cm.

A traditionally decorated sandstone fountain, alongside a cherub and vases on antique red slabs (available from 't Achterhuis in all sizes and colours).

A newly built old-style exterior wall with old bricks, wall clamps and other details. A bluestone door surround and old-fashioned street lighting.

'T ACHTERHUIS
Historic construction materials

> Showrooms and workshops:
> Kreitenmolenstraat 92
> NL – 5071BH Udenhout
> T +31 (0)13 511 16 49
> F +31 (0)13 511 11 42
> www.achterhuis.nl
> info@achterhuis.nl
> Opening hours:
> Monday to Friday, 8.30–5.30.
> Saturday, 10.00–4.00.
>
> Dispatch and warehouse:
> Ambachtsweg 19
> NL – 5071 NS Udenhout
>
> Stone and bricks/warehouse:
> Houtsestraat 119
> NL – 5011 XH Udenhout

Antique railings, an antique fountain and an antique garden statue – there really is a vast selection at 't Achterhuis.

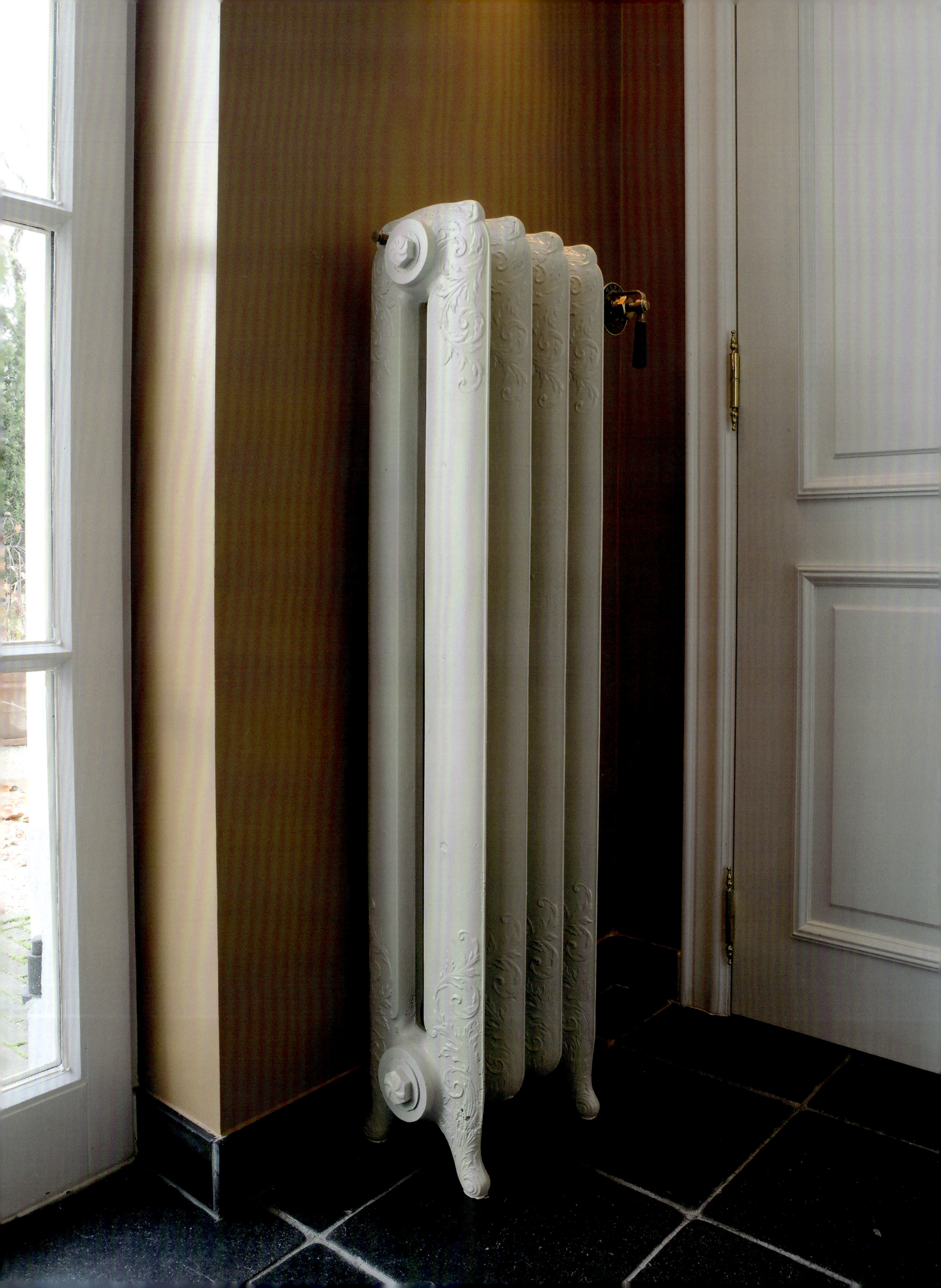

A GLIMPSE OF TIMES GONE BY

Even as a boy, Gunther Mellebeek enjoyed the atmosphere of the past. He takes intense pleasure in every touch of nostalgia that lends extra charm to an interior and creates an atmosphere of warmth.

It was this passion that led him to found his company Classic Comfort.
These faithful reproductions are selected with the utmost care and always offer a glimpse of times gone by, with a sense of nostalgia for our rich architectural history.

Classic Comfort specialises in objects that dealers in historic building materials can stock only sporadically: antique radiators, nostalgic bathtubs, door and window furniture and switches.

In this report, Gunther Mellebeek shows some eye-catching pieces from his collection.

With their exceptional properties of heat exchange, Classic Comfort's radiators (faithful reproductions of authentic 19th- and 20th-century models) give off a gentle and regular heat and react gradually to differences in heat. They are silent, neither creaking nor shaking, and they meet the highest modern standards. At the same time, they introduce an authentic historic touch into the home and radiate a warm and timeless atmosphere.

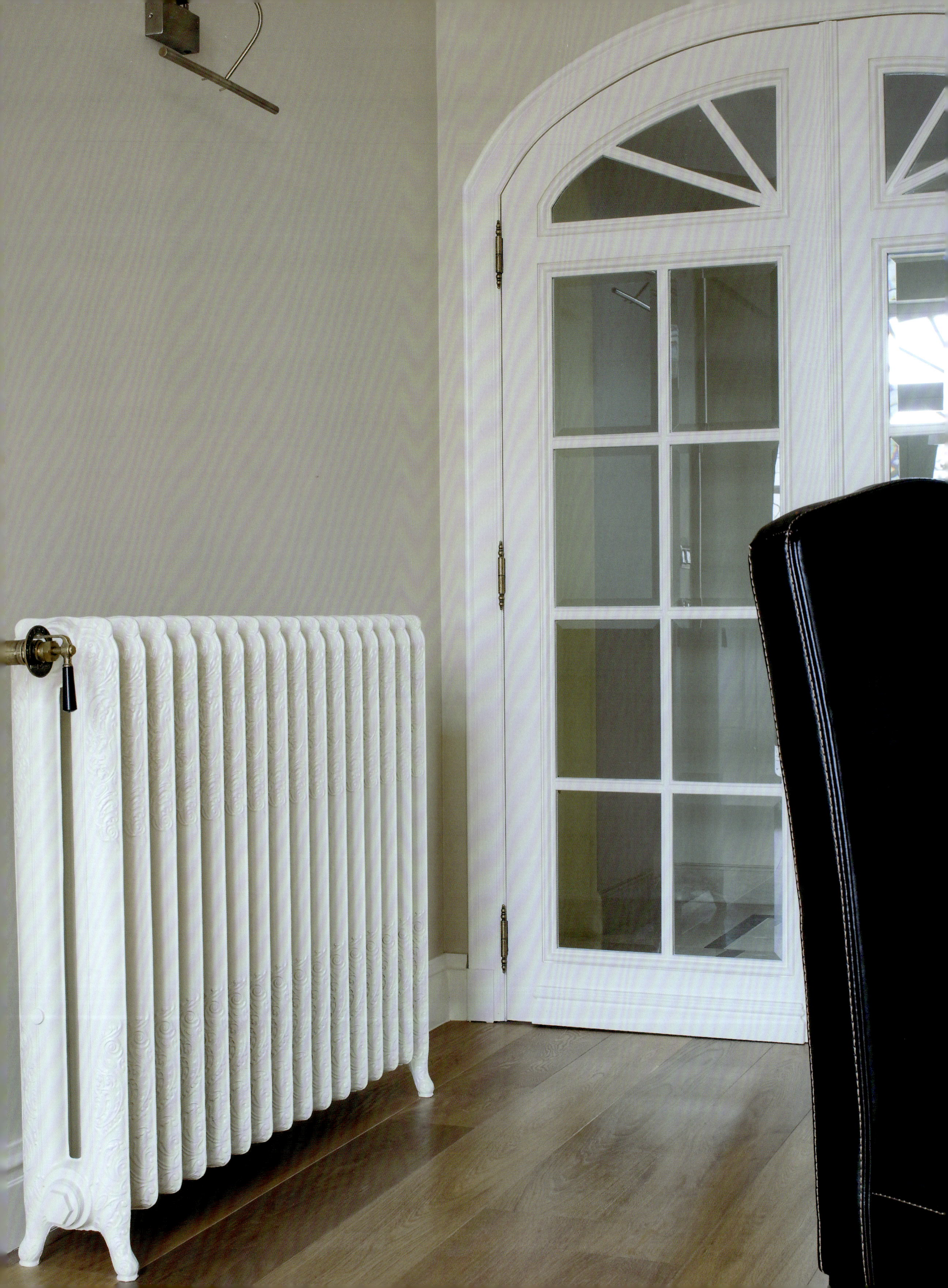

Classic Comfort's radiators are fully cast and finished with time-honoured craftsmanship, making them ideal for both contemporary and classic homes.

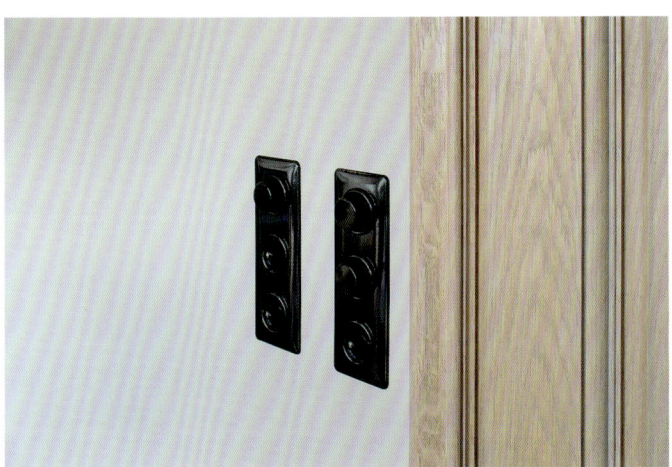

The company's range of switches in bakelite and porcelain lends a timeless elegance to any interior.

Classic Comfort is a distributor of the Giara and Genifer ranges of accessories for furniture, doors and windows.

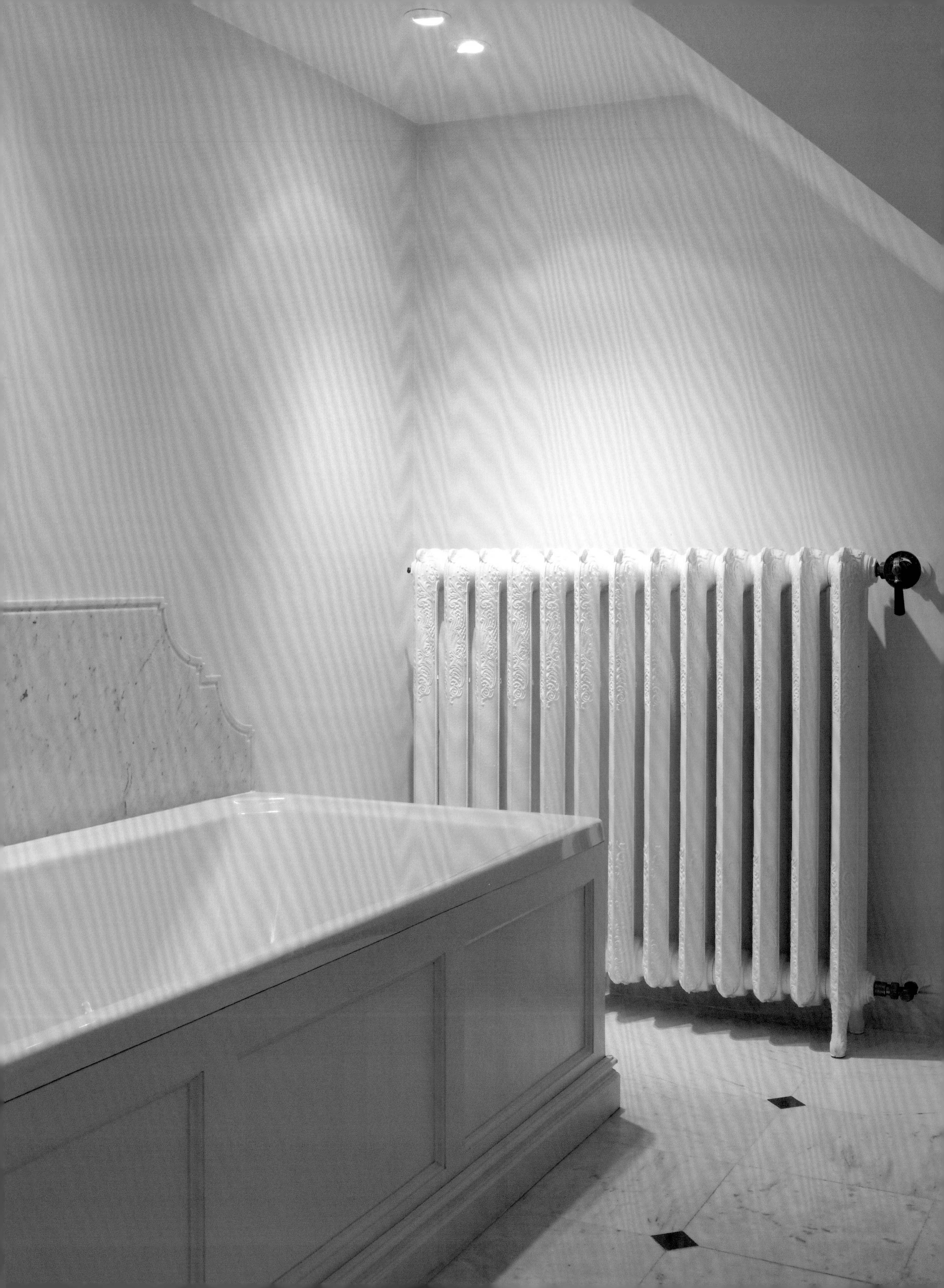

These nostalgic cast-iron radiators by Classic Comfort are available in different heights, colours and models.

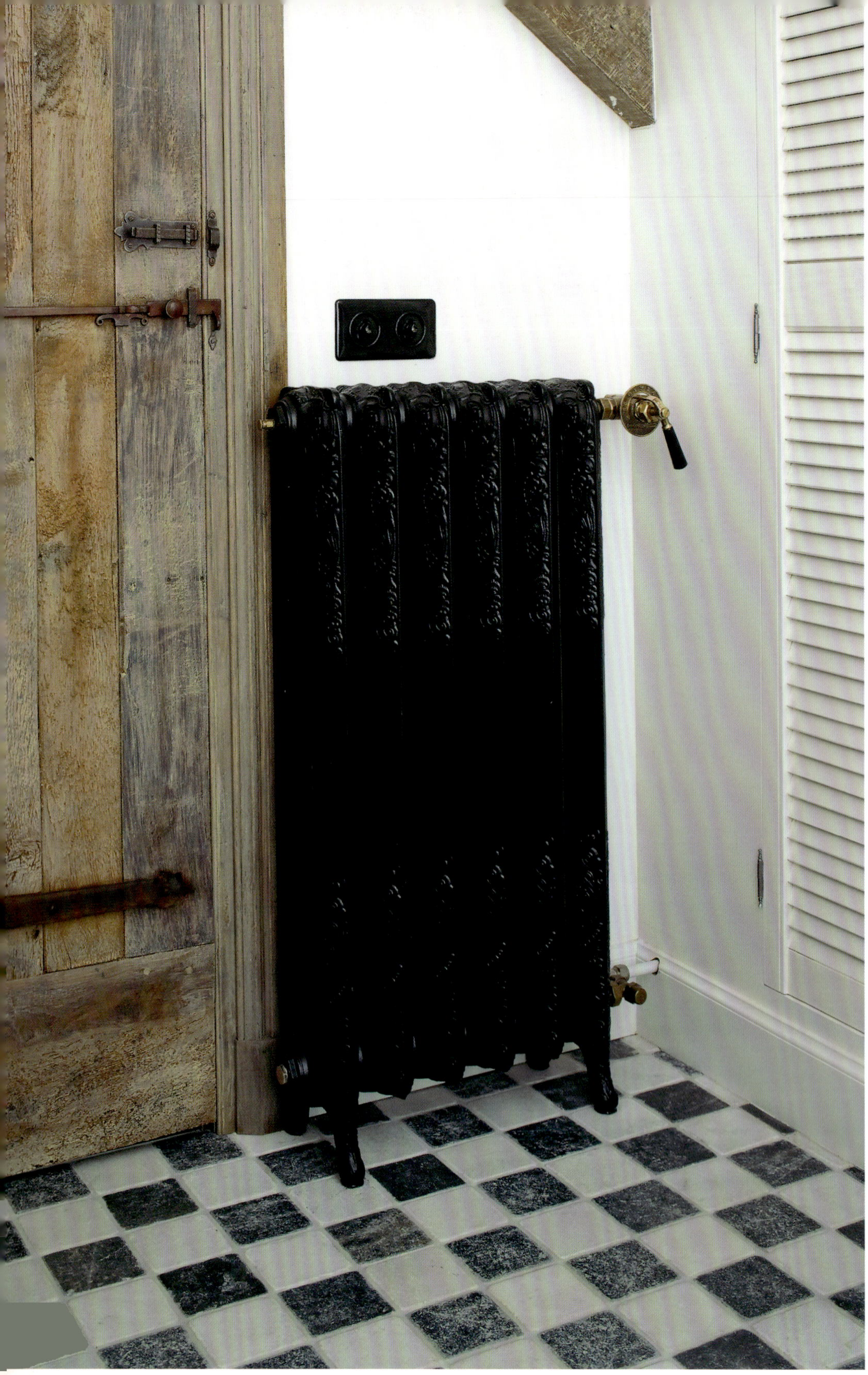

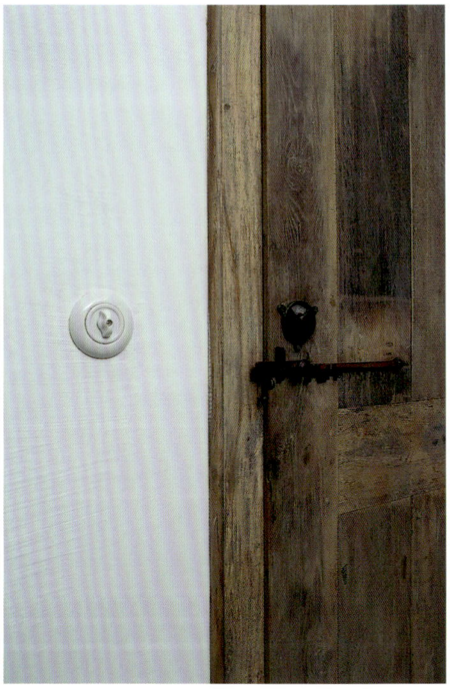

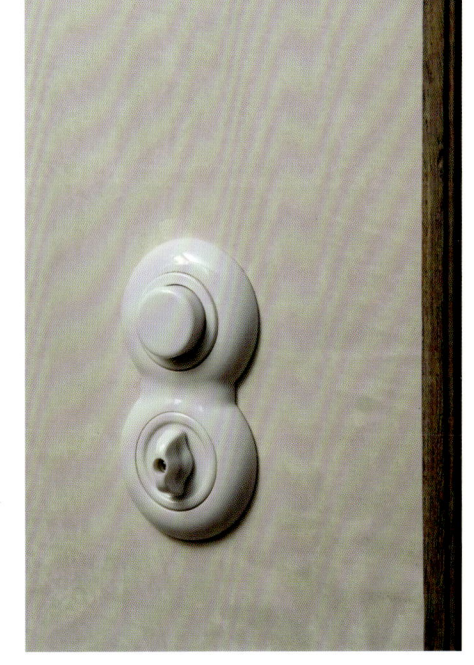

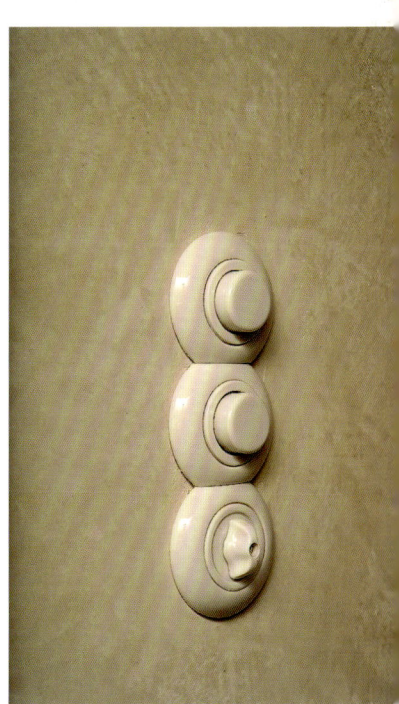

CLASSIC COMFORT

Markestraat 7
B – 2430 Laakdal
MOB +32 (0)494 540 475
www.classiccomfort.be
info@classiccomfort.be
By appointment only.

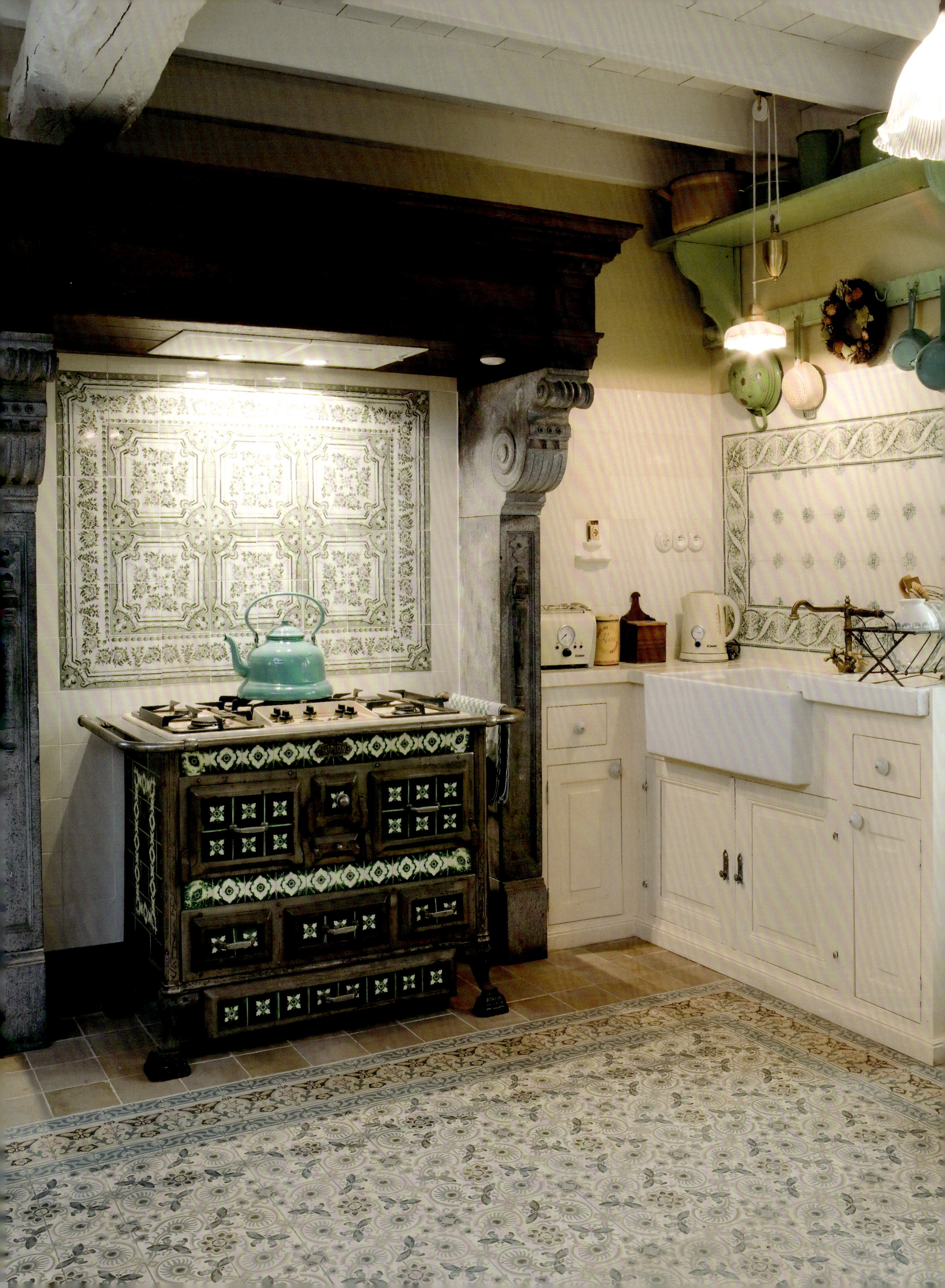

A SPECIALIST IN ANTIQUE VICTORIAN TILED FLOORS AND WALLS

In 1990, Lambert and Dominique Brans started an antiques company in their hometown of Sint-Truiden. After a number of successful years, the couple bought a property with a large display area in Orsmaal-Linter. This turned out to be the ideal location for them to expand upon their passion: collecting and selling antique Victorian, Art Nouveau and Art Deco wall and floor tiles.

The size of their collection is overwhelming: Amfora is now undisputedly Europe's leading supplier of antique tiles from around 1860 to the 1930s. Countless clients from all over the world have used Amfora as a source of inspiration for their renovation and new-build projects: these customers include private individuals and collectors, dealers and architects.

All of Amfora's tiles are authentic pieces that are ready for installation and are created with respect for time-honoured traditions. Every tiled floor has its own history: a glorious past that the enthusiastic Brans family are happy to relate to interested visitors. Their years of experience, their expertise and their client-focused approach ensure that all lovers of antique building materials will find something to their taste at Amfora.

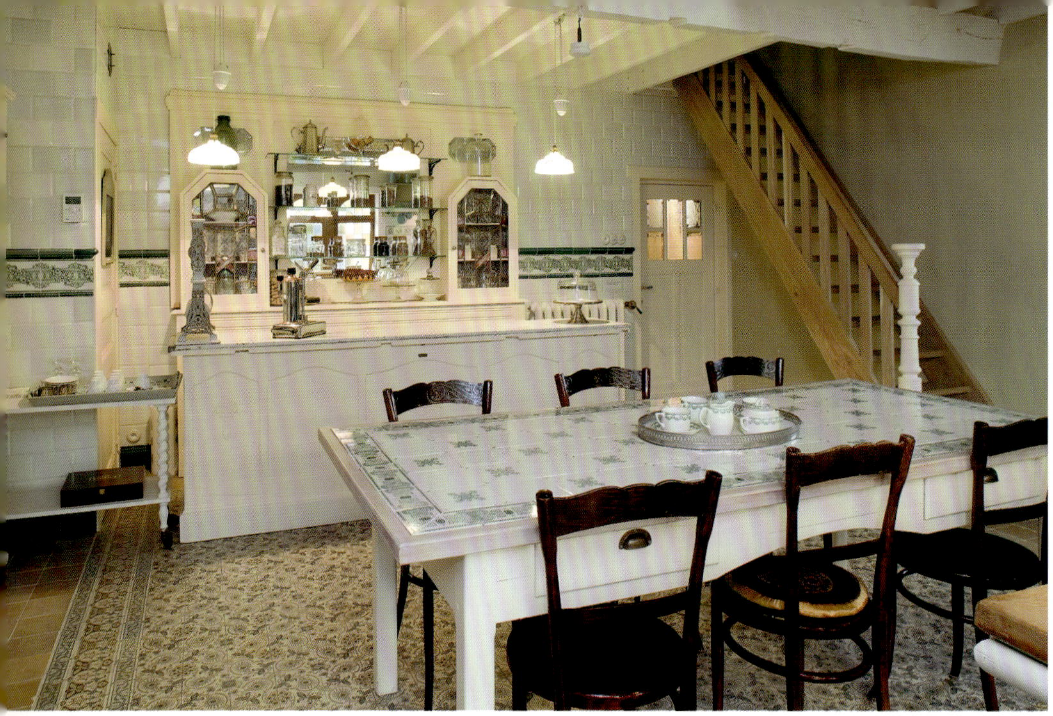
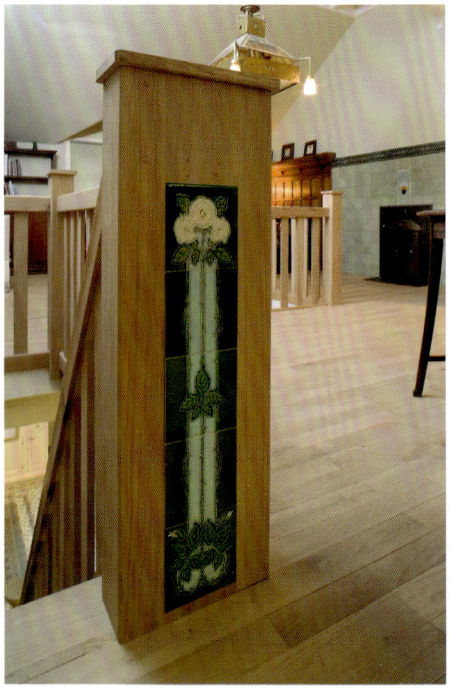
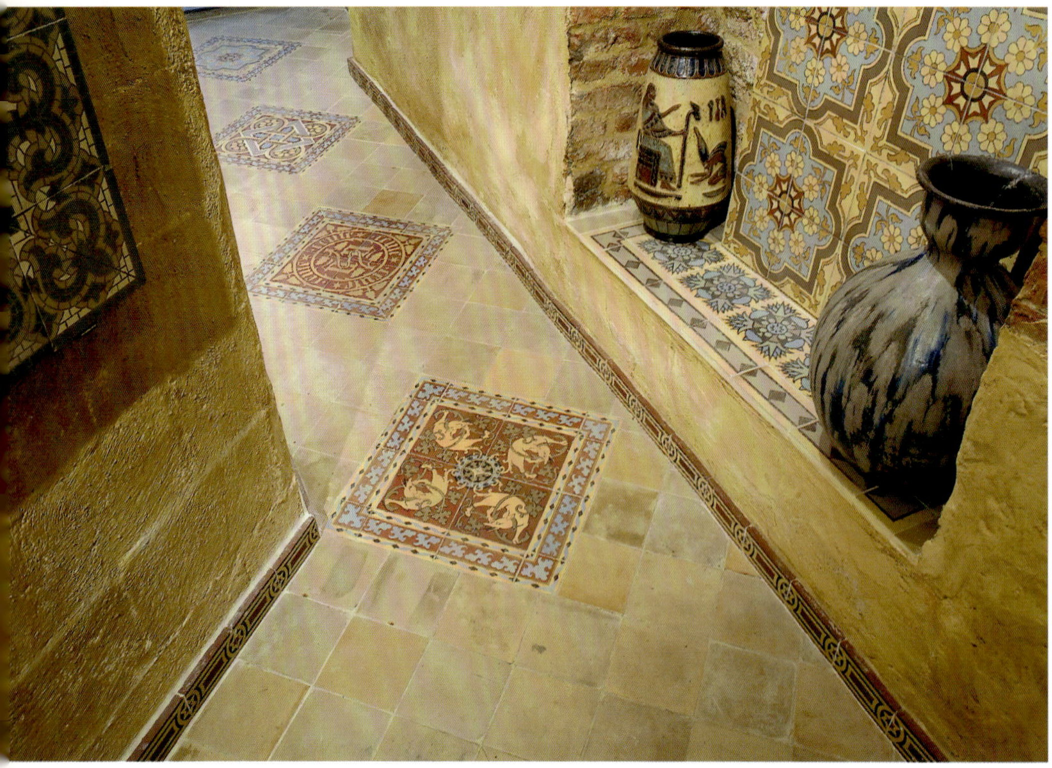
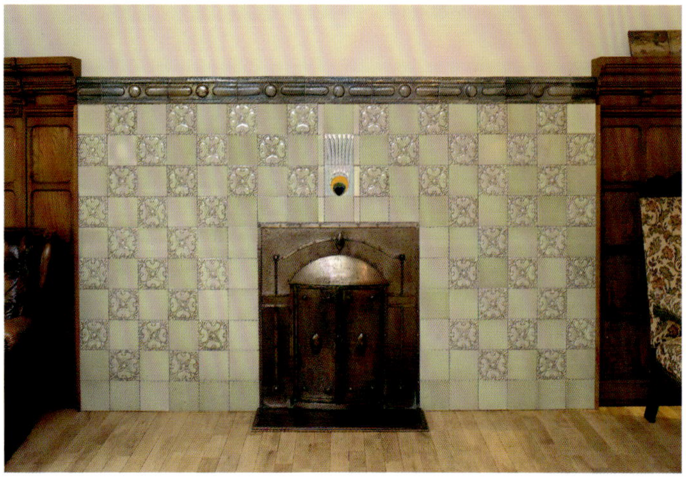
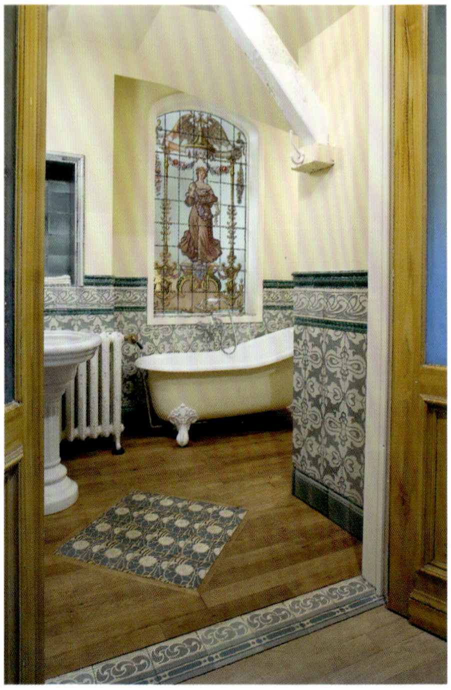

AMFORA

    Sint-Truidensesteenweg 221
    B – 3350 Orsmaal - Linter
    T +32 (0)11 78 43 11
    F +32 (0)11 78 43 11
    MOB +32 (0)495 57 90 67
    www.amfora-antiques.com
    amfora.antiques@skynet.be
    Opening hours:
    Saturday from 10.00 to 6.00
    and Sunday from 2.00 to 4.00.
    Other days by appointment.

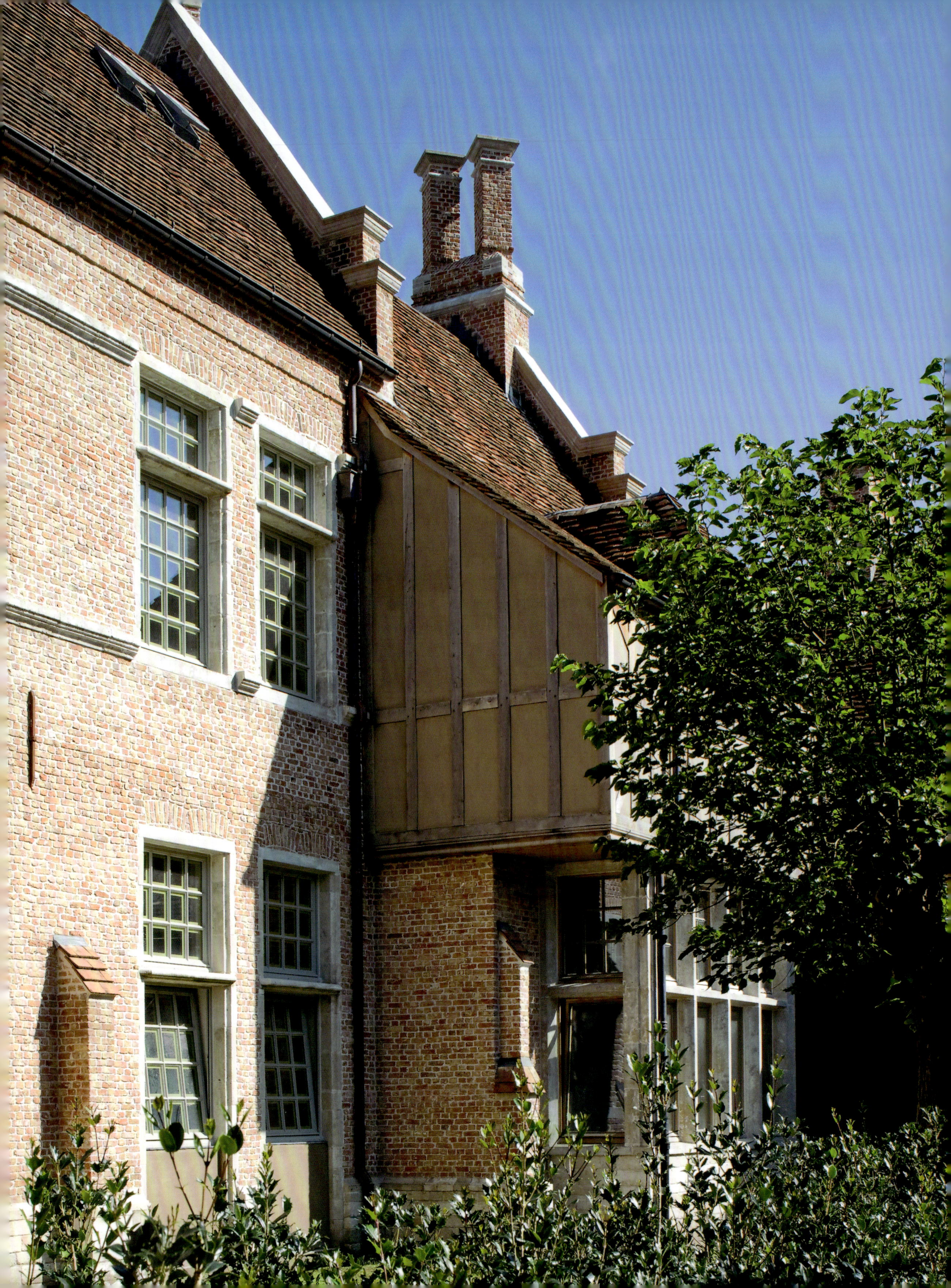

ANTIQUE STYLE AT THE TOP END OF THE MARKET

After decades of experience in the restoration of buildings and exclusive homes, Rik Storms decided to specialise in constructing facades for the homes of private clients. Authenticity and respect for tradition are the key features of his constant search for the most beautiful construction materials.

Top-quality varieties of stone, such as limestone and bluestone (particularly from the 17th and 18th centuries), are restored and adapted in his company's own workshops.

For interior projects, Rik Storms specialises in supplying old floors in natural stone and wood, oak ceilings, fireplaces and doors.
He also offers a wide range of products for the garden and terrace: old terrace floors, steps, doorsteps, clinker bricks and cobbles, handmade garden tables in natural stone and swimming-pool surrounds.

Storms also designs and manufactures washbasins, kitchen sinks and work surfaces in natural stone.

Storms is a famous name for renowned architects, interior designers and private clients at the top end of the market.

p. 214-219

For this project by the Themenos architectural studio, Rik Storms supplied red and grey roof tiles, Balegem stone based on 17th-century designs, and mouldings for the facade and plinth course, also in Balegem stone.

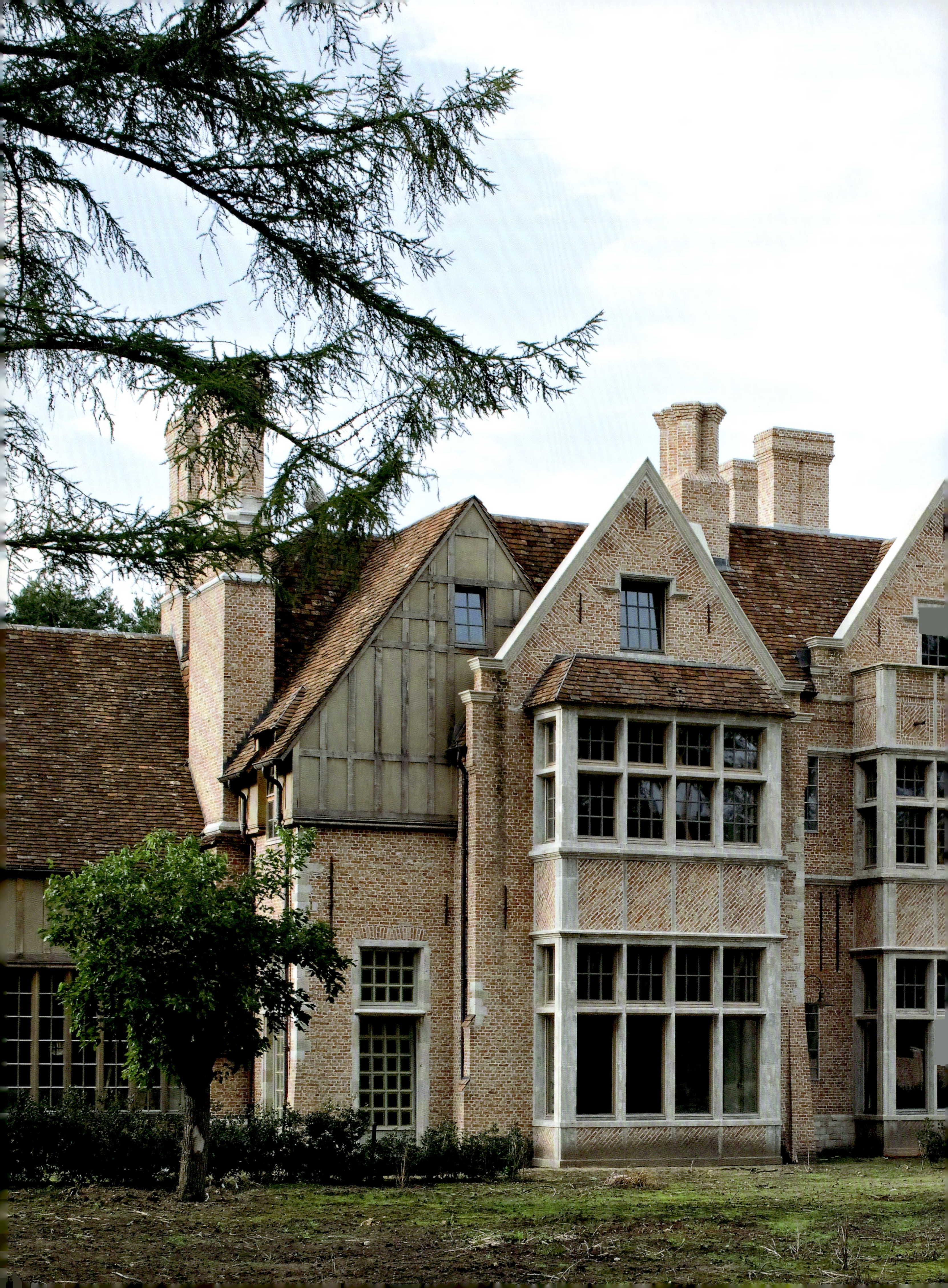

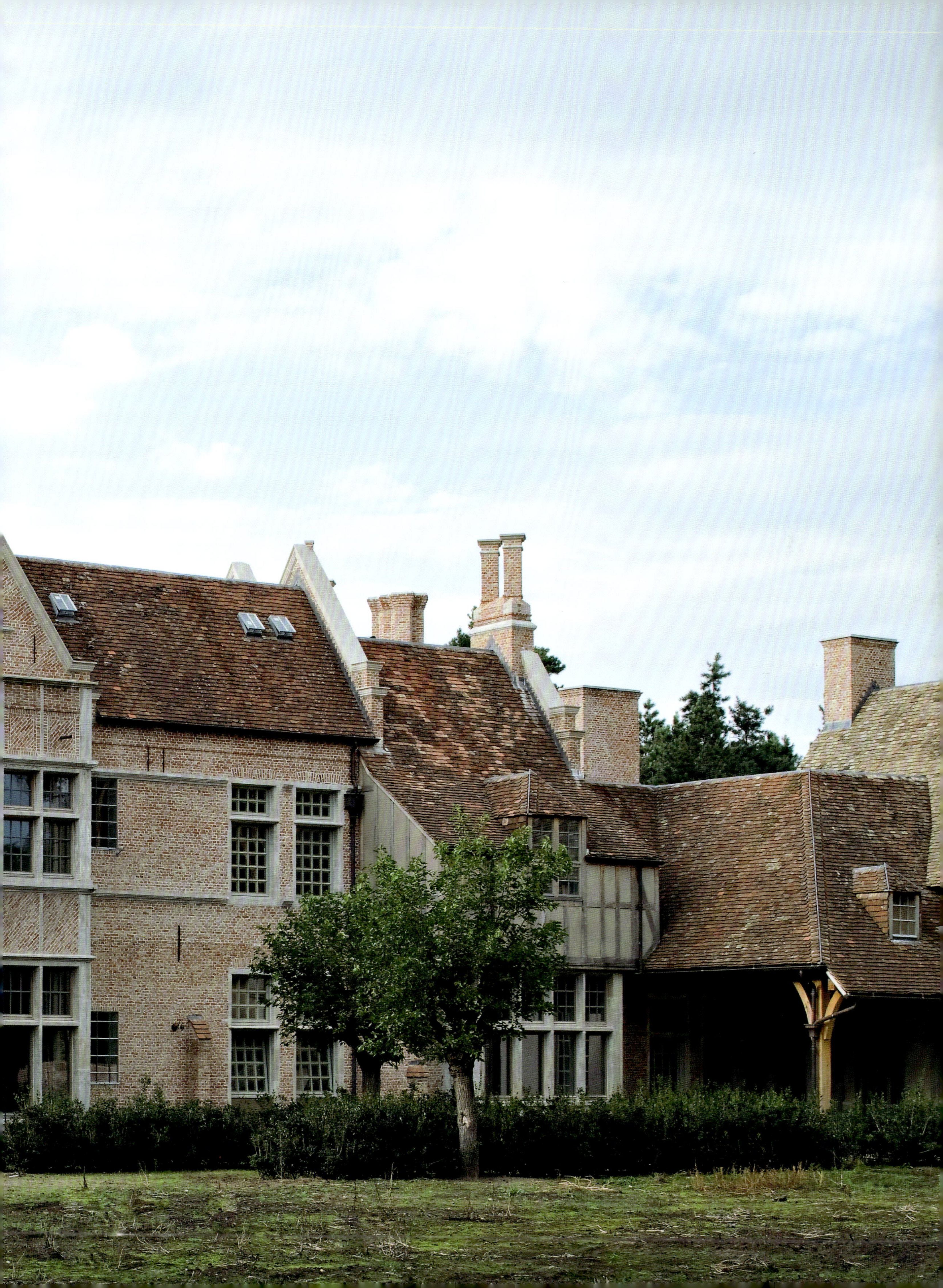

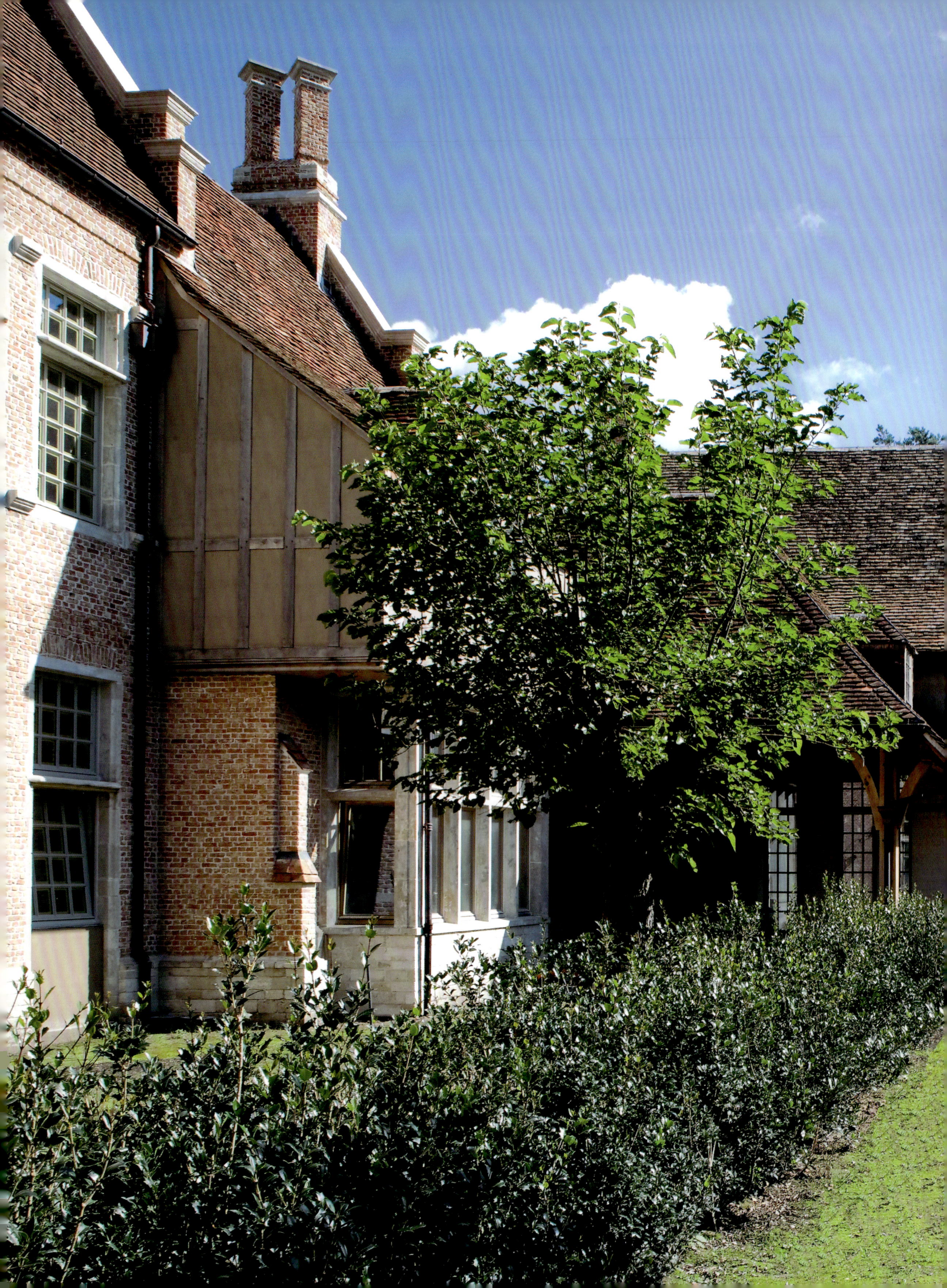

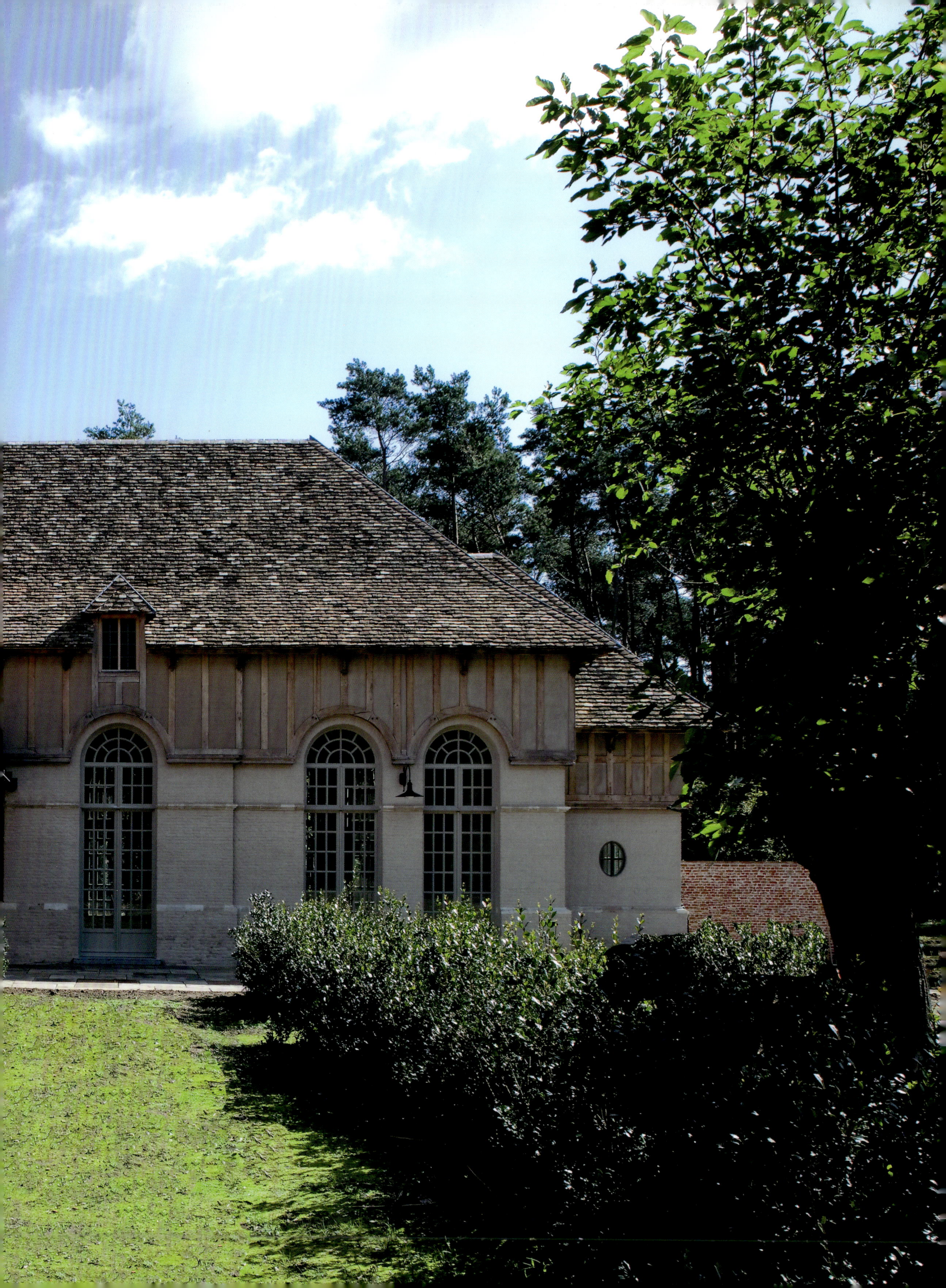

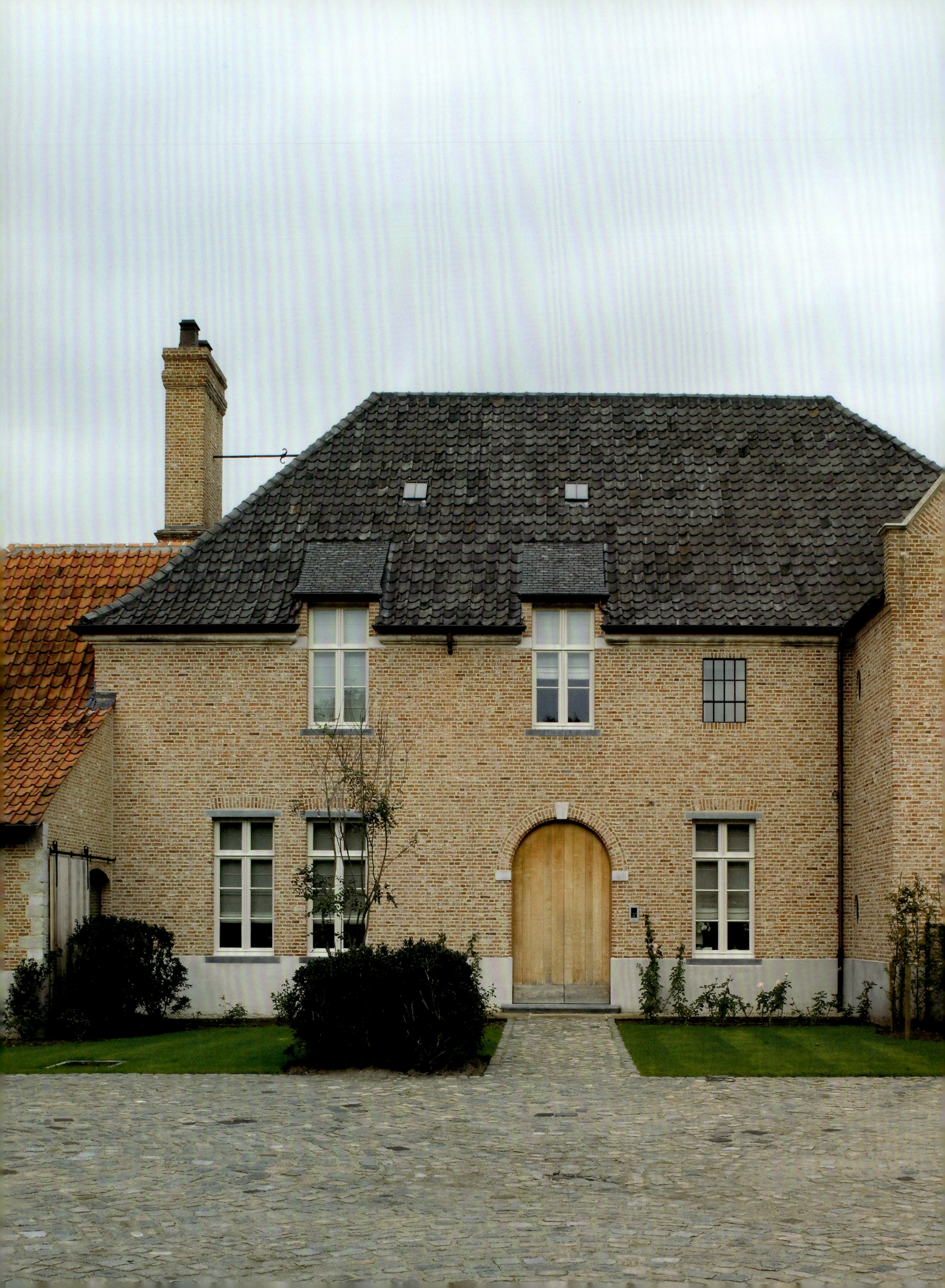

In this project in Flemish Brabant, also by the Themenos architectural studio, Rik Storms provided many exclusive historic construction materials: keystones, cornerstones and window surrounds in Balegem stone based on 17th-century examples, a terrace in Yorkstone and sandstone moulding for the eaves.

An 18th-century Louis XIV fireplace in Pierre de Besançon. Rik Storms always has a number of very special antique fireplaces in stock.

From top: an oak ceiling with 17th-century beams; a bluestone pump basin (19th century) with a new back; and a detail of the old-oak ceiling.

Top photo: a 19th-century entrance gate with statues of the seasons and bluestone slabs.

Bottom left, this page: a sandstone lion (pierre de grès) from the 17th century.

Bottom right two vases on bluestone pedestals (early 19th century) and two vases on the gate (18th century).

A bluestone table, made by Rik Storms to a 17th-century design. Chairs in teak, large bluestone slabs.

RIK STORMS EN C° NV
    Aland 4
    B – 2811 Leest
    T +32 (0)15 71 25 35
    F +32 (0)15 71 41 49
    MOB.: +32 (0)475 77 61 57
    www.rikstorms.com
    info@rikstorms.com

A 19th-century sandstone niche, two bluestone pedestals and bluestone slabs.

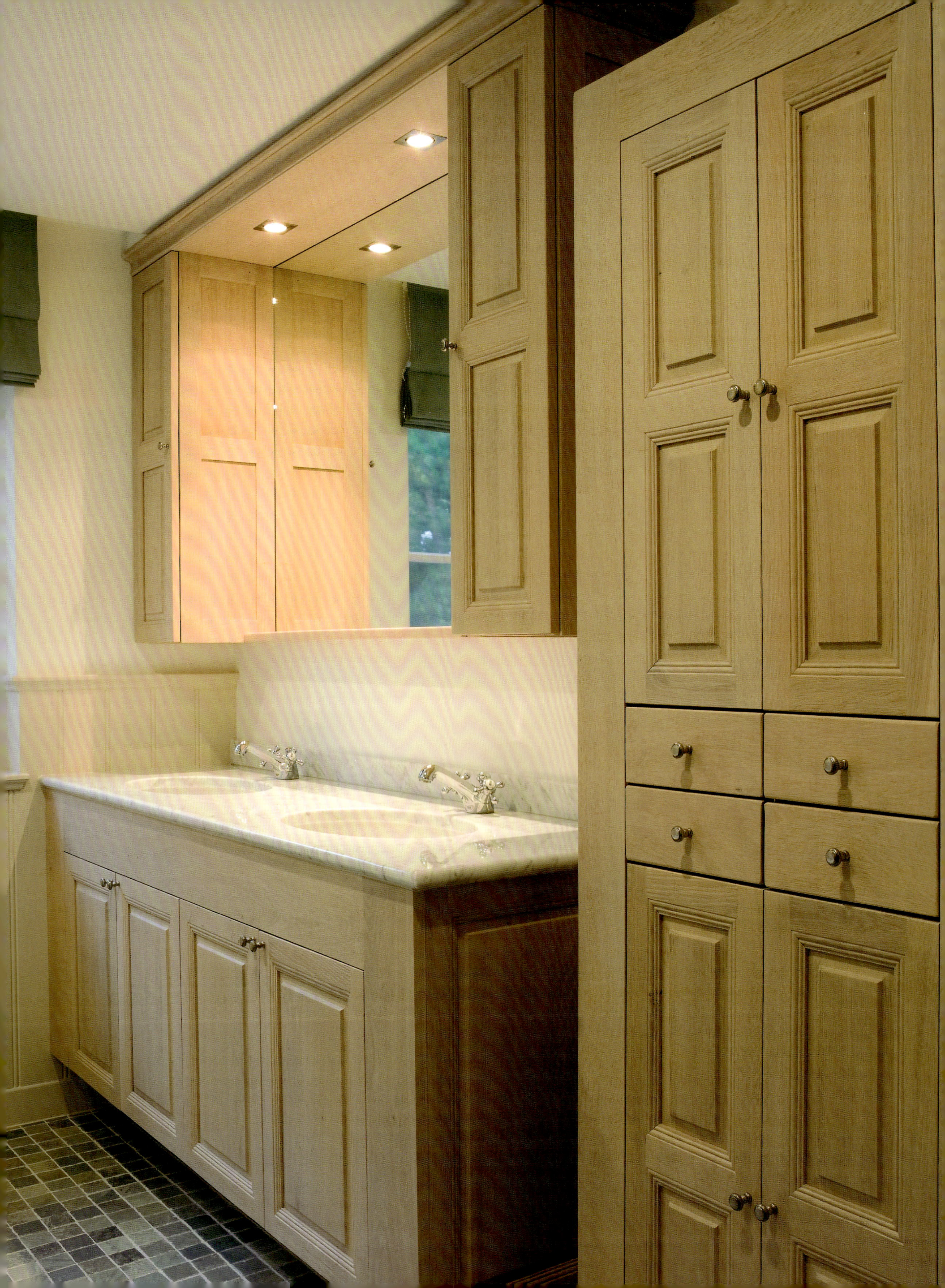

PERFECTION RIGHT DOWN TO THE SMALLEST DETAIL

Dauby nv has been the trendsetter for exclusive door furniture in the Benelux countries for over twenty years.

The company offers a large selection of top-quality articles. They never rest on their laurels and are always on the lookout for stylish, innovative designs, materials and accessories.

Their collection is based on the original, traditionally cast ranges of yesteryear, steering clear of the many imitations that have flooded the market. This means that every Dauby design is unique and exclusive.

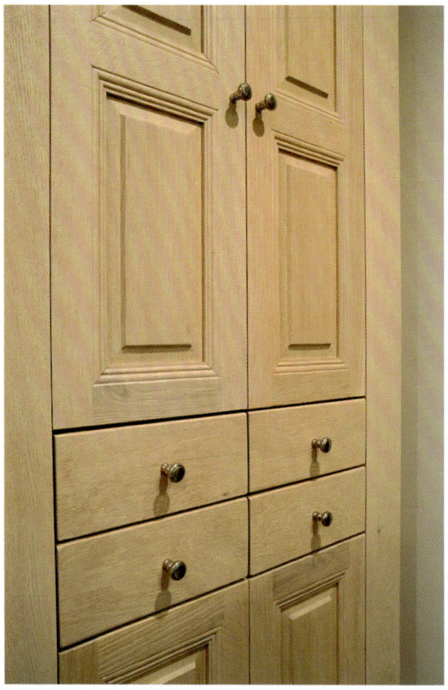
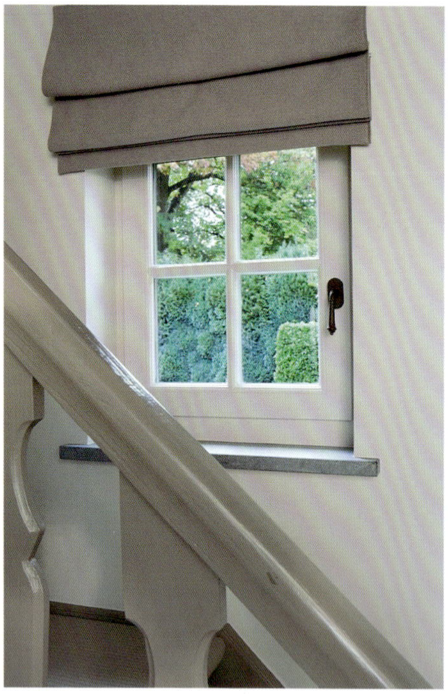
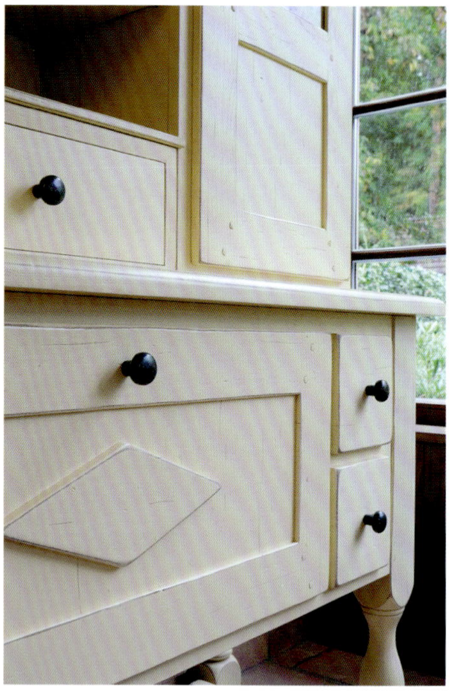
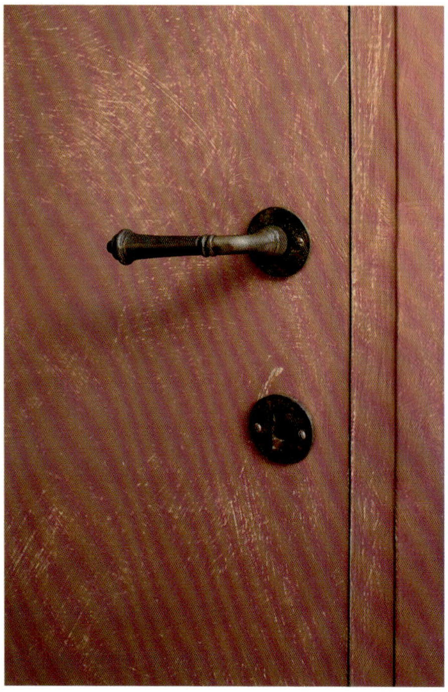
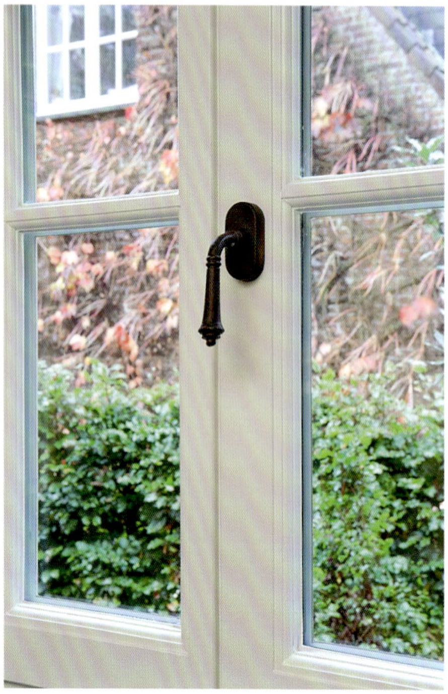
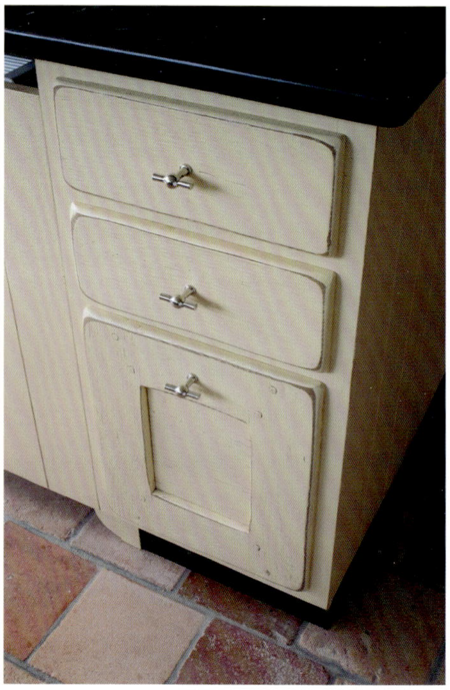

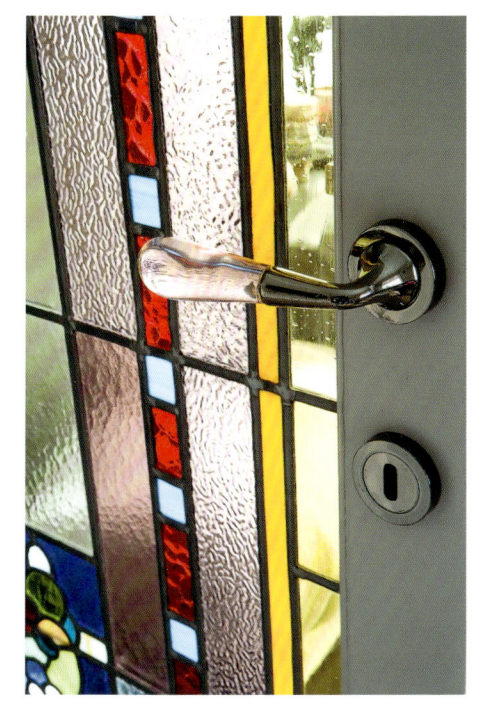

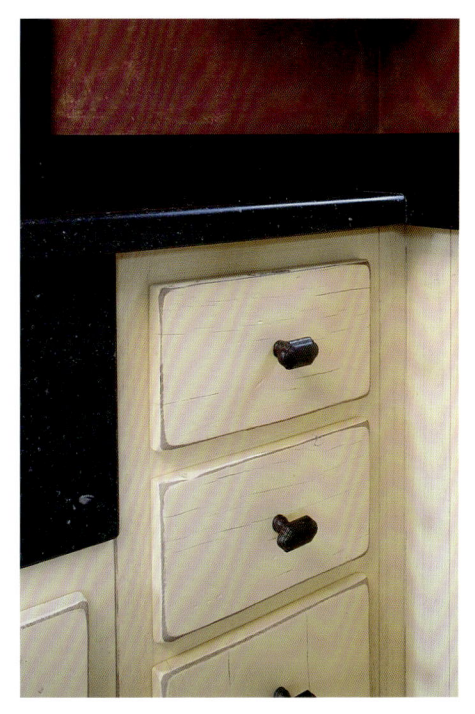

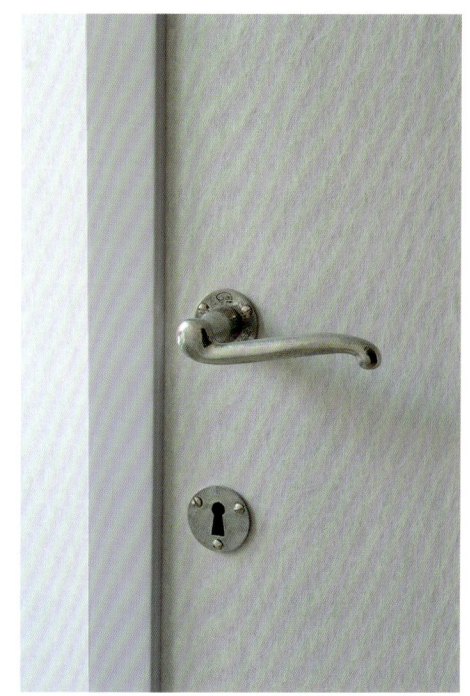

DAUBY nv
Offices and warehouse
Uilenbaan 86
B-2160 Wommelgem
T +32 (0)3 354.16.86
F +32 (0)3.354.16.32
www.dauby.be

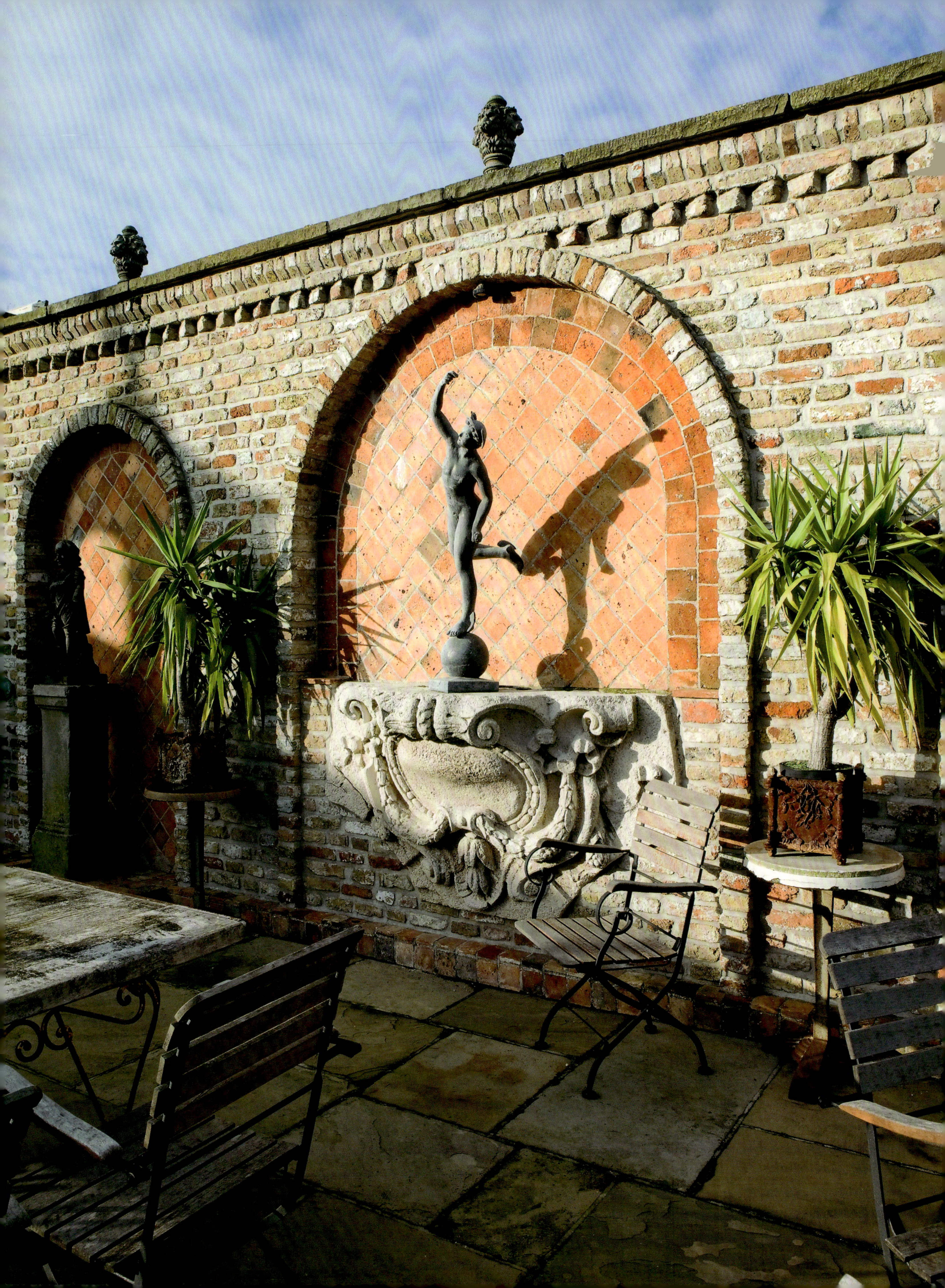

A PASSION FOR ANTIQUE MATERIALS

Fryns-Boret is the perfect address for anyone looking for old and rustic construction materials that are full of character.

This family firm from Gistel always offers a wide selection of old and antique bricks, windows and doors, leaded glass, fencing, wrought iron, floors, flagstones, ornamental bluestone and other distinctive pieces for home and garden.

In this report, Fryns-Boret present some of the large assortment of antique construction materials that can be seen during a visit to the company: this is a must for lovers of antique construction materials.

Fryns-Boret offer a very varied range of old and rustic construction materials for home and garden.

232

FRYNS – BORET
Antique and rustic construction materials
Torhoutsebaan 120
B – 8470 Gistel
T/F +32 (0)59 276 617
T +32 (0)59 267 255
Open: Monday to Friday
from 9.00–12.00 and 1.30–6.00.
Saturday till 5.00. Closed on Sunday.
www.fryns-boret.com
info@fryns-boret.com

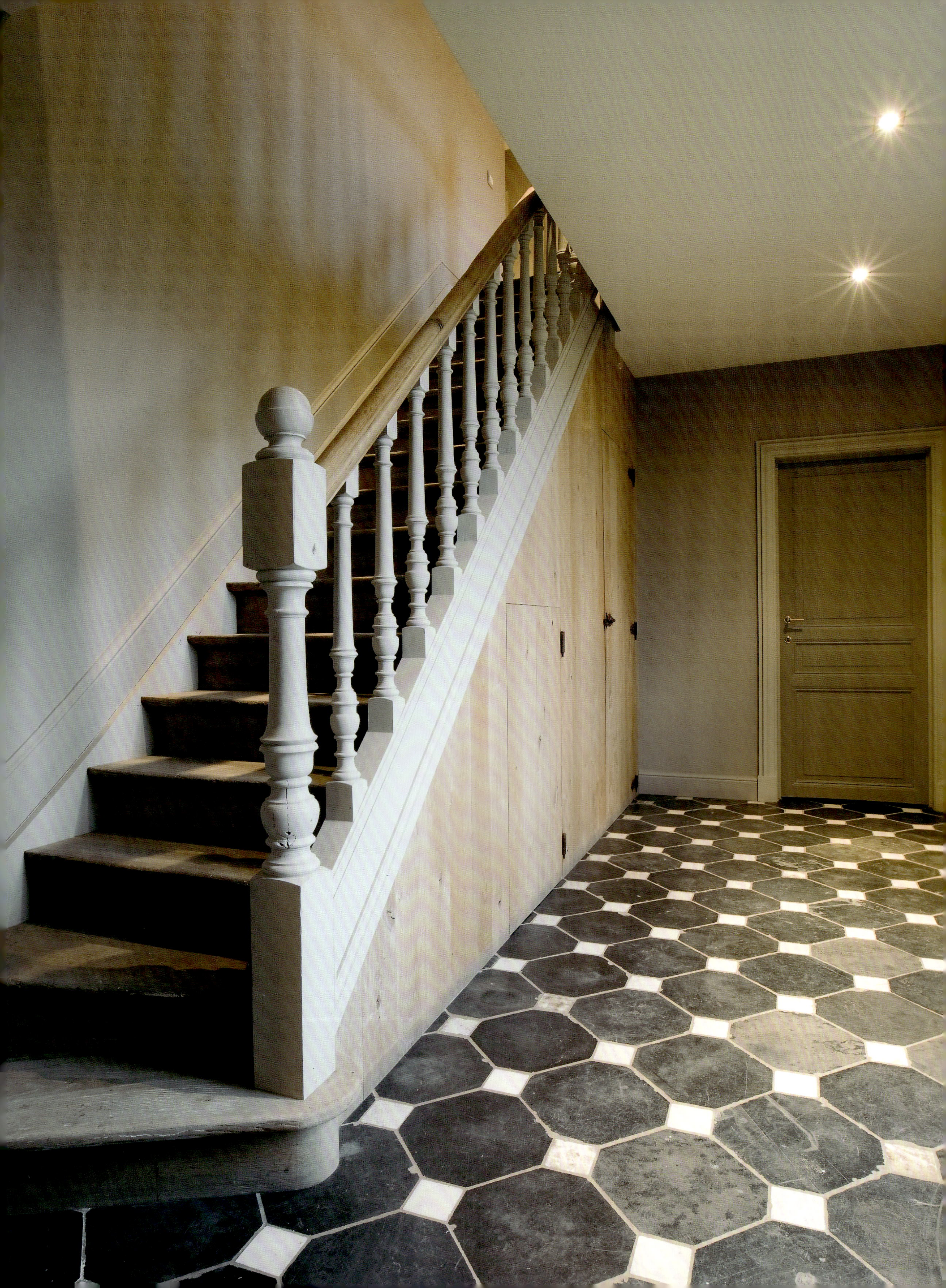

A SPECIALIST IN OLD FIREPLACES AND FLOORS

In a little over three decades, the family firm Deknock has expanded to become one of the leading wholesalers and retailers of antique construction materials in West Flanders.

Deknock's main speciality is the company's large collection of white-stone fireplaces from the 17th, 18th and 19th centuries. In addition to these antique pieces, Deknock make faithful white-stone reproductions in the company workshops.

Deknock also offer a wide range of reclaimed floors, including wooden floors and parquets that are centuries old, magnificent Burgundy slabs, terracotta tiles and church flagstones.

This report features fireplaces, floors and tiles supplied by Deknock for satisfied customers. The photographs strikingly illustrate the high standards of quality that the company constantly aims to achieve.

A floor in old church flagstones with cabochons in white Carrara marble.

An early-18th-century white-stone fireplace (Louis XIV) with antique andirons and hearth plate.

A design by Francis Van Damme, created by Deknock in old Boom klompje bricks.

Kitchen units designed and created by Francis Van Damme.
Floor in antique lavastone.

An oak-plank floor with an aged, grey finish.

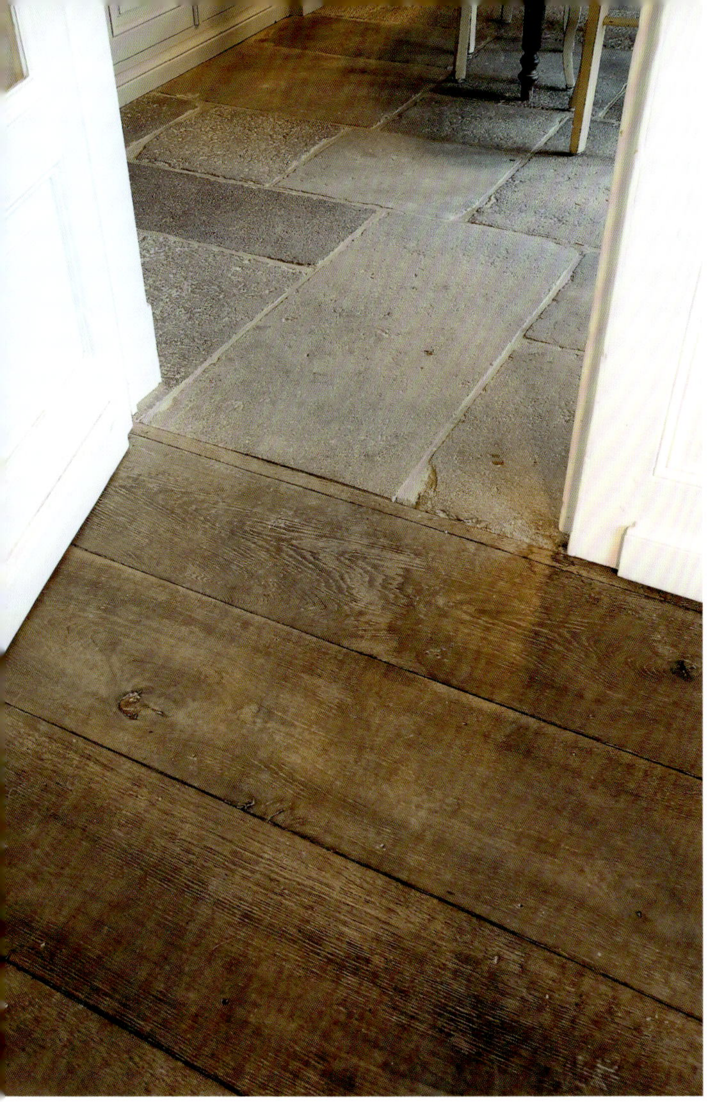

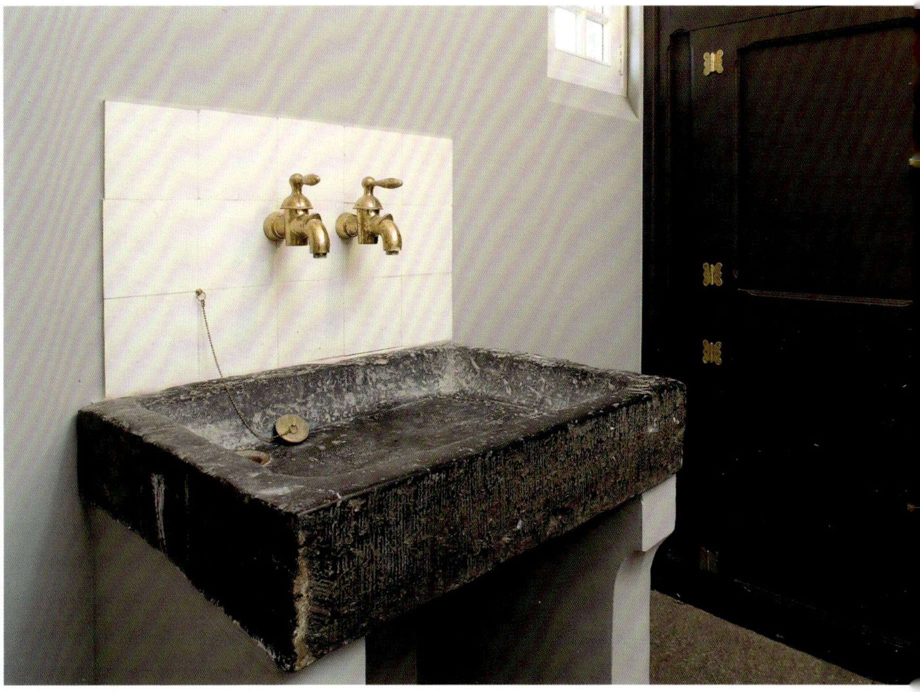

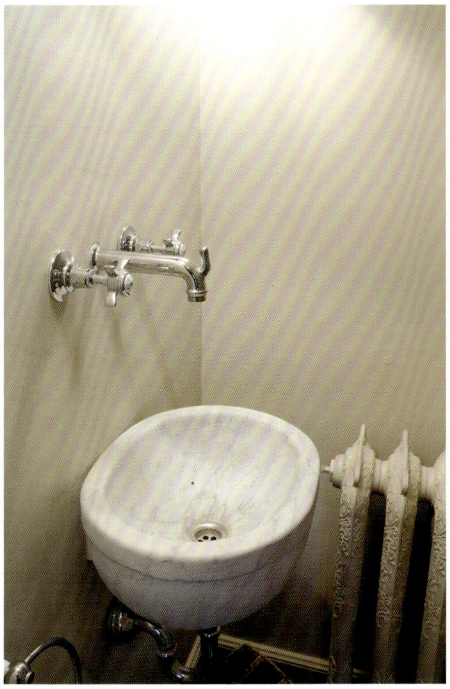

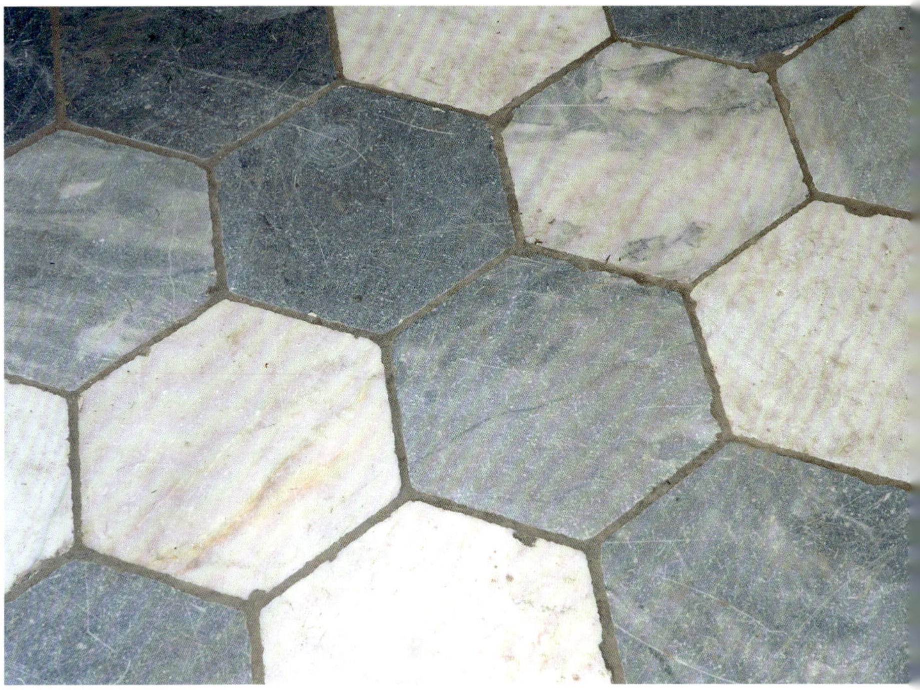

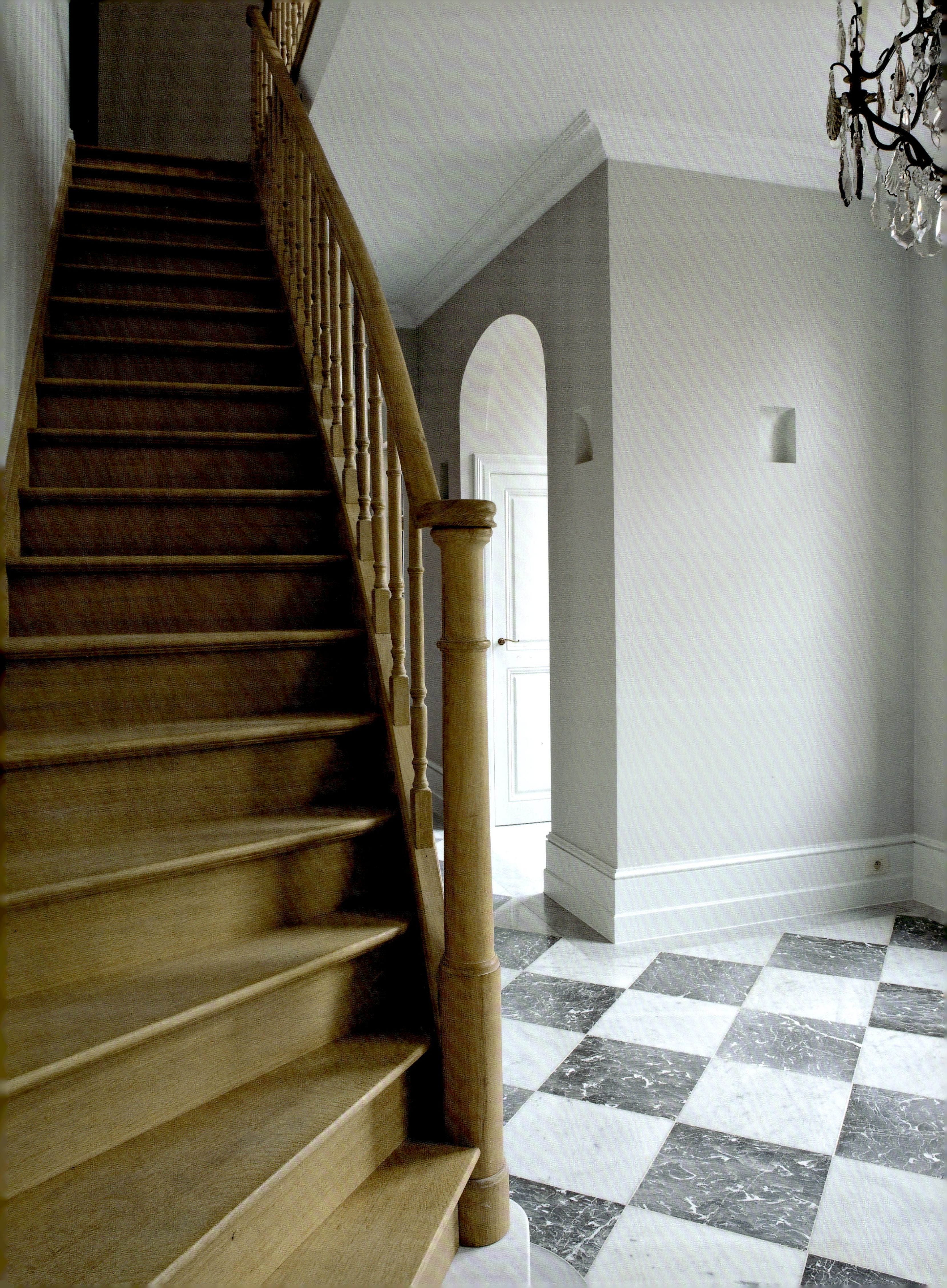

A late-18th/early-19th-century antique fireplace in Belgian St. Anna marble, lined with Boom bricks. An old hearth plate, grate and fireguard.

Deknock supplied this old Carrara and St. Anna marble, arranged in a chessboard design. The oak staircase was also built by Deknock.

A work surface in bluestone, with a smoothed finish and a chiselled edge, also by Deknock.

A work surface in Belgian red marble, made by Deknock.

The oak doors and walls were made by Deknock.

DEKNOCK BVBA
Ruddervoordsestraat 59A
B - 8210 Zedelgem
T +32 (0)50 24 15 30
F +32 (0)50 20 98 05
www.deknock.be
antiek.deknock@pandora.be

Above
A work surface in Carrara marble.

Below left & right
Bath surround in Emperador marble.

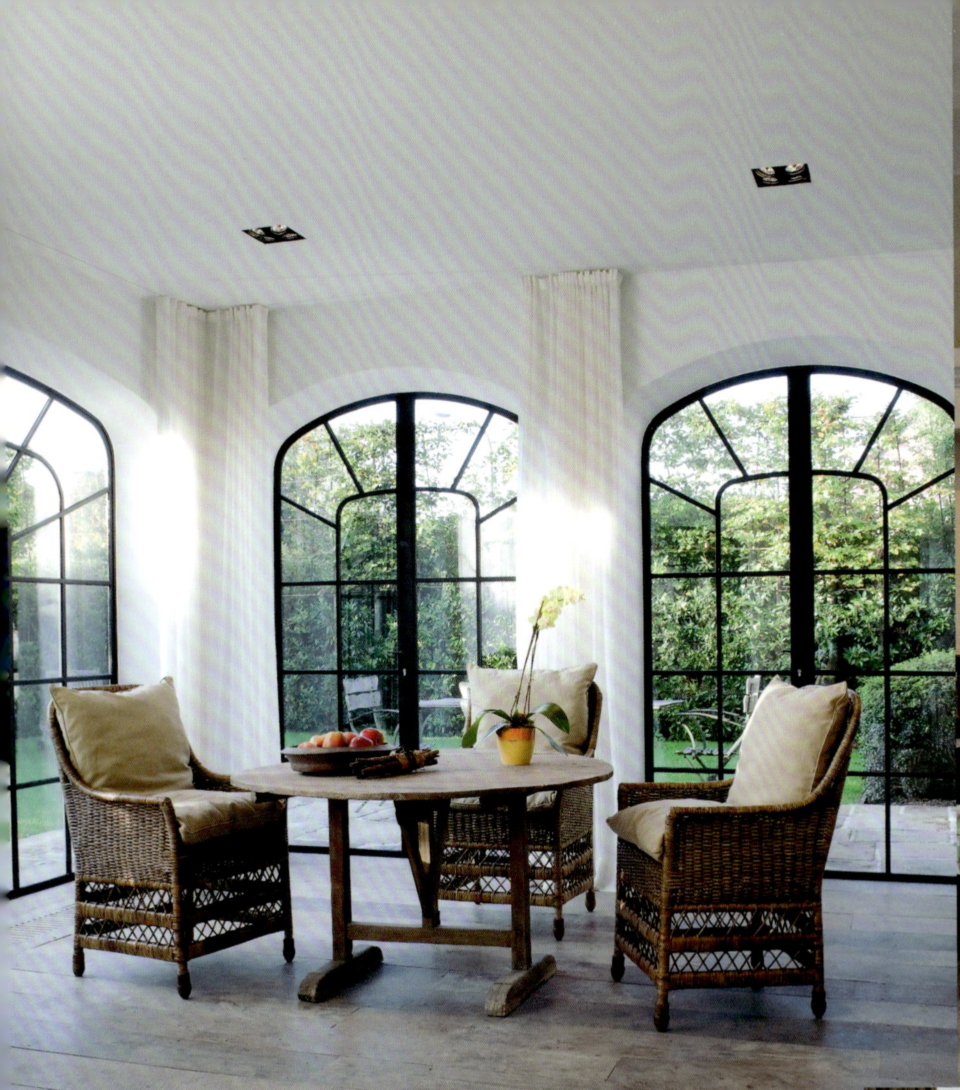
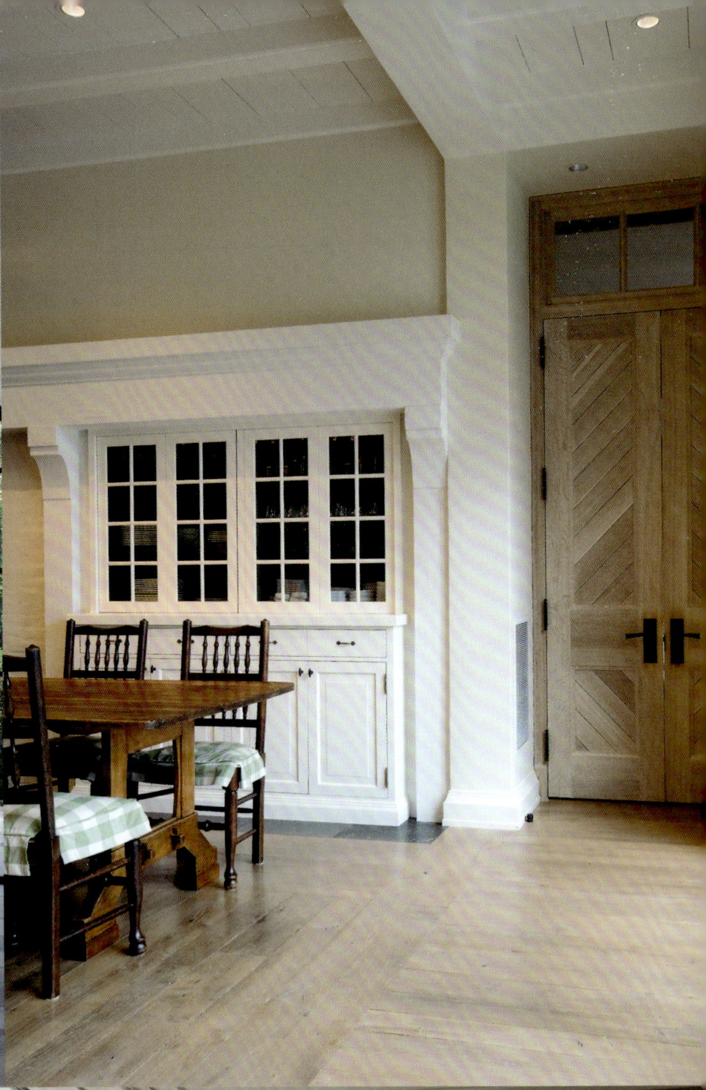
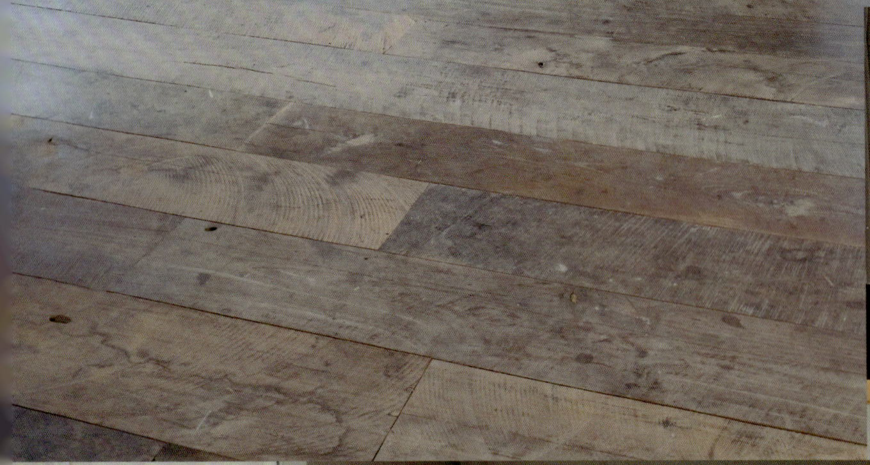
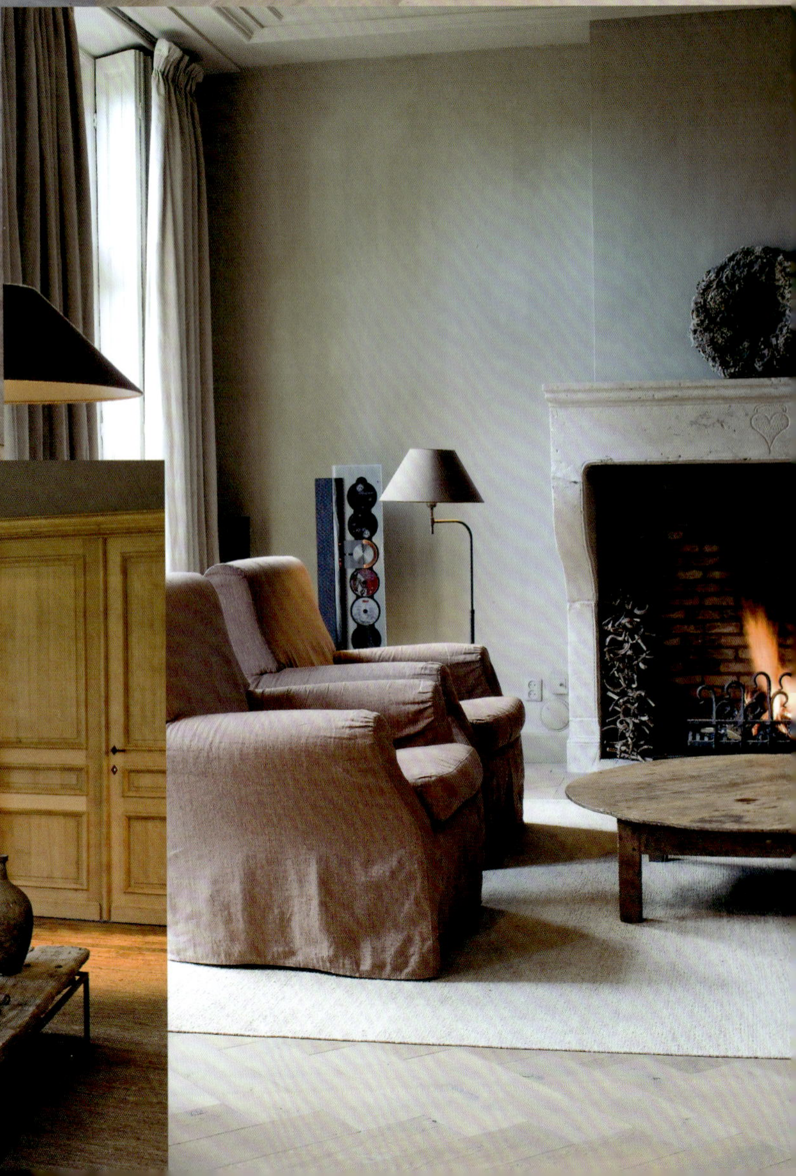
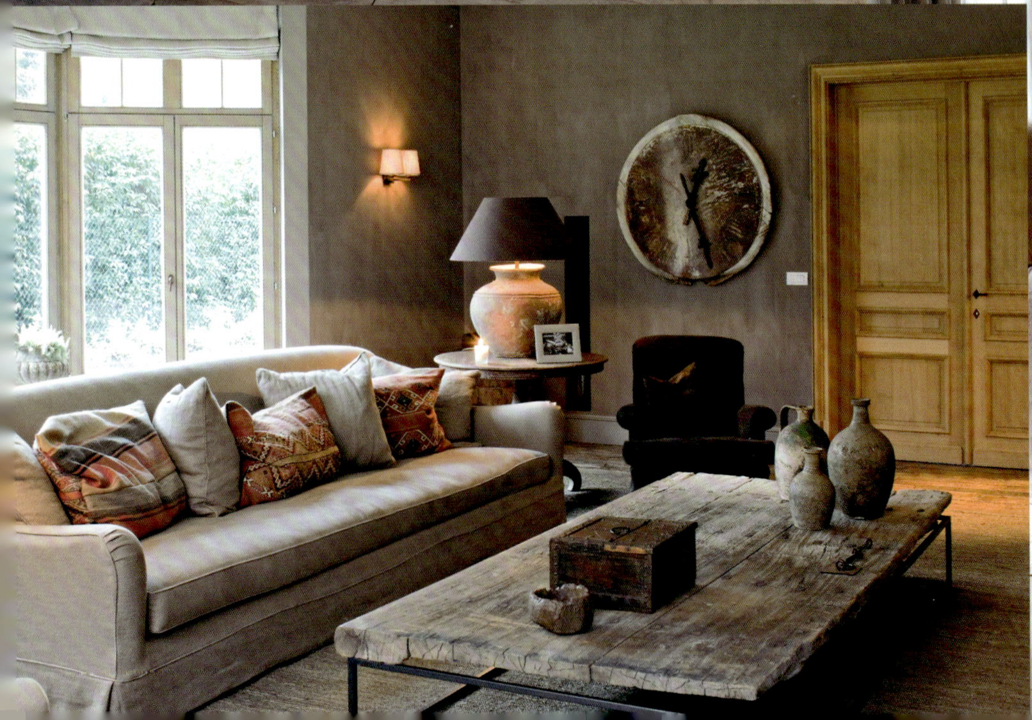

ADDRESSES

't ACHTERHUIS
Reclaimed materials
Showrooms and workplace:
Kreitenmolenstraat 92
NL – 5071BH Udenhout
T +31 (0)13 511 16 49
F +31 (0)13 511 11 42
www.achterhuis.nl
info@achterhuis.nl
Opening hours:
Monday to Friday: 8.30 to 5.30.
On Saturdays from 10 to 4.
Warehouse and transport:
Ambachtsweg 19
NL – 5071 NS Udenhout
Stones / warehouse
Houtsestraat 119
NL – 5011 XH Udenhout
p. 190-201

AMFORA
Sint-Truidensesteenweg 221
B – 3350 Orsmaal - Linter
T +32 (0)11 78 43 11
F +32 (0)11 78 43 11
MOB +32 (0)495 57 90 67
www.amfora-antiques.com
amfora.antiques@skynet.be
Opening hours:
On Saturdays from 10 to 6 and on Sundays
from 2 to 6
Other days by appointment.
p. 210-213

**ARCHITECTURAL ANTIQUES
RIK STORMS EN C°**
Aland 4
B – 2811 Leest
T +32 (0)15 71 25 35
F +32 (0)15 71 41 49
MOB.: +32 (0)475 77 61 57
www.rikstorms.com
info@rikstorms.com
p. 214-225

ANTIQUES & DESIGN
Karel Van Beek / Gert Verhees
Vossendaal 3
B – 2440 Geel
T +32 (0)14 58 42 42
F +32 (0)14 58 15 49
www.antiques-design.be
info@antiques-design.be
p. 60-67

ARCHITECTURAL ANTIQUES THEO EVERS
de Koumen 58
NL – 6433 KD Heerlen-Noord
T +31 (0)45 522 33 33
www.theo-evers.com
info@theo-evers.com
Opening hours:
Thursday and Friday from 10 to 5.
On Saturdays from 10 to 4.
Every first Sunday of the month from 11 to 3.
p. 152-157

ATELIER PASSE PARTOUT
HISTORICAL WOODEN FLOORS
Gallery: St.-Katelijnestraat 41, B – 2800
Mechelen
Postal address: Kazernestraat 15, B – 2801
Mechelen
MOB.: +32 (0)478 56 49 54
www.HistorischeHoutenVloeren.be
p. 158-163

BRUCE BANANTO
145 W. 28th ST.
Suite 803
New York, NY 10001
T +1 212 563 1750
F +1 646 416 6218
p. 96-109

BOENS STEPHANE
Architect
Latemstraat 118
B – 9830 Sint-Martens-Latem
T +32 (0)9 281 02 24
F +32 (0)9 282 99 16
stephane.boens@skynet.be
p. 28-47

CHÂTEAU DE VIERSET
Rue la Coulée 1
B – 4577 Vierset
T +32 (0)85 41 01 70
F +32 (0)85 41 01 50
www.chateaudevierset.be
p. 48-59

CLASSIC COMFORT
Markestraat 7
B – 2430 Laakdal
MOB +32 (0)494 540 475
www.classiccomfort.be
info@classiccomfort.be
Alleen op afspraak.
p. 202-209

CORVELYN
Brugstraat 200
B – 9880 Aalter
T +32 (0)9 325 00 08
F + 32 (0)9 325 00 09
www.corvelyn.be
info@corvelyn.be
p. 164-179

COSTERMANS
Dwarsdreef 52
B – 2970 Schilde
T +32 (0)3 385 02 44
F +32 (0)3 384 29 66
www.costermans-projecten.be
info@costermans-projecten.be
p. 110-125

COUSAERT – VAN DER DONCKT
Furniture design and manufacturing
Stationsstraat 160
B – 9690 Kluisbergen
T +32 (0)55 38 70 53
www.cousaert-vanderdonckt.be
www.keuken-cuisine.be
p. 140-145

DAUBY
Offices and warehouse
Uilenbaan 86
B-2160 Wommelgem
T +32 (0)3 354.16.86
F +32 (0)3.354.16.32
www.dauby.be
p. 226-229

DEKNOCK
Ruddervoordsestraat 59A
B - 8210 Zedelgem
T +32 (0)50 24 15 30
F +32 (0)50 20 98 05
www.deknock.be
antiek.deknock@pandora.be
p. 234-241

EA2
European Architectural Antiques
26 Heistgoorstraat
B – 2220 Antwerpen / Heist op den Berg
T +1 617 894 04 95
info@ea2.be
p. 96-109

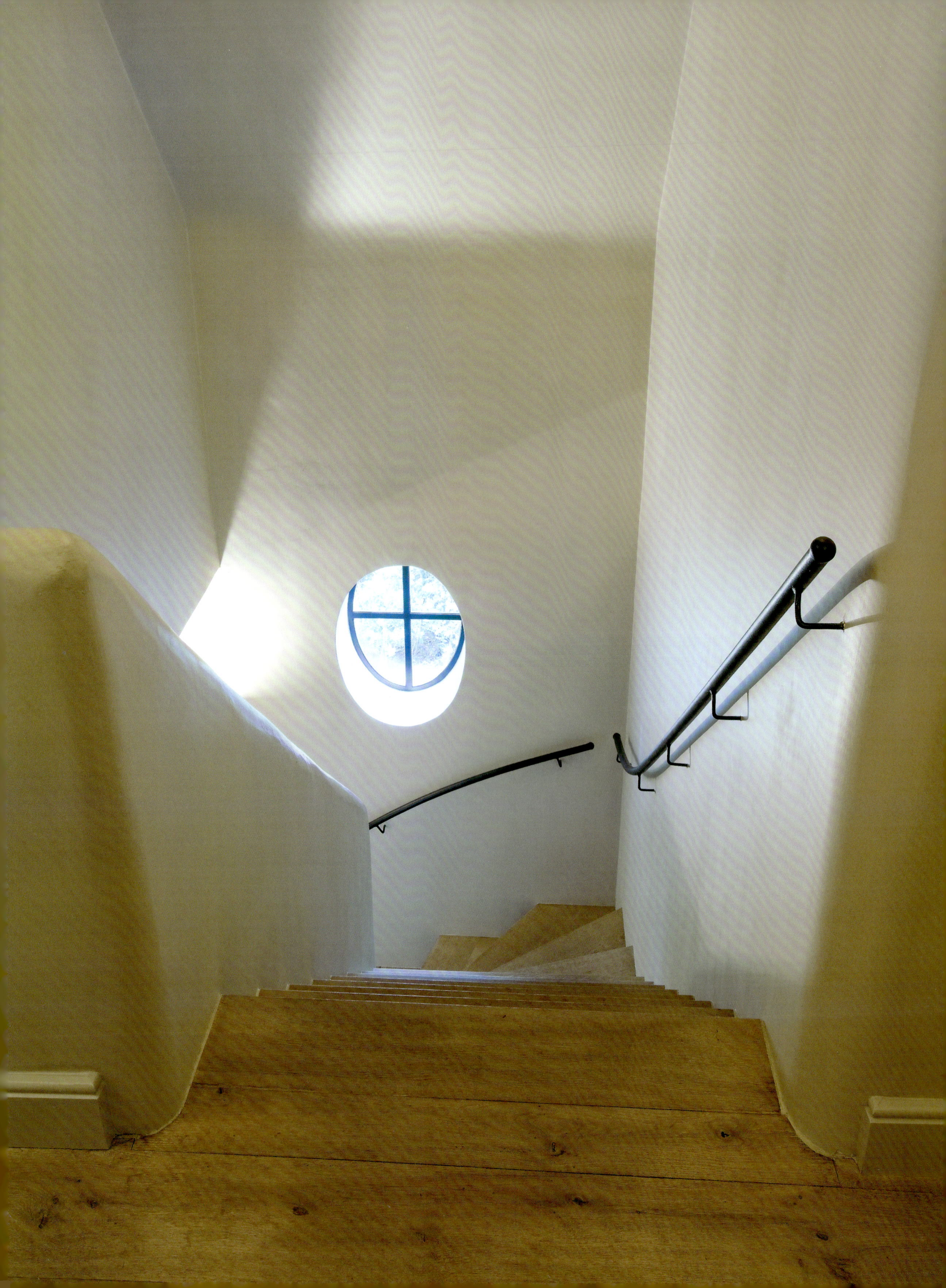

FRYNS – BORET
Architectural antiques
Torhoutsebaan 120
B – 8470 Gistel
T/F +32 (0)59 276 617
T +32 (0)59 267 255
Open: Monday to Friday 9
to 12 and 1.30 to 6.
On Saturdays until 5. Closed on Sundays.
www.fryns-boret.com
info@fryns-boret.com
p. 230-233

NATALIE HAEGEMAN
Anthracite
www.nataliehaegeman-interiors.be
+32 (0)477 24 24 45
+32 (0)3 226 76 06
p. 126-139

KEMPISCHE BOUWMATERIALEN
Bleukenlaan 20
B – 2300 Turnhout
T +32 (0)14 42 04 01
F +32 (0)14 42 34 37
www.kempischebouwmaterialen.be
info@kempischebouwmaterialen.be
Opening hours:
Showroom open from Monday to Friday
8.30 to 12 and 1 to 6.
On Saturdays from 8.30 to 12 and 1 to 3.
p. 180-189

AXEL PAIRON
Antiques / Interiors
Leopoldstraat 35
B – 2000 Antwerp
T/F +32 (0)498 102 815
p. 16-27

PORTE BONHEUR
www.portebonheur.be
Annemie Coppens +32 (0)479 02 99 66
p. 126-139

THEMENOS
Sint-Jansvliet 8
B – 2000 Antwerpen
T +32 (0)3 248 49 93
F +32 (0)3 248 56 23
www.themenos.be
p. 68-95

VANHAELEMEESCH
Veldegemstraat 13
B – 8020 Ruddervoorde
T +32 (0)50 27 71 96
F +32 (0)50 27 56 42
www.vanhaelemeesch.be
info@vanhaelemeesch.be
p. 148-151

A project by Themenos.

PUBLISHER
BETA-PLUS Publishing
Termuninck 3
B - 7850 Enghien (Belgium)
T +32 (0)2 395 90 20
F +32 (0)2 395 90 21
www.betaplus.com
info@betaplus.com

PHOTOGRAPHY
All pictures: Jo Pauwels, except:
p. 140-145 : Moniek Peers

GRAPHIC DESIGN
POLYDEM
Nathalie Binart

TRANSLATION
Laura Watkinson

February 2008
ISBN 13: 978 90 77213 94 0

© All rights reserved. No part of this publication may be reproduced or transmitted in any form or by any means, electronic or mechanical, including photocopy, recording or any other information storage and retrieval system, without prior permission in writing from the publisher.